The IQ Debate

The IQ Debate

A Selective Guide to the Literature

Compiled by
STEPHEN H. ABY
with the assistance of
MARTHA J. McNAMARA

Bibliographies and Indexes
in Psychology, Number 8

GREENWOOD PRESS
New York • Westport, Connecticut • London

Library of Congress Cataloging-in-Publication Data

Aby, Stephen H.
  The IQ debate : a selective guide to the literature / compiled by
Stephen H. Aby, with the assistance of Martha J. McNamara.
    p. cm.—(Bibliographies and indexes in psychology, ISSN
0742-681X ; no. 8)
  Includes indexes.
  ISBN 0-313-26440-6 (alk. paper)
  1. Intelligence levels—Bibliography.   I. McNamara, Martha J.
II. Title. III. Series.
Z7204.I5A29 1990
[BF431]
016.1539'3—dc20   90-13986

British Library Cataloguing in Publication Data is available.

Library of Congress Catalog Card Number: 90-13986
ISBN: 0-313-26440-6
ISSN: 0742-681X

First published in 1990

Greenwood Press, 88 Post Road West, Westport, CT 06881
An imprint of Greenwood Publishing Group, Inc.

Printed in the United States of America

The paper used in this book complies with the
Permanent Paper Standard issued by the National
Information Standards Organization (Z39.48-1984).

10 9 8 7 6 5 4 3 2

Contents

Introduction   vii

PART I: REFERENCE SOURCES   1
  1. Bibliographies   3
  2. Indexes, Abstracts, and Databases   5
  3. Handbooks   11
  4. Dictionaries and Encyclopedias   15

PART II: NONREFERENCE SOURCES   17
  5. Books and Book Chapters   19
  6. Professional Journal Articles   77
  7. Magazine Articles   149
  8. Newspaper Articles   175
  9. ERIC Documents   195
 10. Media Materials   203

Glossary   207
Name Index   213
Subject Index   221

Introduction

SCOPE AND PURPOSE

This selective bibliography is intended to provide students, faculty, librarians, and other researchers with descriptive annotations of 408 of the most relevant sources on the IQ debate. Books, book chapters, professional journal articles, educational documents, popular magazine articles, media materials, and articles from some major newspapers are included, along with a limited number of reference sources. Most of the nonreference sources were published after Arthur Jensen's landmark 1969 article and before the spring of 1990. Selective exceptions have been made, however, for earlier works that are particularly relevant to the historical development of the debate. These include works by Sir Francis Galton, Sir Cyril Burt, Lewis Terman, Walter Lippmann, Robert Yerkes, and Audrey Shuey, among others. Furthermore, in order to keep the bibliography focused, preference is given to sources that explicitly engage in and respond to the debate. Journal articles and books that deal with IQ test construction, reliability, and validity, but that do not explicitly relate their work to the debate, are included much more selectively. This policy should not restrict access to those articles and books; those who do engage in the debate often cite and draw upon that body of research. This literature should also be traceable through some of the bibliography's reference works.

Only works in English are included, and they are drawn primarily from literature in the United States and, to a lesser extent, in Great Britain, Australia, and Canada. The bibliographic citations include such details as the author/editor, title, article title, publication date, pages, publisher, place of publication, and other basic publication information. Citations for Educational Resources Information Center (ERIC) documents that have not been published (such as conference papers) include only author, title, year, page length, and ERIC document number; published ERIC documents have conventional citations, as well as the ERIC document number. Annotations for all entries are descriptive and range in length from 100 to 300 words, with 150 words being typical; all sources have been examined firsthand and have received original annotations.

In order to provide access to literature on all facets of the IQ debate, this bibliography must include all perspectives. Consequently, the works cited represent a cross section of the authors and positions taken in the debate. The selection of entries reflects my exposure to and interest in the topic; another compiler may have added different titles and excluded some that are here. For all entries, I have made every effort to write objective and descriptive annotations, regardless of my opinion of their content. Critical annotations, while perhaps personally gratifying, would limit the user to only my understanding of the issues raised in each source. I have included, later in this Introduction, an "Overview of the IQ Debate," which reflects, somewhat, my more critical opinion of the hereditarian position in the debate.

ORGANIZATION

Entries are arranged in two parts. The first, and smaller, part includes reference sources of relevance to the IQ debate and is arranged by the type of reference source. It covers encyclopedias and dictionaries of psychology; educational and psychological indexes, abstracts, and databases; guides to existing intelligence tests; and related sources. These sources should complement the study of the issues by providing access to related research, to descriptions of existing intelligence tests, and to definitions of key terms.

The second part includes books and book chapters, professional journal articles, popular magazine articles, media materials, newspaper articles, and ERIC educational documents. Within each chapter, entries are arranged alphabetically by author or, lacking this, by title. I chose this method of organization because arrangement by subject headings, broad or narrow, would not do justice to the material. Many of the sources span a number of disciplines and approaches to the debate. Arbitrarily placing these entries under particular subject headings would not make them fully accessible. Furthermore, a large miscellaneous category would still be required. Consequently, this work provides both a comprehensive subject index, with multiple access points for each entry, and a name index. For articles in edited collections, only the article's author is indexed; editors appear in the name index only if their entire volume is annotated separately. For media materials, hosts and primary guests of programs are also considered authors.

Finally, a small glossary of important terms is appended to aid in the reading of the annotations. Although every attempt has been made to write the annotations in clear, nontechnical English, a certain number of technical terms (such as heritability) had to be used. The glossary provides a readily available aid for those not familiar with some of these key terms. In a number of cases, the definitions of some generic technical terms are written to reflect the IQ debate context; hopefully, this does no damage to the more conventional definitions. For terms not in the glossary, one should consult an appropriate dictionary or encyclopedia identified in Part One.

OVERVIEW OF THE IQ DEBATE

History

The publication of Arthur Jensen's article, "How Much Can We Boost IQ and Scholastic Achievement?" in the Winter 1969 issue of the *Harvard Educational Review* created a storm of protest and fueled an ongoing debate in the academic community and the popular media. The source of this furor was Jensen's suggestion that American blacks were, on the average, less intelligent than whites and that this difference was largely genetic in origin. He used this argument to explain what he perceived to be the failure of compensatory education programs such as Head Start; these programs were ignoring inherent intellectual deficiencies, he contended, and thus they were failing.

The arguments that differences in intelligence are inherited, and that races, classes, and ethnic groups differ in their average levels of intelligence, are not new. In 1869 Sir Francis Galton, in *Hereditary Genius*, made the first effort to document "scientifically" the belief that genius or intelligence is inherited. He studied relatives of Britain's elite, and, not surprisingly, found that they too were likely to be among the elite. This indicated to him that ability was inherited. Today it is clear that his explanation had no scientific basis and overlooked environmental factors, and that he was influenced by an upper-class bias. Still, even though Galton's science was flawed, his book marks an unofficial beginning of the

IQ debate and of scientific efforts to explain inequality as being the result of differences in innate ability.

Alfred Binet is credited with having developed the first successful intelligence test in France in 1905. Interestingly, however, his test was intended as a diagnostic tool to discover students who were behind in their studies. There was no suggestion on Binet's part that the test measured the child's innate capacity or ability; in fact, he was critical of the "brutal pessimism" of such an idea. Rather, the test's purpose was to identify students in need of help so that they could then be provided with remediation.

It was not until Binet's test was introduced in the United States, between 1908 and 1920, by Lewis Terman, Henry Goddard, and Robert Yerkes that it was interpreted as a measure of innate intelligence. How did this happen? Critics argue that Terman and the others in the testing movement were eugenicists, and as such, believed in the innate superiority and inferiority of various racial and ethnic groups. The IQ test seemed to provide them with a measure of these innate differences, and thus supported their preexisting biases. In any event, the testing of immigrants at Ellis Island in New York and of American soldiers in World War I helped to legitimize both the intelligence test and the field of psychology. The findings from these testing efforts confirmed for these early mental testers that certain racial, ethnic, and immigrant groups were intellectually inferior. These results, as well as the influence of the mental testers and eugenicists, contributed to the passage of the racist Immigration Restriction Act of 1924, which limited immigration from countries whose citizens were deemed less intelligent. From these early beginnings, the tests spread into the schools as a seemingly scientific means of identifying students' native abilities and of tracking them into different and unequal educational experiences.

In this period, the IQ debate surfaced in its earliest public forum. Lewis Terman and Walter Lippmann, in a series of popular magazine articles in the 1920s, engaged in a debate over the results and interpretation of the World War I army intelligence tests. Lippmann was critical of the methods and findings of the army mental tests and, more generally, of intelligence testing. His critique foreshadowed many of the arguments that resurfaced after Arthur Jensen's article in 1969. For example, he accused the mental testers of misunderstanding the concept of mental age and of attributing to it a fixedness that violated Binet's intent. Lippmann also raised questions about the representativeness of the American population sample (400 Californians) on which Binet's test was standardized for American use. He questioned further whether the testers even knew what intelligence was and criticized their willingness to believe in it simply because they had test scores for it. He also examined biases in the test's construction, as well as its poor correlation with other indicators of success.

The years of the World War II era were quiet ones for the IQ debate. The horror of Nazism, with its lethal ideology of the inferiority of various racial, ethnic, and religious groups, very probably contributed to the low profile of eugenics and hereditarianism in this period. At the same time, the field of psychology was gradually moving away from hereditarianism and towards environmentalism. Still, data relevant to the later IQ debate were being collected. For example, an often-cited twin study by Newman, Freeman, and Holzinger was published in 1937. Similarly, Cyril Burt in England was amassing data on an increasingly large sample of identical twins reared apart, although it would be discovered later that the data were fraudulent. All of these historical threads became newly relevant when Arthur Jensen published his controversial article in 1969.

The Current Debate

Much of Jensen's article was a summary and analysis of previous research. In particular, he focused on studies of identical twins reared apart (twin studies), kinship correlations, and adoption studies. In Jensen's estimation, the instances of genetically identical twins reared in different environments offered the opportunity to discover the relative influence of genetics and environment on intelligence. If the twins showed significantly similar IQ scores, despite being raised in different environments, this would indicate, he felt, that one's intellectual ability was determined primarily by genetic endowment. Similarly, with the kinship correlations, if the scores of closely related individuals were more highly correlated than those of distant relatives, this would indicate the role of genes in intelligence differences. Adoption studies, too, were considered useful on this point. If, despite their rearing environment, the IQs of adopted children were less like those of their adopted siblings and parents and more like their natural parents, then this would indicate the effect of genes on intelligence.

After reviewing this and other research, Jensen suggested that intelligence is 80% heritable; that is, 80% of the differences among individual IQ scores in a population is attributable to genes, not environment. If intelligence is 80% heritable within the black and white populations, he argued, then it is not unreasonable to assume that the differences between blacks and whites are mostly genetic in origin as well. Jensen argued further that blacks and whites differed in the way they were best able to learn. Blacks and whites were comparable in associative or rote learning abilities, while whites were superior in cognitive or abstract learning abilities. He indicated that schools would be more successful if they taught students in a manner consistent with their learning styles.

The possible social, educational, and policy implications of Jensen's arguments were obvious. If, as Jensen argued, intelligence is a major determinant of success in school and life, and if differences in intelligence are largely inherited, then social and educational inequality is seemingly unavoidable. Furthermore, if blacks are, on the average, less intelligent than whites, then racial inequality is ultimately reducible to biological differences, not to problems of social policy. In a country with a history of racism, Jensen appeared to be providing scientific evidence of racial inferiority, and his theory seemed to rationalize racial inequality. Furthermore, he was undermining compensatory education programs intended to help correct past social and educational injustices. His suggestion that blacks were generally rote learners raised the spectre that many of them would be given a terminal, non-academic education. It is not surprising that the article generated such strong reaction, especially in that period of the civil rights movement and social activism.

Jensen estimated that approximately 120 articles were written in response to his article in just the first few years after its publication. Interestingly, these responses were not limited to the academic community. In 1973 *Newsweek* published an article entitled "Born Dumb?" that addressed the issue. *Time, U.S. News and World Report, New Republic, The New York Times*, and many other popular publications covered the controversy as well. In 1975, CBS News presented an hour special, hosted by Dan Rather, called "The IQ Myth." Few academic disputes have received such extensive and prolonged coverage in the popular media. The IQ controversy is different because it touches on a pivotal social issue in American society: How do we explain persistent social and racial inequality in a country that espouses the rhetoric of equality of opportunity?

The controversy has continued unabated since the early 1970s. Proponents of Jensen's position, as well as Jensen himself, have defended and expanded his arguments. Jensen has since argued that certain physiological measures, such as "evoked potentials" (brain wave activity) or choice reaction time (the amount of time that passes after a subject is shown a stimulus, before selecting a correct response) correlate with intelligence measures. This, he argues, indicates that intelligence differences are innate and physiologically based.

Some of Jensen's supporters have generated their own controversy. For example, in his book *IQ in the Meritocracy*, published in 1973, Richard Herrnstein argued that poor people in general, regardless of race, were less intelligent than the rich, thus resulting in their poverty. Furthermore, he argued that if the less intelligent continued to intermarry, they would become a virtual caste, enslaved by their genetically determined intellectual deficiencies. In an even more controversial argument, William Shockley, the late Nobel-prize-winning physicist from California, argued that women on welfare should be offered cash incentives to undergo sterilization; that way, they would not reproduce their genetically inferior offspring and further populate the welfare roles.

The Critics

Critics have attacked IQ theory for a variety of reasons. Some attack the very motivation for conducting such research. In a society with a long history of both individual and institutional racism, why investigate the alleged innate deficiencies of an oppressed population? Why not, instead, research the damaging role of oppressive social institutions? These critics argue that the rationale for investigating intelligence differences is rooted in racism and that this fuels support for the theory to this day. In effect, focusing on the victims of racism and their alleged deficiencies excuses the social institutions that have perpetuated racial inequality. This, they argue, is the hidden political agenda of IQ theory: the justification of continued social inequality.

Others critics have attacked the quality of the research on IQ, disputing the methodological soundness of the key studies (such as the twin studies, kinship correlations, and adoption studies) and the cultural fairness of the IQ tests. In effect, their point is that the hereditarians rely upon bad science, and therefore, have no basis for any explanation of differences in IQ scores. Take the twin studies, for example. For twin studies to be useful, the twins must be raised in significantly different environments. Only then could one attribute a similarity in their IQ scores to genetics. According to critics such as Leon Kamin, however, this methodological requirement has not been met; twins are often raised in environments too similar to separate out genetic versus environmental causes for their similar scores. Even more spectacularly, Kamin and others have demonstrated that much of the twin data published by Sir

Cyril Burt were fraudulent. This argument has come to be accepted by most participants in the IQ debate. The hereditarians respond that Burt's data are not essential to their position and that there are other, more acceptable, data on twins to prove the point. Robert Joynson, in a 1989 book-length defense of Burt, suggests that Burt's data were not fraudulent at all.

Of course, the argument over the causes of differences in intelligence presumes that we know what intelligence is and how to measure it. Some critics accept neither of these propositions. Is intelligence the single, underlying ability that hereditarians make it out to be (that is, "g" or general intelligence)? Or do people possess a variety of intelligences that are the consequence of their own unique history? Furthermore, is intelligence an innate entity or thing that can be identified and measured, or is it a collection of behaviors that are defined as intelligent by one's culture? And if the latter is the case, who does the defining? Are intelligent behaviors in the subcultures (that is, blacks and other minorities) valued as much as the behaviors of the dominant cultural groups? Even if one accepts that an innate intelligence exists, there is the problem of how to measure it in a manner that is fair to all cultures. Many critics argue that this problem has not been overcome and that the tests rely upon knowledge and information that are more likely to have been learned by middle-class whites.

In response, hereditarians ask how environmentalists can explain the fact that middle-class blacks still score worse than middle-class whites, and that American Indians, who are more impoverished than blacks, do better on intelligence tests than blacks. Critics state that research on intelligence has not adequately controlled for environmental differences. In a society that still has segregated housing and schooling and that reflects an entrenched racism, a middle-class black person has not had the same environmental experience as a middle-class white person, despite their ostensibly similar class standing. And while American Indians are poorer than blacks, do we know that this is the only relevant environmental difference that could explain IQ test performance? It is this inadequacy of our understanding that has prompted research into more subtle environmental factors by such critics as Jane Mercer, Zena Blau, and Elsie Moore.

Another focus for the critics is Arthur Jensen's assumption that compensatory education has failed. This, after all, was his basis for suspecting that the targeted students lacked the innate ability to benefit from such programs. The critics question whether, in fact, compensatory programs have ever been sufficiently attempted. The essence of their point is that sending an impoverished minority child to a preschool program for a few hours a day for a summer is not going to place those children on an even footing with middle-class white children. It is unrealistic to assume that it would. What is needed are more comprehensive efforts to improve the whole constellation of family and environmental factors that can have an impact on one's opportunities. Beyond this, the implication that blacks need to be made more like whites suggests a rather colonial attitude toward black culture.

Still other critics challenge a central idea in the IQ argument, the assumption that intelligence is a key determinant of success in school and life. They challenge this on at least two different levels. Samuel Bowles and Herbert Gintis, for example, argue that it is one's social class background, not one's intelligence level, that is most determinative of one's success. Other critics challenge the connection between intelligence and inequality with a more basic question: Even if individuals do inherit different levels of intelligence, why do they have to receive unequal social rewards as a result? This, the critics argue, is not inevitable, but rather, is a value choice by those with the power to choose. A society could just as well respond to unequal intelligence levels by showering more, not less, support and services on the "less intelligent." The point is, one's intelligence level need not dictate the social rewards one receives.

The response of the hereditarians to these criticisms has been varied. In many cases, they have responded to substantive criticisms in kind, arguing point by point on the theory and methods of intelligence testing. They have also, on occasion, accused their critics of censorship and violations of academic freedom when they have been publicly or professionally harassed for their position. The suggestion is that it is unacceptable in a marketplace of ideas to suppress legitimate academic research simply because it violates cherished liberal beliefs or ideologies. According to the hereditarians, research into intelligence differences is a legitimate subject of inquiry, and it should be evaluated on its scientific, not ideological, merits. Again, however, the issues are not quite so clear cut. Some critics, such as Steven Selden, argue that the selection of "problems" for research is influenced by one's values and ideologies, and therefore, is not scientifically neutral. Bias can affect not only how one does research but also what one researches.

Important questions, then, are raised by the IQ debate. How much of our behavior is learned, as opposed to being innate? What is intelligence, and what does it mean to be intelligent? Are people born with different amounts of intelligence, or can we learn to behave intelligently? If intelligence is inherited, do races, ethnic groups, and social classes inherit significantly different amounts of it? If so, how does one prove this? If there are different levels of intelligence, does this necessarily lead to social inequality? What is the history of IQ theory and research, and how does this relate to the current debate?   How well has IQ research been carried out? Do IQ tests actually measure intelligence, whatever it is? Are there political interests that benefit by the different positions taken in the debate? Does this affect support for IQ research? Is IQ research opposed because critics do not like the implications of some of its findings? If so, is this censorship? All of these questions, and more, are discussed in the material relating to the debate.

Because the literature on the IQ debate has mushroomed during the last 20 years, and because it overlaps the fields of education, psychology, and sociology, there is a need for focused access to the most relevant material. This annotated bibliography provides that access, and, in so doing, supports and promotes study of the issues. Furthermore, this debate is part of the broader nature versus nurture debate that attempts to identify the relative contributions of genes and environment to human behavior. Consequently, the types of arguments and evidence used in the IQ debate recur in other debates, such as those over sex-role behavior and crime. Here, too, the issue is whether behavioral differences (such as between men and women, criminals and noncriminals) are the result primarily of genetic or environmental differences. Familiarity with the IQ debate should enhance one's ability to understand and critique these variations on the nature-nurture debate.

ACKNOWLEDGMENTS

A number of people contributed to the completion of this bibliography, whether it was through reading drafts, suggesting sources, obtaining books and articles from other libraries, editing, printing the final copy, or broadening my understanding of the topic. Hoping that nobody has been left out, I would like to thank Susan Franzosa, Bill Thomas, Don Martin, Peter Sola, Gene Grabiner, Roger Woock, Bob Lingard, Susan Yates, John Ball, Sarah Lorenz, Joan Robinson, Sue Shellhorn, Tom Bennett, Vickie Evans, Margaret Maybury, Lisa Reichbach, Patricia Meyers, Sally Scott, Mildred Vasan, and Russell Curtis, who first taught me about the IQ debate in 1971. Special thanks go to Martha McNamara, who helped edit the work and also contributed some of the newspaper article annotations. Because of their help, this bibliography is much better than it otherwise would have been. Of course, the remaining deficiencies are my responsibility alone.

I   REFERENCE SOURCES

1 Bibliographies

1. *A Review of Head Start Research Since 1970 and an Annotated Bibliography of the Head Start Research Since 1965.* Washington, D.C., Department of Health and Human Services; distr., Washington, D.C., GPO, 1983. 600p.

   The Head Start compensatory education programs have loomed large in the IQ debate. Their alleged failure with the disadvantaged prompted some academics, like Arthur Jensen, to suspect genetic causes. This book provides a review of the Head Start research up to 1982, as well as an annotated bibliography of articles, books, and other sources of research on Head Start. The entries in the bibliography are accessible by either the author index or the general subject index.

2. Rosenfield, Geraldine, and Howard Yagerman. *The New Environment-Heredity Controversy: A Selected Annotated Bibliography.* New York, Information and Research Services, American Jewish Committee, 1973. 52p.

   This is a short bibliography of 55 books and articles on the nature vs. nurture debate. The entries are arranged under four chapter headings: 1) the hereditarians, 2) the environmentalists, 3) the synthesizers, and 4) the policy and morality debate. Since the IQ debate is one aspect of the nature vs. nurture debate, much of this material should be useful background reading. In addition, the bibliography includes some of the early responses to Arthur Jensen's 1969 article in the *Harvard Educational Review.*

3.   Watson, Robert I., Sr., ed. *Eminent Contributors to Psychology*. New York, Springer, 1976. 2v.

This bibliography is a guide to some 12,000 primary sources and 50,000 secondary sources by and about 500 major figures in the development of psychology. Consequently, it is a good source of citations on the early intelligence testers, such individuals as Alfred Binet, Sir Francis Galton, James McKeen Cattell, Henry Goddard, Edward Thorndike, Robert Yerkes, and Lewis Terman. The primary sources are in volume one, and are arranged alphabetically by the psychologist; secondary sources, arranged alphabetically by psychologist, then by author, appear in volume two.

4.   Wright, Logan. *Bibliography on Human Intelligence*. Washington, D.C., National Clearinghouse for Mental Health Information; Washington, D.C., GPO, 1969. 222p.

This is a bibliography of books, monographs, book chapters, and articles on the testing and measurement of intelligence. Over 67,000 citations are arranged alphabetically by author. The cutoff date for inclusion was around 1965. Also, the bibliography excludes works on the structure of intellect, specific intelligence tests, and the psychological testing controversy.

Subject access is provided by a hierarchical index of citations and a topical index. The former lists the citation numbers for works under broad subject outline categories. The latter is a more conventional subject or keyword index, which refers the user to the appropriate page in the index of citations.

Major categories in the index of citations cover historical antecedents, related concepts, theoretical works, the nature of intelligence, factors influencing intelligence, and group intelligence tests. Works by many early figures in the IQ testing movement are included.

2 Indexes, Abstracts, and Databases

5. *Australian Education Index*. Hawthorn, Victoria, Australian Council for Educational Research, 1958- . quarterly, with annual cumulation.

    This is a guide to journal articles, conference papers, theses, research reports, newspaper articles, parliamentary debates, and other materials on education. Australian and some international materials are included; some of the entries are accompanied by abstracts. There is subject and author access in one alphabetical arrangement; subject headings are drawn from the Library of Congress list of subjects. This is also available as an online database through AUSINET.

6. *British Education Index*. Leeds, England, University of Leeds/Education Library, 1961- . 3 quarterly issues plus an annual cumulation.

    The *British Education Index* identifies articles in approximately 250 British and, to a lesser extent, international journals "published or distributed in the British Isles" (preface, vol. 15). It includes a brief subject index, a subject list of articles with citations, and an author index (with citations). References on the IQ debate can be found under the major headings "Intelligence" and "Intelligence Tests," plus their subheadings. The online database version of the index also includes British and Irish theses; it is available on the DIALOG database service.

7.   *Canadian Education Index.* Toronto, Canadian Education Association, 1965- . 3 issues/year, including an annual cumulation.

This indexes Canadian books, pamphlets, journal articles, and reports on education.   There are both subject and author indexes, with entries in both English and French.   Entries on the IQ debate can be found under such headings as "Intelligence" or "Intelligence Levels."

8.   *Comprehensive Dissertation Index.*   Ann Arbor, Mich., University Microfilms International, 1973- . annual.

This is an easy-to-use source for locating dissertations by either subject or author.   An eight volume base set covers the years 1861-1972, and another multi-volume set covers 1973-1977; after that, there are annual volumes.   These yearly volumes, which cover either the "Social Sciences and Humanities" or the "Sciences," are subdivided further by discipline.   Dissertations within each discipline are arranged by their relevant keywords.   The citations are complete, and also include a reference to *Dissertation Abstracts International* (entry #10), where one can find an abstract.   The dissertations can also be located in the author index, whose entries include complete citations.

9.   *Current Index to Journals in Education.*   Vol. 1- , No. 1- . Phoenix, Ariz., Oryx Press, 1969- . monthly, with semi-annual cumulations.

The *Current Index to Journals in Education* (CIJE) is an index to articles in approximately 780 education and education-related journals.   Its companion index, *Resources in Education* (entry #16), indexes research reports, conference papers, books, manuscripts, and other less accessible educational materials; these sources are made available on microfiche.   Both the RIE and CIJE include subject and author indexes, as well as abstracts describing the cited sources.   RIE also permits searching by institution name and type of publication (e.g. book, dissertation); CIJE offers an additional journal contents index.

Subject searching in both indexes is aided by the *Thesaurus of ERIC Descriptors* (entry #21), which lists the subject terms used by ERIC. There are a number of subject headings relevant to the IQ debate: "Intelligence," "Intelligence Differences," "Intelligence Quotient," "Intelligence Tests," "Intelligence Factors" (used until 1980), "Intelligence Level" (used until 1980), and "Nature Nurture Controversy." One can also search the author index under the names of key participants in the debate (e.g. Jensen, Eysenck, Kamin, Lewontin, Scarr). The debate is also searchable on the **ERIC** online (entry #12) and CD-ROM databases, which are the computer database equivalents to both the CIJE and the RIE.

10.   *Dissertation Abstracts International.* Ann Arbor, Mich., University Microfilms International, 1969- . monthly, with annual author indexes.

This provides complete citations and abstracts, written by the author, of dissertations from the United States and Europe. The volumes cover the humanities and social sciences (Part A), the sciences and engineering (Part B), or with European dissertations (Part C). Within a volume, the abstracts are arranged by broad subject and subtopic, then alphabetically by author. The dissertations can also be located with the keyword-in-title index and the author index. Older dissertations can be found using *Dissertation Abstracts* or *Microfilm Abstracts*. *Dissertation Abstracts International* is also available for computer searching through major database vendors such as DIALOG or BRS, as well as on CD-ROM.

11.   *Education Index.* New York, H. W. Wilson, 1929- . monthly, except July and August, with quarterly and annual cumulations.

This is one of the major indexes to articles in education. Complete article citations are arranged alphabetically by subject and author; there is also a separate index section to book reviews. Articles on the IQ debate can be found not only under the names of key individuals, but also under such subject headings as intelligence; efficiency, mental; heredity of intelligence; intelligence tests; and intelligence quotient. This index is available online through *Wilsonline*, and on CD-ROM through *Wilsondisc*.

12.   *ERIC.* Washington, Educational Resources Information Center, 1966- . monthly updates.

This is the comprehensive, database equivalent to both the *Current Index to Journals in Education* (entry #9) and *Resources in Education* (entry #16), which are the two print ERIC indexes. The CIJE covers approximately 780 education and education-related journals back to 1969; the RIE includes educational documents (conference papers, research reports, etc.) back to 1966. This database is available on both the DIALOG and BRS database services, as well as on CD-ROM.

13.   *PsycALERT*. Washington, D.C., American Psychological Association. weekly updates.

The *PsycALERT* database complements *PsycINFO* (entry #15) by offering online access to the most recent published articles in psychology. These articles are later placed into the *PsycINFO* database with complete indexing and access.

14.   *Psychological Abstracts*. Arlington, Va., American Psychological Association, 1927- . monthly, with quarterly, annual, and triennial cumulative indexes.

This is the major index for finding articles and dissertations in psychology and its related fields. The citations, which are accompanied by descriptive abstracts, are classified into any of 16 broad subject categories and their subheadings. However, the subject or author indexes provide a more specific means of searching. Subject index headings are drawn from the *Thesaurus of Psychological Index Terms* (entry #22). There are a number of headings that are particularly useful for searching on the IQ debate. These include intelligence, intelligence measures, mental age, intelligence quotient, culture fair intelligence test, and intellectual development. Besides the monthly indexes, there are quarterly, annual, and triennial indexes. *Psychological Abstracts* is also available online through the *PsycINFO* and *PsycALERT* computer databases (see entries #13 and #15) and on CD-ROM format.

15.   *PsycINFO*. Washington, D.C., American Psychological Association, 1967- . monthly updates.

This database is the online equivalent to *Psychological Abstracts* (entry #14). It routinely includes books, articles, and other sources on psychology published worldwide; it also selectively covers dissertations from *Dissertation Abstracts In-*

ternational (entry #10). Available on the DIALOG and BRS database services, *PsycINFO* is complemented by its current information service database, *PsycALERT* (entry #13). It also comes out on CD-ROM.

16. *Resources in Education.* Phoenix, Ariz., Oryx Press, 1966- . monthly, with annual cumulations.

   See *Current Index to Journals in Education* (entry #9).

17. *Social Sciences Index.* New York, H. W. Wilson, 1974- . quarterly, with annual cumulations.

   This indexes articles in over 300 journals in the various social sciences and related disciplines, including sociology, psychology, and education. Article citations are arranged alphabetically by author or subject. Those relating to the IQ debate can be found under such terms as "Intelligence," "Intelligence Tests," "Intelligence Quotient," and "Nature and Nurture." Located at the end of each index volume is a book review section, which is arranged alphabetically by the name of the book's author. This index is also available online through the *Wilsonline* database service and on CD-ROM through *Wilsondisc.*

3   Handbooks

18.   Buros, Oscar Krisen, ed. *Intelligence Tests and Reviews: A Monograph Consisting of the Intelligence Sections of the Seven Mental Measurements Yearbooks (1938-72) and Tests in Print II (1974)*. Highland Park, N.J., Gryphon Press, 1975. 1129p.

This is a guide to descriptions and reviews of intelligence tests identified in editions one through seven of the *Mental Measurements Yearbook* (entry #19). The focus here is on the statistical and methodological evaluation of specific intelligence tests; there is no explicit discussion of the IQ debate. However, this would be a useful source for those wanting to review and examine particular tests. The tests are arranged first by the edition of *Mental Measurements Yearbook* (MMY) or *Tests in Print* (entry #20) in which they appear, then by whether they are group or individual tests. The test descriptions usually mention the target group, cost of the test, time of administration, and the name of the test developer. If the test has been reviewed in either *Mental Measurements Yearbook* or *Tests in Print*, the reader is directed to that review. Tests can also be located by using the title, name, publisher, and subject (scanning) indexes.

19.   Conoley, Jane Close, and Jack J. Kramer, editors. *The Tenth Mental Measurements Yearbook*. Lincoln, Nebraska, Buros Institute of Mental Measurements, University of Nebraska-Lincoln; distr., Lincoln, Nebraska, University of Nebraska Press, 1989. 1014p.

This is the single best print source for finding reviews of standardized tests in general and intelligence tests in particular. Tests are arranged alphabetically, and the citations usually include the test's target group, publisher, cost, and other basic information. There are also references to earlier editions of this yearbook where reviews of the test can be found. Additional access to the tests is provided by name, title, score, acronym, publisher, and classified subject indexes. The tenth edition of the yearbook covers tests that are new or revised since the previous edition; other tests can be identified using earlier editions of the *Mental Measurements Yearbook* or *Tests in Print* (entry #20). This information is also available online through the BRS database service.

20.   Mitchell, James V., Jr., ed. *Tests in Print III: An Index to Tests, Test Reviews, and the Literature on Specific Tests.* Lincoln, Nebraska, University of Nebraska Press, 1983. 714p.

This is a cumulative listing of and index to available tests that are found in earlier editions of *Tests in Print* and *Mental Measurements Yearbook* (entry #19). For each test cited, there is information on the appropriate target group, publisher, cost, and other test-related details. The citation also tells the user in which of the earlier editions, if any, the test was reviewed. Over and above their arrangement by broad subject or type of test, tests can be located by using the name, title, subject (scanning), and publisher indexes.

21.   *Thesaurus of ERIC Descriptors.* 11th ed. Phoenix, Ariz., Oryx Press, 1987, c1986. 588p.

This is the list of official subject categories used by ERIC to classify the articles and documents found in *Current Index to Journals in Education* (entry #9), *Resources in Education* (entry #16), and the ERIC databases (online and CD-ROM). Consulting this list of terms can help identify the most appropriate term or terms for one's topic. The thesaurus not only directs the user from unused terms to preferred terms, but also lists broader terms, related terms, and narrower terms. There is also a list of descriptor words in context (the rotated display), a hierarchical listing, and a group listing.

22.   *Thesaurus of Psychological Index Terms.* 4th ed. Washington, D.C., American Psychological Association, 1985. 263p.

This provides the alphabetical list of preferred subject terms for use in *Psychological Abstracts* (entry #15), as well as its online and CD-ROM equivalents. Arranged alphabetically, the terms are often accompanied by lists of broader, narrower, and related terms. The thesaurus also directs the user from terms that are not used to their recommended form. Like the ERIC thesaurus, it provides a list of descriptor words in the context of a complete subject heading.

23. Wolman, Benjamin B., ed. *Handbook of Intelligence: Theories, Measurements, and Applications.* New York, John Wiley and Sons, 1985. 985p.

Wolman has assembled a broad range of articles on various theories, measurements, and applications of intelligence. The first group of articles, on theories of intelligence, discuss different models of intelligence, as well as research on genetic, neurological, and cognitive aspects of intelligence. The second section, on measuring intelligence, includes articles on the validity of intelligence tests; environmental influences; the assessment of children, minorities, the culturally different, and the mentally retarded; and group intelligence tests. The articles in the final section address clinical and educational applications of intelligence tests. While the entire collection addresses issues underlying the IQ debate, there are also frequent discussions of more specific aspects of the debate itself.

4   Dictionaries and Encyclopedias

24.   Corsini, Raymond J. *Encyclopedia of Psychology*. New York, John Wiley & Sons, 1984. 4v.

This includes definitions and essays on over 2,000 terms, theories, tests, and individuals in the field of psychology. The entries, which are written by experts in the various subject areas, range from 200 to 9,000 words in length; they may also include cross-references to related terms, as well as suggestions for further reading. Many of the key technical terms, theories, and individuals in the IQ debate are defined and discussed. Volume 4 includes the name and subject indexes and a collective bibliography for the first three volumes.

25.   Wolman, Benjamin B., comp. and ed. *Dictionary of Behavioral Science*. 2d ed. San Diego, Academic Press, 1989.

This dictionary provides mostly brief definitions to thousands of terms in the behavioral sciences. Many key technical terms used in the IQ debate are included. There are also biographies of well known psychologists, including some of key figures in the history of the IQ debate (e.g. Cyril Burt, Francis Galton, Alfred Binet, Lewis Terman, Henry Goddard, Robert Yerkes). When listing multiple word terms, the dictionary gives preference to nouns (e.g. "concurrent validity" is listed as "validity, concurrent"). "See" references are used sparingly, so the user may need to look up variant wordings of the term.

II NONREFERENCE SOURCES

5   Books and Book Chapters

26.   Aronowitz, Stanley. "The Trap of Environmentalism."
      Schooling and Capitalism: A Sociological Reader. Edited by
      Roger Dale, Geoff Esland, and Madeleine MacDonald.
      London, Routledge and Kegan Paul, 1976. pp. 102-104.

      In criticizing the hereditarian position on intelligence, en-
      vironmentalists are trying to equalize the opportunities for
      minority groups and the poor; they are seeking fairness and
      equity in the selecting and sorting process by which people
      attain their position in the economy. According to
      Aronowitz, however, this will not bring about real social
      equality. Our social class structure is characterized by a
      pyramid-shaped division of labor, with relatively few highly
      rewarded, powerful positions at the top, and many positions
      with less of these qualities at the bottom. Equalizing op-
      portunities in such an unequal division of labor will not bring
      about social equality. Until the distribution of power and
      rewards in the division of labor is equalized, individuals will
      be competing to become unequal. Because of these con-
      straints in the larger class structure, Aronowitz believes that
      inequalities of race and sex will persist.

27.   Bereiter, Carl. "Genetics and Educability: Educational Im-
      plications of the Jensen Debate." *The IQ Controversy: Criti-
      cal Readings*. Edited by N. J. Block and Gerald Dworkin.
      New York, Pantheon, 1976. pp. 383-407.

      While accepting that IQ tests measure some form of innate in-
      telligence, Bereiter argues for better instruction for those with

below average IQ scores. Although these students do not possess the thinking abilities needed to do well on IQ tests or to respond to conventional methods of instruction, they can learn. Bereiter says that efforts should be made to develop instructional techniques, such as rote learning or programmed instruction, that demand less "thinking" (i.e. facility with "abstract, verbal cognitive abilities" p. 385). These techniques should capitalize on low IQ students' associative (rote) learning abilities.

Bereiter argues that a radical redistribution and improvement of existing environmental conditions for low IQ students 1) could dramatically improve the mean IQ of the population, but 2) would probably not affect the unequal distribution of scores. "Bright" students, who are innately more able thinkers, will still do better and learn more than those who are less bright. In fact, general improvement in the environment would probably increase individual differences in IQ. Bereiter suggests that it is "wishful thinking to suppose that, through conventional ameliorative efforts, we will ever stumble upon environmental variations that will interact with genetic factors in such a way as to produce dramatic compensatory effects" (pp. 395-396). It is also possible that improvements in environments reach a threshold, beyond which they have little additional effect. And improvements in educational environments may, as Jensen suggests, have only a slight effect.

28.   Biesheuvel, S. "An Examination of Jensen's Theory Concerning Educability, Heritability and Population Differences." *Race and IQ*. Edited by Ashley Montagu. New York, Oxford University Press, 1975. pp. 59-72.

Biesheuvel argues that Jensen's hypothesis is based upon the false premise that genetic racial differences in IQ are scientifically verifiable. In fact, they are difficult to verify because 1) behavior is the result of a genetic/environment interaction, 2) one cannot really control "all the relevant environmental variables" (p. 61), 3) "the measuring devices are themselves culture bound" (p. 61), and 4) we do not fully understand "the genetic basis of behavior" (p. 61).

Biesheuvel shows how Jensen does not adequately consider the subtle mechanisms by which social and nutritional environments can affect intellectual development. Furthermore, Jensen controls for gross environmental variables cross-sectionally, at one point in time, rather than longitudinally; this approach underestimates a number of environmental affects which occur earlier in a child's development. Biesheuvel also criticizes Jensen for treating IQ, an abstraction, as if it were real, and for not appreciating that heritability estimates are relative to specific, and often homogeneous, environments.

29. Blau, Zena Smith. *Black Children/White Children: Competence, Socialization, and Social Structure.* New York, Free Press, 1981. 283p.

Blau argues that her study of racial differences in intellectual competence provides "strong evidence that the sources of these differences are social, not genetic, in origin" (p. xv). Based upon data collected among black and white mothers of fifth- and sixth-grade children, she identifies the social structural and socialization variables that account for racial differences in intellectual competence. Blau looks at such variables as the mother's socioeconomic origins, religious affiliation, "marital status, number of children, duration of employment, and organizational memberships" (p. 57) to determine their affect on children's IQ and achievement test performance. She also examines socialization variables, such as the type of discipline used with the children, the valuation of education, and "the investment of time and other resources in the child" (p. 11).

30. Block, N. J., and Gerald Dworkin, eds. *The IQ Controversy: Critical Readings.* New York, Pantheon, 1976. 557p.

This is a collection of mostly reprinted articles written by many well known figures in the IQ debate. It is divided into four major parts. Part 1 is primarily a historical section that includes an exchange of articles written by Walter Lippmann and Lewis Terman in the 1920s, as well as a more recent article by David McClelland. Part 2 addresses the genetic contribution to differences in IQ; it includes articles by Arthur Jensen, Richard Lewontin, Sandra Scarr-Salapatek, and Leon Kamin, among others. Part 3 treats the social and political consequences of the hereditarian position on IQ; this includes articles by Richard Herrnstein, Carl Bereiter, Noam Chomsky, Mary Jo Bane and Christopher Jencks, Leon Kamin, and

Clarence Karier. Part 4 contains a lengthy analysis of the debate written by Block and Dworkin. While some of the articles (e.g. Jensen, Herrnstein) are supportive of a hereditarian position in the debate, most are critical of that perspective.

31.   Blum, Jeffrey M. *Pseudoscience and Mental Ability: The Origins and Fallacies of the IQ Controversy.* New York, Monthly Review Press, 1978. 240p.

Pseudoscience entails inadequate "attempts at verification" and the wide dissemination of "unwarranted conclusions drawn from such attempts" (p. 12). According to Blum, the belief that mental abilities are inherited is pseudoscience. His critique is organized into three major parts and 13 chapters. Part one provides a historical discussion and critique of the origins of the eugenics movement and psychometrics. Part two tackles some of the major issues in the current IQ debate: IQ test validity, the heritability of intelligence, racial/ethnic differences in IQ test performance, and creativity tests. Part three provides a broader discussion of how pseudoscience is possible. It also discusses the political and ideological functions served by the belief in inherited intelligence. In his final chapter, Blum puts forth an alternative view of how mental abilities should be understood.

32.   Bodmer, W. "Genetics and Intelligence: The Race Argument." *Heredity & Environment.* Edited by A. H. Halsey. New York, Free Press, 1977. pp. 312-322.

Bodmer identifies a number of issues in the IQ debate that are difficult to resolve. While Jensen and others may consider IQ tests to be a good measure of general intelligence, other researchers argue that such tests do not tap all of the dimensions of intelligence. Furthermore, intelligence "is dependent on a combination of the effects of environmental factors and the product of many different genes" (p. 315); this makes it hard to isolate their relative influences. It is also difficult to define races genetically; most genetic differences occur within races, not between them. Beyond that, our current research techniques cannot prove that the IQ differences between races are genetic in origin. In any event, Bodmer points out, IQ has been shown to be relatively insignificant in the overall determination of success. Finally, since racial differences in IQ are based on group averages, they should not be allowed to affect the equitable treatment of individuals.

33. Bowles, Samuel, and Herbert Gintis. "Education, Inequality, and the Meritocracy." *Schooling in Capitalist America: Educational Reform and the Contradictions of Economic Life.* New York, Basic Books, 1976. pp. 102-124.

The chapter is similar in many respects to the authors' "IQ in the U.S. class structure" (entries #34 or #295). Bowles and Gintis argue that the function of education in a capitalist economy is to reproduce the inequality needed in an unequal economy. The resulting inequality is accepted because both the economy and the schools are supposedly meritocracies, with everyone having an equal chance to succeed. Those who do not succeed are alleged to lack either the innate ability or the effort. In schools, unequal IQ scores help to justify the unequal educational results, which in turn are used to explain social and economic inequality. However, the authors demonstrate through statistical analysis that "IQ is not an important criterion for economic success" (p. 122). The meritocracy argument is, they argue, primarily a means of justifying or legitimating inequality.

34. Bowles, Samuel, and Herbert Gintis. "IQ in the U.S. class structure." *Identity and Structure: Issues in the Sociology of Education.* Edited by Denis Gleeson. Nafferton, England, Nafferton Books, 1977. pp. 67-102.

See entry #295.

35. Brace, C. Loring, and Frank B. Livingstone. "On Creeping Jensenism." *Race and IQ.* Edited by Ashley Montagu. New York, Oxford University Press, 1975. pp. 151-173.

The authors criticize Jensen's theory as being part of a long line of theories used to rationalize unequal treatment of certain groups based upon their physical differences from the dominant social group. More specifically, they argue that Jensen does not clearly distinguish between "individual and population performance" (p. 155) and that he does not fully control for influences of the environment. To underscore their criticism on the latter point, Brace and Livingstone discuss the importance of one specific environmental factor-- nutrition. Although stature is a highly heritable trait, improvements in nutrition improved height in Sweden and other countries by almost two standard deviations in only 100 years.

Why, the authors argue, couldn't one expect a similar effect
of nutrition on IQ or mental development? The authors discuss ways that poor nutrition could affect such development.
Jensen is also criticized for underestimating the influence of
environment in adoption studies and for assuming that two
populations would surely differ on intelligence since they differ on so many other physical characteristics.

36.   Brigham, Carl C. *A Study of American Intelligence.* Princeton, Princeton University Press, 1923. 210p.

The first part of this book is a description of the army intelligence tests administered to recruits in World War I.
Brigham reviews both the alpha (group) and beta (individual)
tests, including their administration and test items. The second part of the book is Brigham's analysis of the data, with
particular emphasis on intelligence differences between different races or nationality groups. He finds that there has
been a decline in the level of intelligence of immigrants com-
ing to the United States. This coincides, he argues, with a
decrease in the proportion of Nordic immigrants, who are
more intelligent, and an increase in the proportion of Alpine
and Mediterranean immigrants, who are less intelligent. Because of this change, as well as the inevitability of inter-
marriage between all groups, Brigham predicts a gradual
decline in the level of national intelligence. He suggests that
selective immigration restriction and other measures are
needed "to preserve or increase our present intellectual capacity" (p. 210).

37.   Bronfenbrenner, Urie. "Is Early Intervention Effective?
Some Studies of Early Education in Familial and Extra-
Familial Settings." *Race and IQ.* Edited by Ashley Montagu.
New York, Oxford University Press, 1975. pp. 287-322.

Bronfenbrenner reviews the results of a number of studies on
the effectiveness of intervention programs. He finds that
group-oriented pre-school programs are not particularly effective at producing long-term improvements in IQ. However, those that are most effective are more structured and
cognitively oriented. Bronfenbrenner suggests that many of
the problems with these programs may reside "beyond the
doors of the school" (p. 301).

The most successful programs that Bronfenbrenner reviews are those that are home-based. These programs are successful at producing long-term gains in IQ because, he argues, they entail ecological intervention (i.e. they transform the family environment), they actively involve the family in the child's development, and they involve a sequence of environments and experiences that promote child development. However, implementation of such child development strategies is dependent on our society's willingness "to make conditions of life viable and humane for all its families" (p. 317).

38. Cancro, Robert, ed. *Intelligence: Genetic and Environmental Influences.* New York, Grune & Stratton, 1971. 312p.

This is a collection of 15 papers from a conference on intelligence held at the University of Illinois. For pedagogical reasons, Cancro has separated the papers into three sections, although he acknowledges that the understanding of intelligence necessarily overlaps all three section topics. Section one addresses the theory and measurement of intelligence, and includes papers by David Wechsler and Raymond B. Cattell, among others. Section two focuses on genetic contributions to intelligence, and its seven papers include articles by Jerry Hirsch and Bruce Eckland. The papers in section three address primarily environmental contributions to intelligence; Edmund W. Gordon and J. McVicker Hunt are among the contributors.

39. Chapman, Paul Davis. *Schools as Sorters: Lewis M. Terman, Applied Psychology, and the Intelligence Testing Movement, 1890-1930.* New York, New York University Press, 1988. 228p.

Chapman analyzes the major factors leading to the establishment of intelligence testing as a selecting and sorting mechanism in the schools. The first factor was the development of the field of psychology. Chapman traces the role of Lewis Terman and other early psychologists in demonstrating the socially useful applications of this new field. The mental testing of World War I recruits helped greatly in legitimizing psychology in general and mental testing in particular. Pioneering projects in certain California schools further laid the groundwork for the widespread adoption of mental tests. The second contributing factor was the growing diversity of the public school population, primarily as a result of increased immigration. Mental testing offered a means of sorting a growing student population that varied both by cultural background and, so the psychologists believed, by innate ability. Finally, underlying the converging agendas of psychologists and school administrators was the Progressive Era belief in social reform and social efficiency.

40.   Chomsky, Noam. "IQ Tests: Building Blocks for the New Class System." *Shaping the American Educational State: 1900 to the Present.* Edited by Clarence J. Karier. New York, Free Press, 1975. pp. 393-406.

Chomsky is responding critically to Richard Herrnstein's 1971 *Atlantic* magazine article entitled "IQ" (entry #316). Herrnstein's basic argument is that the United States is gradually becoming a "stable hereditary meritocracy," with the innately intelligent occupying the most important and well-paid positions in society.

Chomsky takes issue with a number of Herrnstein's assumptions. For example, Herrnstein assumes that the only way to motivate the intelligent to undertake important jobs is by the lure of material gain. But why, Chomsky asks, must this necessarily be so? If work were undertaken for its intrinsic rewards, then unequal material rewards would not be necessary. Furthermore, Chomsky disputes the assumption that the most socially important positions receive the highest rewards. In an unequal, free market society, the highest rewards go to those who serve the needs and interests of the wealthy and powerful. Chomsky also questions Herrnstein's assumption that those attaining "social success" do so primarily because of their intelligence. Other traits, such as being "ruthless, cunning, avaricious, self-seeking, lacking in sympathy and compassion, subservient to authority" (p. 400) may be equally or more important.

Finally, Chomsky addresses the social consequences and scientific usefulness of research into the correlation between race and IQ. In a racist society, such research would surely lend support to racists, even if that were not the researcher's intent. Therefore, it is incumbent upon researchers to weigh such factors against the scientific significance of the research. In fact, Chomsky does not find research into the race/IQ correlation inherently interesting, certainly not any more so than the relationship of height and IQ. It is only the existence of racism, and the mistreatment of individuals according to their racial category, that makes the subject interesting.

41. Cravens, Hamilton. "Mental Testing." *The Triumph of Evolution: American Scientists and the Heredity-Environment Controversy 1900-1941*. Philadelphia, University of Pennsylvania Press, 1978. pp. 224-265.

Cravens reviews some of the history of the mental testing debate in the United States as it reflects the broader heredity vs. environment controversy. The debate centered around three basic issues: racial and ethnic differences in intelligence, the relationship between intelligence and crime, and the relationship between intelligence and social status. Relying upon the World War I army data, hereditarians like Carl Brigham and Robert Yerkes argued that there were inferior and superior races and nationalities. Others argued that low intelligence led not only to crime and immoral behavior, but also to low social status. However, Cravens explains that still other psychologists, who identified methodological problems with the hereditarian research, found social and environmental explanations for some of the observed correlations. Ultimately, the interaction and interdependence of nature and nurture became the more favored position in psychology.

42. Eckberg, Douglas Lee. *Intelligence and Race: The Origins and Dimensions of the IQ Controversy*. New York, Praeger, 1979. 275p.

Eckberg critically examines four major assumptions in the hereditarian position on IQ: 1) that intelligence tests actually measure a unitary intelligence; 2) that individuals can be ranked on this "global mental ability;" 3) that intelligence is socially important for success and achievement; and 4) that intelligence is genetically determined. The first part of the book demonstrates that these assumptions are theoretically and empirically weak. The last half of the book is a historical analysis of how these assumptions came to be embedded in hereditarian psychology and of how they became taken for granted by both supporters and many critics of the hereditarian perspective.

43.   Eckland, Bruce K. "Social Class Structure and the Genetic Basis of Intelligence." *Intelligence: Genetic and Environmental Influences.* Edited by Robert Cancro. New York, Grune & Stratton, 1971. pp. 65-76.

Eckland argues that social class inequality may be due not simply to unequal opportunities, but to social class differences in intelligence. This follows from a number of related points. First, our society is a meritocracy in which educational and occupational success is based upon rewarding those who are more able or intelligent. Second, parents pass on 50% of their genes to their offspring, accounting for a certain amount of similarity in intelligence. Third, the fact that people tend to marry those like themselves (i.e. assortative mating) further increases the genetic, intellectual similarity between parents and children. Consequently, those who are intelligent and successful will be likely to have more intelligent children, who in turn will be more likely to achieve a high social class position. Eckland suggests that as equality of opportunity becomes widespread, social class differences may be increasingly explained by genetic differences in intelligence.

44.   Ehrlich, Paul R., and S. Shirley Feldman. *The Race Bomb: Skin Color, Prejudice, and Intelligence.* New York, Quadrangle, 1977. 207p.

Ehrlich and Feldman address six basic issues: 1) are there biological races?; 2) what are the implications of socially defined races?; 3) what is intelligence and what do intelligence tests measure?; 4) is IQ inherited?; 5) are there racial differences in intelligence?; and 6) even if there are racial differences in inherited IQ, what difference does it make? They argue that race is not a valid biological category. However, it does have a social reality, and scientific racism helps to justify prejudice and discrimination based on race. The authors dispute the hereditarian evidence from the major twin and adoption studies and counter with studies of racial admixture and transracial adoptions that support an environmental explanation of racial differences in IQ. They then outline major environmental factors that affect IQ; these include such factors as test bias, language differences, motivation, test administration, family environment, nutrition, and educational inequities.

45. Elliott, Rogers. *Litigating Intelligence: IQ Tests, Special Education, and Social Science in the Courtroom.* Dover, Massachusetts, Auburn House, 1987. 226p.

Elliott reviews and analyzes two major court cases challenging the use of IQ tests in placing minority children in classes for the educable mentally retarded: Larry P. v. Riles in California, and PASE v. Hannon in Chicago. Elliott examines the testimony, the legal strategies, the social and political contexts in which the trials took place, and the behavior of the judges. He not only attempts to explain the different outcomes of the two trials, but also addresses whether the plaintiffs were well served by the decisions. Finally, Elliott explores whether the courtroom's adversarial environment can allow for the objective consideration of social science research.

46. Evans, Brian, and Bernard Waites. *IQ and Mental Testing: An Unnatural Science and its Social History.* London, Macmillan, 1981. 228p.

The first part of this book is a critical analysis of the historical development of the mental testing movement in Britain. The authors trace the establishment of psychometric theory, as well as the influence of both eugenics and the fears of a declining national intelligence. The analysis then shows the contribution of mental testing toward the rationalization of vocational selection and educational inequality. In the latter area, the authors explain the role of mental testing in Britain's 11+ exams and the related tracking of students. Part two of the book deals with many of the scientific and methodological issues in the IQ debate. In particular, the authors are critical of the concept of general intelligence ("g") and of the kinship, twin, and adoption studies used to support heritability estimates.

47. Eysenck, H. J. "The Biological Basis of Intelligence." *Human Abilities in Cultural Context.* Edited by S. H. Irvine and J. W. Berry. Cambridge, Cambridge University Press, 1988. pp. 87-104.

Eysenck argues that current evidence supports Sir Francis Galton's view that there is a general factor of intelligence underlying all intelligent behavior and that intelligence is innate. In fact, current theorists distinguish between Intelligence A (innate intelligence), Intelligence B (intelligence A reflected in practical behavior), and Intelligence C (measures of intelligence). However, it has been difficult to measure innate intelligence, and current IQ tests tap both innate intelligence and acquired knowledge. For Eysenck, two of the most promising efforts to measure Intelligence A are measures of reaction time and of evoked potentials. Both of these biological measures seem to correlate well with IQ and may be good cross-cultural measures of intelligence. Eysenck briefly touches on how these data would fit into a general theory of intelligence.

48.   Eysenck, H. J. *The Inequality of Man.* San Diego, EdITS Publishers, 1975. 288p.

Writing for a popular audience, Eysenck attempts to document the genetic basis for many human behaviors and inequalities. In particular, he focuses on intelligence, personality, mental illness, and crime. The first three chapters deal with intelligence. Eysenck reasserts and demonstrates the existence of a general factor of intelligence, "g." The following chapter reviews the various lines of evidence (e.g. twin studies, adoption studies) that show that intelligence differences are largely hereditary in origin. In the final chapter on intelligence, Eysenck argues that educational achievement and social class standing are a result, in large part, of one's innate intelligence. He disputes the contention that differences in school variables, social class background, teacher expectations, or other environmental variables account for much of one's school and social success.

49.   Eysenck, H. J. *Race, Intelligence and Education.* London, Temple Smith, 1971. 160p.

Eysenck's defense of the hereditarian research and findings of Jensen and others centers around five chapters: "The Jensenist heresy"; "What is race?"; "What is intelligence?"; "The intelligence of American negroes"; and "Changing human nature." He first defends the appropriateness of Arthur Jensen's research into hereditary differences in intelligence, including racial differences. Eysenck then reviews and justifies the validity of definitions of race and intelligence; he also shows how intelligence is instrumental in achieving educational and occupational success. Drawing upon the research review of

Audrey Shuey, Eysenck supports the contention that blacks are, on the average, less intelligent than whites. Eysenck concludes by calling for further research. He is not optimistic about changing the genotypic basis of intelligence and intelligence differences. However, he does see the possibility and value of new discoveries in environmental manipulation.

50. Eysenck, H. J., and Leon Kamin. *The Intelligence Controversy.* New York, John Wiley and Sons, 1981. 192p.

Hans Eysenck and Leon Kamin are each given approximately half of this book to argue their case either for (Eysenck) or against (Kamin) the hereditarian position on intelligence. The bulk of the volume is devoted to each author's major essay. Eysenck's essay discusses such issues as the origin of IQ tests, their relationship to achievement, the regression to the mean, racial and cultural differences in IQ, and the influence of environment. Kamin critiques not only the historical development of IQ testing and the work of Sir Cyril Burt, but also the adoption studies, twin studies, and kinship correlations. The last, and smaller, portion of the book consists of each author's rejoinder to the other's essay. This volume was published in Britain under the title *Intelligence: The Battle for the Mind* (entry #51).

51. Eysenck, H. J., and Leon Kamin. *Intelligence: The Battle for the Mind.* London, Macmillan, 1981. 192p.

This is identical to *The Intelligence Controversy.* See entry #50.

52. Fancher, Raymond E. *The Intelligence Men: Makers of the IQ Controversy.* New York, W. W. Norton, 1985. 269p.

Fancher provides a historical overview of the IQ debate by focusing on the biographies and ideas of key individuals in the evolution of the debate. The individuals covered include John Stuart Mill, Francis Galton, James McKeen Cattell, Alfred Binet, Charles Spearman, William Stern, Henry Goddard, Robert Yerkes, Lewis Terman, David Wechsler, Cyril Burt, Arthur Jensen, and Leon Kamin. For each individual, Fancher attempts to identify the historical and biographical circumstances that generated their interest in the topic. Fancher also relates each person's research to the work which had preceded it and to some broad stages in the evolution of the debate. These stages include the early nature-nurture controversy, the invention and redefinition of intelligence tests, the rise of intelligence testing, and the research on twins and the genetics of intelligence.

53.   Farber, Susan L. *Identical Twins Reared Apart: A Reanalysis*. New York, Basic Books, 1981. 383p.

Farber reanalyzes previous twin studies in light of recent research and current, more rigorous methodological requirements. Specifically, she reviews twin data relating to such factors as appearance and other normative traits, physical symptoms, psychosis, IQ, and personality. Regarding IQ, Farber finds the process of pooling the twin data, and even the data themselves, questionable. Her reanalysis suggests the untenability of the hypothesis that IQ differences are determined primarily by heredity. On the whole, Farber finds that most of the earlier twin studies do not meet acceptable methodological standards; they suffer from a "biased and limited sample and the inconsistent quality of data" (p. 268). The influence of environment was significantly underestimated, owing to such factors as mutual contact or lack of separation of the twins. While not dismissing the role of heredity, Farber suggests that we should focus on patterns of development, as suggested by Piaget, rather than on the inheritance of specific, stable traits like intelligence.

54.   Fine, Benjamin. *The Stranglehold of I.Q.* Garden City, N. Y., Doubleday & Co., 1975. 278p.

Fine makes a broad range of criticisms of intelligence tests. He finds fault not only with the definition of intelligence, but also with the tests' method of construction, their questions, and their use in schools for the tracking of students. Fine counters the argument that intelligence is mostly hereditary by discussing specific cases and studies showing the significant effect of school and family environments on children's IQ scores. He also contends that a low IQ score can unfairly lead to a self-fulfilling prophecy, in which a child's educational treatment and achievement suffer. Consequently, Fine recommends the abolition of not only intelligence tests, but also all standardized tests, which "too often are inaccurate, invalid, and misleading" (p. 138). He favors, instead, criterion-based tests constructed by the teacher.

55. Flynn, James R. *Race, IQ and Jensen*. London, Routledge & Kegan Paul, 1980. 313p.

Flynn concedes that Arthur Jensen has constructed a very strong case for the hereditarian explanation of racial differences in intelligence. Its strength comes from Jensen's two-pronged attack, in which he 1) provides evidence of the heritability of racial differences in intelligence and 2) discredits suggested environmental causes for that difference. Flynn's critique is that there exists direct evidence, as opposed to Jensen's indirect evidence, of environmental causes of racial differences in IQ. This evidence includes the Minnesota adoption study, studies of racial admixture, and research on occupation children of mixed marriages in Germany. Flynn explores a number of environmental variables, such as nutrition, parent-child interaction, self-image, and early childhood stimulation, which might explain racial differences in IQ.

56. Galton, Sir Francis, F.R.S. *Hereditary Genius: An Inquiry Into Its Laws and Consequences*. New York, Horizon Press, 1952. 379p.

Galton's purpose is to demonstrate that genius is innate. He rejects emphatically the idea "that babies are born pretty much alike..." (p. 12). After all, since many physical attributes are distributed among the population along the lines of the normal curve, would not the same hold true for the distribution of intelligence? To prove his argument, he attempts to show that eminent men have eminent kin. "Eminence" for Galton means that one's reputation and achievements are matched by only one in 4,000 men. He argues that an eminent reputation is a reflection of natural abilities, not of opportunities afforded by accident of birth. Social advantages cannot keep those with "moderate ability" (p. 36) in the eminent category, nor can social obstacles thwart the eventual success of the truly eminent.

Galton identifies "eminent" men from among judges, statesmen, literary men, scientists, and others. For these individuals, Galton shows the high number of eminent relatives. This, he argues, demonstrates that the qualities needed for achieving eminence are hereditary.

57.   Garber, H., and F. R. Heber. "The Milwaukee Project: In-
       dications of the Effectiveness of Early Intervention in Pre-
       venting Mental Retardation." *Research to Practice in Mental
       Retardation: Volume I, Care and Intervention.* Edited by
       Peter Mittler. Baltimore, University Park Press, 1977. pp.
       119-127.

       Garber and Heber summarize some of the tentative findings
       of their Milwaukee Project, which was an experimental inter-
       vention program aimed at preventing mild mental retardation.
       They suggested that children coming from disadvantaged
       backgrounds, who had mothers with IQs less than 80, were at
       the greatest risk of mild mental retardation. An experimental
       group of such children was identified, and the family was
       subjected to an intensive and comprehensive family rehabili-
       tation program; the hope was that this intervention would "al-
       low normal intellectual development" (p. 120). In fact, Gar-
       ber and Heber found this to be the case, with the experimen-
       tal children having significantly higher IQ scores than the
       control group by the time they entered school. This suggested
       to the authors that mild mental retardation was preventable
       and was not primarily determined by genetics. The authors
       caution that family interventions need to be sensitive to the
       varying needs of each family. Furthermore, school-age expe-
       riences can undermine the effects of these intervention pro-
       grams.

58.   Garber, Howard L., and Rick Heber. "The Efficacy of Early
       Intervention with Family Rehabilitation." *Psychosocial In-
       fluences in Retarded Performance: Volume II, Strategies for
       Improving Competence.* Edited by Michael J. Begab, H. Carl
       Haywood, and Howard L. Garber. Baltimore, University Park
       Press, 1981. pp. 71-87.

       This is a report of the findings and follow-up assessment of a
       family intervention and rehabilitation project, the Milwaukee
       Project. Its purpose was to identify at an early age children
       at risk of mental retardation and to intervene in their family
       and educational experiences so as to avert that retardation.
       The experimental group of at-risk children, as well as their
       mothers, were subjected to intensive intervention programs
       and services for approximately six years, until the children
       entered school. After the intervention, Garber and Heber
       found the experimental group's IQ scores to be approximately

30 points higher than the control group's scores (120.7 vs. 87.2). Four years later, there still remained a 20 IQ point advantage for the experimental group. The authors caution that at-risk families are different in important ways, so the interventions should be tailored to each family's circumstances. Furthermore, more needs to be known about how to sustain the improvements within the environments of the disadvantaged.

59. Gartner, Alan, Colin Greer, and Frank Riessman, eds. *The New Assault on Equality: IQ and Social Stratification.* New York, Harper and Row, 1974. 225p.

This is a collection of eight articles critical of IQ, most of which were originally published in the journal *Social Policy*. The contributors include Samuel Bowles and Herbert Gintis (entry #295), Noam Chomsky (entry #40), Ross A. Evans, Jerome Kagan, George Purvin, David McClelland (entry #98), Stanley Aronowitz (entry #26), and Frank Riessman. The editors envisioned the articles as a counter to what they called the "contemporary meritocratic illusion mechanism" (pp. 5-6), the IQ test. By this, they meant that the tests gave the appearance of rewarding the intelligent. The reality, however, was that the tests rationalized limiting "the opportunities of immigrants, blacks, and third world people" (p. 1)

60. Gould, Stephen Jay. *The Mismeasure of Man.* New York, Norton, 1981. 352p.

Gould's book is a critique of a number of theories that fall under the general category of scientific racism. The last half of the book focuses on the theory that intelligence is inherited. Specifically, Gould chronicles the establishment and misuse of the concept of innate intelligence by psychologists in the U. S. and Britain.

The first part of this critique looks at the roles of H. H. Goddard, Lewis M. Terman, R. M. Yerkes, and C. C. Brigham in the early intelligence testing movement in the United States. According to Gould, these theorists misused Alfred Binet's work on intelligence, primarily as a result of their preexisting eugenic beliefs. Where Binet saw the intelligence test as a diagnostic tool to be used in identifying students needing remedial help, Terman et al. converted it into a test of innate

abilities and limitations. Yerkes' use of the test on World War
I army recruits helped to legitimize both the test and the field
of psychology. Providing apparent scientific evidence of the
intellectual inferiority of certain nationalities and races, the
test was consequently used to help pass the Immigration
Restriction Act of 1924. Gould criticizes not only the content
of the test and the conditions under which it was administered, but also the interpretation of the results.

The second part of Gould's critique examines the work of Sir
Cyril Burt, Charles Spearman, L. L. Thurstone, and Arthur
Jensen. Gould's criticism is that these theorists reified the
concept of intelligence. That is, they took an abstract concept, intelligence, and treated it as if it were a real entity.
They did this through the use of factor analysis; the misuse of
this statistical technique allowed them to find a factor --
called "g" or general intelligence -- that seemed to run
through one's performance on all intelligence tests. Gould
points out, however, that this was a consequence of the
statistical technique used. To consider such an abstraction
real, as these theorists did, was not scientifically justified.
His discussion of the work of L. L. Thurstone, and Thurstone's disagreement with Burt and Spearman, highlights this
problem.

61.   Gould, Stephen Jay. "Racist Arguments and IQ." *Ever Since
Darwin: Reflections in Natural History*. New York, Norton,
1979. pp. 243-247.

The idea that races are genetically endowed with different
levels of intelligence is, Gould argues, unsupported by
scientific evidence. Still, proponents of the position managed
to gain passage of the Immigration Restriction Act of 1924,
which limited immigration of those from allegedly less intelligent races and countries. The position persists currently
in the arguments of Arthur Jensen.

Gould says that Jensen's 1969 *Harvard Educational Review* article, "How Much Can We Boost I.Q. and Scholastic Achievement?" is wrong on three different levels. First, Jensen assumes that IQ scores measure intelligence. Yet while IQ
scores do correlate with school success, this does not prove
that they measure intelligence. Rather, they could be measuring how middle-class a child is, or how good an "apple-

polisher" the child is; it may be these factors, not "intelligence," that contribute to success in school.

Second, Gould says Jensen is wrong about the assumed heritability of IQ and the implication that it cannot be affected environmentally. Other clearly inherited characteristics can be changed environmentally (e.g. poor vision is highly heritable, yet it is easily corrected with glasses); why couldn't the same be true of intelligence? Furthermore, the evidence supporting the heritability of IQ is flawed. Leon Kamin has shown that Sir Cyril Burt's research data on identical twins raised apart are implausible, if not fraudulent. Also, subsequent twin studies did not account for the fact that twins' scores will correlate because of age and sex similarities.

Third, Jensen is confused about variations within and between groups. Even if IQ scores are 80% heritable within a group (e.g. whites), this does not mean that the 15 point difference between whites and blacks is therefore genetic in origin.

Gould contends that the genetic argument persists for political, not scientific, reasons. In the face of continuing poverty and inequality, it is politically expedient to blame the victims for their genetic deficiencies rather than to blame the system.

62.   Halsey, A. H., ed. *Heredity & Environment*. New York, Free Press, 1977. 337p.

This edited collection of articles treats the nature vs. nurture or heredity vs. environment debate. However, the last two sections focus more specifically on the issue of IQ. The articles in part three, "IQ and social stratification," generally address the issue of environmental and genetic factors in inequality; most of these articles predate the resurgent IQ debate that followed Jensen's 1969 article. Part four, "IQ, genetics, and race," contains articles specifically on the race and IQ debate. The four articles in this section were contributed by Arthur Jensen (entry #72), Phillip V. Tobias (entry #131), G. Smith and T. James (entry #118), and W. Bodmer (entry #32).

63.   Hearnshaw, L. S. "Posthumous Controversies." *Cyril Burt: Psychologist*. Ithaca, Cornell University Press, 1979. pp. 227-261.

Burt has been accused of fabricating data in his research on
the IQs of twins, IQ and social mobility, and declining national intelligence. In reviewing the evidence, Hearnshaw
finds seriously flawed and fabricated data in each case.
However, he agrees with Nicholas Wade's assessment that it is
difficult to determine how many of the flaws are due to
"fraud,...carelessness, or something in between" (p. 237).
Hearnshaw concludes that it is unfair and overly simplistic to
call all of Burt's work fraudulent.

64.   Henderson, Paul. "Class Structure and the Concept of In-
      telligence." *Schooling and Capitalism: A Sociological
      Reader*. Edited by Roger Dale, Geoff Esland, and Madeleine
      MacDonald. London, Routledge and Kegan Paul, 1976. pp.
      142-151.

According to Henderson, the argument over whether intelligence is determined by heredity, environment, or both,
misses the point. He argues that the more fundamental issue
is to explain the social basis of the conception of intelligence.
Where did this conception come from, and what purpose does
it serve? Henderson's point is that "intelligence" is a middle-
class construction, embodying the values, characteristics, and
behaviors of that class. As a result, this conception of intelligence serves to restrict upward social mobility to those individuals having these traits. This, of course, favors the middle class, and thus, helps to perpetuate the existing social class
structure.

65.   Herrnstein, R. J. *I.Q. in the Meritocracy*. Boston, Atlantic
      Monthly Press, 1973. 235p.

This book is a much expanded version of Herrnstein's article
on I.Q. from the *Atlantic Monthly* magazine (#316). After
recounting the reactions to his work both by the left and by
liberal, environmentally-oriented academics, he addresses historical, scientific, and policy-related aspects of I.Q. The first
two chapters discuss the historical origins of intelligence testing and the evolution of definitions of intelligence, respectively. Chapter three treats the uses of intelligence, with
Herrnstein suggesting that intelligence correlates with and
probably determines educational and social success. Chapter
four covers the nature vs. nurture debate, with Herrnstein
supporting the "nature" or hereditarian perspective. He

presents research data on foster children, identical twins, and others showing that intelligence is approximately 80% heritable. Herrnstein concludes by suggesting that as environmental inequities are eliminated, our society will become a meritocracy in which inequality is based on hereditary differences in ability.

66.   Hirsch, Jerry. "Behavior-Genetic Analysis and Its Biosocial Consequences." *The IQ Controversy: Critical Readings.* Edited by N. J. Block and Gerald Dworkin. New York, Pantheon, 1976. pp. 156-178.

After a brief overview of some historical examples of scientific racism, Hirsch discusses the scientific difficulties in determining the heritability of intelligence.   He cautions that 1) heritability estimates apply only to a specific population, 2) there are many sources of environmental variation, and 3) gene frequencies, and therefore heritability, can vary across generations. These and related considerations demonstrate the wide variety of ways that genes and environments can interact; this makes heritability estimates very problematic, if not "deceptive and trivial" (p. 168).

Hirsch identifies two "conceptual blunders" involved in trying to compare races on their inherited intelligence. First, heritability estimates for a population tell us nothing about the specific contributions of genes and environments to any particular individual in that population. Second, even a highly heritable trait can potentially be improved in different environments. Hirsch finishes by reviewing some research that provides useful models for studying the effects of genes and environments on human behaviors.

67.   Hunt, J. McV. *Intelligence and Experience.* New York, Ronald Press, 1961. 416p.

Hunt challenges the traditional beliefs that intelligence is fixed and that its development is predetermined. While conceding that genes impose broad limits on intelligence, Hunt contends that various lines of research demonstrate the role of experience in intellectual development. This research includes findings from neuropsychology, animal learning studies, stimulus-response methodology, computer programming, and the work of Jean Piaget. According to Hunt, this evidence

makes the belief in fixed intelligence and predetermined development untenable, and supports efforts "to discover ways
to govern the encounters that children have with their environments, especially during the early years of their development, to achieve a substantially faster rate of intellectual development and a substantially higher adult level of intellectual
capacity" (p. 363).

68.   Jensen, Arthur R. *Bias in Mental Testing*. New York, Free
       Press, 1980. 786p.

Jensen systematically defends mental tests (achievement, aptitude, and intelligence) against the charge that they are
biased. The first chapter categorizes and reviews the variety
of criticisms made against mental tests in general and against
intelligence tests in particular. The second chapter reviews
the court decisions which have, for the most part, limited the
use of intelligence tests for employee selection and educational placement. Subsequent chapters address issues that relate to potential bias in mental tests. These include such
topics as the distribution of mental ability, mental test items,
whether IQ tests measure intelligence, the validity and
reliability of mental tests, correlates of mental tests, internal
criteria and external sources of bias, sex bias, and culture-
reduced tests. The various lines of evidence indicate, according to Jensen, that mental tests "are not biased with respect to
any native-born, English-speaking minority groups in the
United States" (p. 715).

69.   Jensen, Arthur R. *Educability and Group Differences*.
       London, Methuen, 1973. 407p.

Jensen challenges what he perceives to be the dominant, environmental expalantions of group, including black-white,
differences in intelligence. After a preface in which he dis
cusses the legitimacy of scientific research on this topic,
Jensen proceeds to address many of the technical and political
issues and attempts to refute some of the environmentalists'
criticisms on these topics. The issues include intelligence and
educability, within-group vs. between-groups heritability,
race and social class differences in intelligence, teacher expectations, the culture bias of IQ tests, inequality of schooling, and studies of racial hybrids or racial admixture, among
others.

70.   Jensen, Arthur R. *Genetics and Education.* New York, Harper & Row, 1972. 379p.

This is a collection of previously published articles written by Arthur Jensen treating the issue of genetic differences in intelligence. The articles deal with such issues as intelligence and mental retardation, heritability estimates and twins, and ethics and genetic research. Also included is Jensen's *Harvard Educational Review* article, "How Much Can We Boost IQ and Scholastic Achievement?" (see entry #207), a preface reviewing the controversy surrounding that article's publication, and a bibliography of articles written about the article. There is an additional bibliography of articles and books written by Jensen on the issue of genetics and individual differences.

71.   Jensen, Arthur R. "Heredity, Environment, and Intelligence." *The Encyclopedia of Education.* Vol. 4. Lee C. Deighton, editor-in-chief. New York, Macmillan Company and The Free Press, 1971. pp. 368-380.

After defining intelligence and explaining its key role in educability and achievement, Jensen discusses a method for estimating its heritability. Heritability refers to the amount of variation in a characteristic (e.g. intelligence) that is attributable to genetic differences. Jensen presents a formula for estimating heritability and analyzes its genetic and environmental components. He then addresses some of the common misconceptions about heritability. Following this, he reviews the major empirical findings from twin studies, adoption studies, and kinship studies that suggest intelligence is approximately 80% heritable. The educational implications of these findings are that schooling should provide "a range and diversity of educational methods, programs, and goals, and of occupational opportunities, just as wide as the range of human abilities" (p. 379).

72.   Jensen, Arthur R. "Race and mental ability." *Heredity & Environment.* Edited by A. H. Halsey. New York, Free Press, 1977. pp. 215-262.

Arthur Jensen's article begins by reviewing evolutionary and genetic mechanisms that can create group differences in behavioral traits (e.g. intelligence). He then presents evidence supporting a genetic explanation of black/white differences in intelligence; he also refutes environmental explanations of the difference, including theories of cultural deficit, test bias, and language deprivation.

73.   Jensen, Arthur R.   "Race and the Genetics of Intelligence: A Reply to Lewontin." *The IQ Controversy: Critical Readings.* Edited by N. J. Block and Gerald Dworkin. New York, Pantheon, 1976. pp. 93-106.

Responding to a critique by Richard Lewontin (see entry #85), Jensen asserts that the research indicates consistent deficiencies by blacks on IQ tests and in school performance and that compensatory education programs did not alter these deficiencies. These programs failed, he contends, because they did not take into account "individual differences in developmental rates, patterns of ability, and learning styles" (p. 95). Not all students have the same levels of intelligence (i.e. abstract reasoning abilities), even though they are similar in associative (rote) learning capabilities. Teaching should be geared to a student's strengths and should not assume that all students are basically the same.

Jensen reasserts that there are average differences in intelligence between the social classes and races. Furthermore, the higher reproductive rate of blacks with lower average IQs represents a "dysgenic trend." As a result, genetic differences in intelligence between whites and blacks could become worse. Jensen points out that he knows of no educational or psychological intervention that can raise IQs. Defending his use of heritability in explaining black-white differences in intelligence, Jensen maintains that the magnitude of the heritability of intelligence within a population makes it probable that the difference between the groups is genetic. Lastly, in criticizing an environmental explanation, he points out that American Indians do better than blacks on IQ and achievement tests despite having worse environmental conditions.

74.   Jensen, Arthur R.   *Straight Talk About Mental Tests.* New York, Free Press, 1981. 269p.

Written for the general reader, this book represents Jensen's overview of the key issues and evidence in the IQ debate. Chapter one addresses the nature of intelligence, the development and uses of intelligence tests, and their validity and reliability. Chapter two focuses on the structure of mental abilities, with special emphasis on the existence of general intelligence or "g". Chapter three concentrates on the principles of genetics and various types of research demonstrating the inheritance of intelligence (e.g. kinship correlations, twin studies). Chapter four deals with the issue of test bias in general and racial bias in particular. Chapter five reviews the sources of environmental influence on IQ, while chapter six discusses the evidence for racial and social class differences in IQ. Chapter seven includes Jensen's responses to numerous questions put to him in correspondence. Throughout, Jensen affirms his position that intelligence differences are approximately 70% heritable and that mental tests are valid, reliable, and unbiased.

75. Joseph, Andre. *Intelligence, IQ and Race--When, How and Why They Became Associated.* San Francisco, R & E Research Associates, Inc., 1977. 142p.

The first part of the book focuses on Alfred Binet's intelligence tests, which were intended to be diagnostic in nature. Joseph then discusses how Binet's work was adapted to the United States. In this adaptation, American intelligence testers reinterpreted the test as a measure of innate ability; this, according to Joseph, was consistent with their eugenic beliefs in the superiority and inferiority of different races or ethnic groups. Joseph also reviews various explanations of the relationship between race and intelligence. This relationship has been confounded by difficulties in defining and establishing one's race and by the influence of ethnicity and social class. He also discusses different models of Black socialization used to explain the social position of Blacks; these include the deficit model, the cultural difference model, and the bicultural model. Joseph calls for more culturally sensitive tests and for a return to their constructive use as diagnostic tools.

76. Joynson, Robert B. *The Burt Affair.* London, Routledge, 1989. 347p.

Joynson defends Sir Cyril Burt against the accusations that significant parts of his research and writing were fraudulent. Specifically, Joynson addresses three major charges: 1) that

Burt misrepresented his own role, and thus minimized Charles Spearman's role, in the application of factor analysis to the field of psychology; 2) that Burt fabricated data, and even invented research assistants, in his kinship and twin studies; and 3) that Burt fabricated data both on educational standards and on the relationship between intelligence and occupational class. After reviewing the charges and evidence, Joynson argues that Burt has not received fair consideration and that there are reasonable explanations and defenses for Burt's behavior and findings. Joynson also defends Burt against the charge that he became mentally unstable in his later years, and that this led to his alleged fraudulent behavior. Finally, Joynson reconstructs and criticizes the events leading both to the charges of fraud and to their general endorsement.

77.   Juel-Nielsen, Niels. *Individual and Environment: A Psychiatric-Psychological Investigation of Monozygotic Twins Reared Apart.* Copenhagen, Munksgaard, 1965. 158p. and 292p. in two parts.

This is a Danish study of 12 twin pairs (nine female, three male) who ranged in age from 22 to 77. Juel-Nielsen interviewed, tested, and examined the twins on a variety of medical, psychological, personality, and psychometric characteristics, including intelligence, with the intent of further understanding the relative contributions of heredity and environment to "phenotypical differences" (e.g. personality, intelligence). According to Juel-Nielsen, the intelligence test scores of the twins were similar enough, in light of their separated rearing environments, to suggest that genes play a considerable and predominant role in intelligence. The first half of the book discusses the study's methods, findings, and limitations, as well as its relation to other twin studies; the last half comprises the appended and detailed case material on each twin pair.

78.   Kamin, Leon J. "Heredity, Intelligence, Politics, and Psychology: II." *The IQ Controversy: Critical Readings.* Edited by N. J. Block and Gerald Dworkin. New York, Pantheon, 1976. pp. 374-382.

This is a brief critique of some of the origins of the intelligence testing movement in the U.S. and of the underlying prejudices of the movement's early promoters. Specifically,

Kamin documents the racial and ethnic biases of such early testers as Henry Goddard, Robert Yerkes, and Lewis Terman. These individuals supported, through research and/or eugenics societies, restrictions on immigration into the U.S. of people from certain countries. The ultimate reflection of their influence on this issue was the passage of the restrictive immigration law of 1924.

79. Kamin, Leon J. *The Science and Politics of I.Q.* Harmondsworth, England, Penguin, 1974. 252pp. index.

Kamin criticizes the pioneers of the IQ testing movement in the U.S. as being biased by their beliefs in the innate intellectual inferiority of certain races, nationalities and ethnic groups. These prejudices were reflected in the restrictive immigration policies of the 1920s. The bulk of Kamin's analysis is a critique of the three major types of research used to support a hereditarian explanation of intelligence differences: twin studies, kinship correlations, and adoption studies. For all three types of research, Kamin finds flaws in the evidence and its interpretation; hereditarian explanations are promoted, he argues, while plausible environmental explanations are ignored. Finally, Kamin discusses the danger of so many IQ researchers relying uncritically on secondary sources. He also disputes other claims about the harmful effect of intrauterine experience and inbreeding on later IQ.

80. Krasner, William. *Labeling the Children.* Rockville, Md., U.S. Department of Health, Education, and Welfare, National Institute of Mental Health, Mental Health Studies and Reports Branch; Washington, GPO, 1977. 21p.

Krasner reviews Jane Mercer's research finding that schools harm students when IQ tests are used to identify the mentally retarded. In an eight year study in Riverside, California, Mercer found that schools were basing their diagnoses of mental retardation almost exclusively on IQ tests. However, these tests were unfair to minorities and ethnic groups, whose cultural experiences were different from those of the dominant culture. Consequently, an inordinately large number of these ethnic and minority students were incorrectly diagnosed as being mentally retarded. This labeling, in turn, resulted in a restriction of the students' learning opportunities. As a result, Mercer created SOMPA (System of Multicultural

Pluralistic Assessment), which is a multi-faceted and more culture-fair model for assessing children and identifying mental retardation.

81.   Lawler, James M. *IQ, Heritability and Racism.* New York, International Publishers, 1978. 192pp.

Lawler offers a wide-ranging philosophical, historical, and methodological critique of IQ testing. He criticizes the hereditarians for assuming that intelligence 1) is fixed at birth, and 2) is distributed among the population unequally, along the lines of the normal curve. Lawler's historical analysis contrasts the diagnostic purposes for which Alfred Binet intended the intelligence test with the hereditarian and eugenic goals of Sir Francis Galton and Lewis Terman. Lawler also criticizes the reliability and validity of intelligence tests. Throughout, Lawler provides a Marxist analysis not only of the sources of individual differences in performance in schools, but also of ways of addressing these differences.

82.   Layzer, David. "Science or Superstition?: A Physical Scientist Looks at the IQ Controversy." *The IQ Controversy: Critical Readings.* Edited by N. J. Block and Gerald Dworkin. New York, Pantheon, 1976. pp. 194-241.

According to Layzer, Jensen's measures of the heritability of IQ do not meet all of the formal, methodological requirements of a polygenic theory of inheritance. Layzer also draws upon the work of Christopher Jencks to find fault with the heritability estimates used by Jensen. Furthermore, even if IQ were highly heritable within groups, this would have "no direct bearing on the issues of educability or of genetic differences between ethnic groups" (p. 202). Layzer is also critical of the twin studies and of the hereditarians' lack of understanding of the complex ways in which culture and environment can affect IQ. Finally, Layzer cites evidence showing that the cognitive skills of low IQ children are not fixed and that their IQ scores can be raised. He also cites evidence supporting the argument that whites and blacks cannot be scientifically shown to be genetically different in terms of intelligence.

83.   Lewontin, Richard C. "The Analysis of Variance and the Analysis of Causes." *The IQ Controversy: Critical Readings.*

Edited by N. J. Block and Gerald Dworkin. New York, Pantheon, 1976. pp. 179-193.

This is a fairly technical discussion of some limitations of using a particular statistical technique, the analysis of variance, in the analysis of causes in human genetics. Lewontin argues that because genes and environments interact in complex ways, it is difficult to quantify their relative contributions to an individual case. The analysis of variance, studying the deviation of a value from the mean, is often used to circumvent this difficulty. However, studying the "deviation of phenotypic value from the mean" (p. 184) is different from studying the value itself. Lewontin discusses, and provides some examples of, some of the problems that follow from this. His conclusion is that while an analysis of causes can be used to modify and intervene in human environments, the analysis of variance is useless from a practical standpoint.

84. Lewontin, Richard C. "Further Remarks on Race and the Genetics of Intelligence." *The IQ Controversy: Critical Readings.* Edited by N. J. Block and Gerald Dworkin. New York, Pantheon, 1976. pp. 107-112.

Lewontin accuses Jensen of having written an ideological work springing from a "professionalist bias" and "an elitist and competitive world view" (p. 108). This is reflected in Jensen's concern with "dysgenic trends" among low IQ blacks and in his comparing the education of blacks to turning base metals into gold. Lewontin also finds fault with Jensen's mention of authorities in order to bolster the weight of his arguments. Also, Lewontin reiterates his point that Jensen has misused the concept of heritability; high heritability of a trait within two populations tells us nothing about the cause of an average difference between them. As for Jensen's concern over the disproportionate reproduction of low IQ blacks, Lewontin explains that it is based on incorrect and outdated evidence. Lewontin's final point is that even if intelligence differences are genetic in origin, the policy implications of this are determined by our social attitudes and values. For previous articles in the exchange between Lewontin and Jensen, see entries #73 and #85.

85. Lewontin, Richard C. "Race and Intelligence." *The IQ Controversy: Critical Readings.* Edited by N. J. Block and Gerald Dworkin. New York, Pantheon, 1976. pp. 78-92.

This is a reprint of an article written by Lewontin in 1970 criticizing Arthur Jensen's *Harvard Educational Review* article. Jensen's position, according to Lewontin, is that the lower average score of blacks on IQ tests, and the failure of compensatory education programs to erase this difference, probably reflects lower levels of inherited intelligence. Jensen supports the argument, says Lewontin, by asserting that 1) intelligence is stable after about eight years of age, and 2) intelligence scores are distributed along the lines of the normal curve. The implication is that these assertions reflect the genetic origin of differences in intelligence.

Lewontin argues that the stability of IQ after age eight could reflect not the influence of genetics, but rather the consistency of one's educational experience. As for the normal distribution of scores, Lewontin says there is no law of genetics which states that normal distributions are necessarily genetic in origin. Lewontin's main criticism focuses on the concept of heritability, which he accuses Jensen of misusing. Heritability refers to the degree to which the variance of a trait within a population is due to genetics. According to Lewontin, Jensen mistakenly assumes that if intelligence is 80% heritable within the white population, then the difference between blacks and whites (15 points) is also 80% heritable. Lewontin also points out that a trait's being highly heritable does not mean that it cannot be changed environmentally.

86.   Lewontin, R.C., Steven Rose, and Leon J. Kamin. "IQ: The Rank Ordering of the World." *Not in Our Genes: Biology, Ideology, and Human Nature.* New York, Pantheon, 1984. pp. 83-129.

According to the authors, the early IQ testing movement had a hereditarian bias, reflected in the work of Lewis Terman in the U.S. and Cyril Burt in Great Britain. A practical outcome of this bias in the U.S. was the Army psychological testing in WWI and its contribution to the Immigration Restriction Act of 1924.

New IQ tests are constructed to correlate with other, established intelligence tests and with school performance. The authors argue, however, that there is no independent proof that the tests are valid measures of innate intelligence. In fact, test items seem riddled with culturally specific and learned information. Also, the tests arbitrarily define and measure intelligence, treating it as if it were a real entity. The tests are also arbitrarily constructed to make results conform to a normal curve. Furthermore, IQ correlates with social/economic success only indirectly; both variables are dependent upon one's family background.

The authors devote a great deal of their analysis to the subject of the heritability of intelligence. First, saying that a trait is highly heritable or genetically determined does not mean that it is unchangeable by environmental conditions. Second, much of the early research allegedly proving the heritability of intelligence was conducted by Sir Cyril Burt; this research has since been shown to be fraudulent. Third, more recent studies of IQ correlations of twins reared apart and of adopted children do not prove that intelligence is inherited; their major flaw is that these studies did not ensure that the effect of environment was controlled for. Fourth, the assertion that different races have different levels of intelligence misuses the concept of race. Besides being difficult to define, "race" does not account for much genetic variation among humans. By far, the greatest genetic variation is between members of any particular race.

87.   Lippmann, Walter. "The Abuse of the Tests." *The IQ Controversy: Critical Readings.* Edited by N. J. Block and Gerald Dworkin. New York, Pantheon, 1976. pp. 18-20.

This is another in a series of articles written by Lippmann in the early 1920s criticizing intelligence testing. His argument here is that the tests may be quite good at grading students and at diagnosing those who are not progressing as expected. A more appropriate or successful "fit" of the student to the school environment could result from this diagnosis. However, there is the danger that parents and school administrators may conclude that the tests reveal some inherent intellectual limitation. Rather than see the tests as an indication of which students need help, "the less sophisticated or the more prejudiced will stop when they have classified and forget that their duty is to educate" (p. 20). Lippmann is pessimistic about an educational process controlled by individuals with this belief; an intellectual caste system could result.

88.   Lippmann, Walter. "A Future for the Tests." *The IQ Controversy: Critical Readings.* Edited by N. J. Block and Gerald Dworkin. New York, Pantheon, 1976. pp. 26-29.

According to Lippmann, intelligence testers use a "statistical illusion" to make it appear that intelligence is a fixed entity established by one's "germplasm." That is, rather than show how much a student learns each year in absolute amounts, the testers provide scores (i.e. the intelligence quotient) that are relative to the average. This minimizes or conceals the amount of learning and development that takes place. As an analogy, Lippmann talks about a child's gaining weight. That child might gain 20 to 25 pounds each year for a few years, but his or her relative ranking--the weight quotient--wouldn't change if other children grew at the same pace. This may give the impression that no development had taken place. Lippmann makes the same point with respect to intelligence. The intelligence quotient is generally constant, thus giving the mistaken impression that one's intelligence may also be fixed or constant.

Lippmann suggests that the self-interest of intelligence testers is involved here. The more successfully they assert that their tests measure fixed intelligence, the more power and influence they may come to have. Lippmann believes that the intelligence testers' claims for their tests will pass because they are without foundation. At that point, the tests could be put to more practical use. For other articles written by Lippmann in the 1920s, and for a reply by Lewis Terman, see entries #87,#89-93, and #125.

89.   Lippmann, Walter. "The Great Confusion: A Reply to Mr. Terman." *The IQ Controversy: Critical Readings.* Edited by N. J. Block and Gerald Dworkin. New York, Pantheon, 1976. pp. 39-42.

Lippmann wrote a series of articles in the early 1920s that were critical of intelligence testing (see #87-93). A critical response to these was written by Lewis Terman (#125). This article represents Lippmann's response to Terman. Here, Lippmann reasserts his point that the results of the army tests of intelligence are more representative of adult intelligence than are the results of the Stanford-Binet. This is because the former were administered to a much larger, more representative group. Also, contrary to Terman's argument, Lippmann shows that giving the recruits more time to do the tests would have made significant improvements in their scores. Though their relative ranking might not have altered, their overall scores would have gone up. This refutes the idea that only 5% of recruits were "A" men (i.e. officer material). Had recruits been given double the time to do the tests, many more of them would have been classified "A" men. Finally, Lippmann does not deny the possible role of heredity in intelligence. However, he contends that the evidence to confirm this position does not yet exist.

90. Lippmann, Walter. "The Mental Age of Americans." *The IQ Controversy: Critical Readings.* Edited by N. J. Block and Gerald Dworkin. New York, Pantheon, 1976. pp. 4-8.

This is one of a series of articles written by Lippmann in the early 1920s in which he criticizes the practice of intelligence testing (see also entries #87-89, #91-93). Here, he ridicules Lothrop Stoddard's argument that the mental age of Americans is 14 years old. This argument, says Lippmann, results from Stoddard's prejudice and his misunderstanding of the results of the WWI army intelligence tests.

Lippmann's criticism focuses first on Stoddard's misunderstanding and misuse of the concept of "mental age." As Lippmann points out, Alfred Binet's early attempts to define intelligence gave way to more practical efforts to devise diagnostic tests that could identify "normal" and "backward" schoolchildren. Test items were arbitrarily selected; when 65% to 75% of children in an age group could do these tests, that was considered normal.

Lewis Terman was responsible for standardizing Binet's test for Americans, and the adult version of the test was standardized on some 400 Californians. It is to the latter standard that 1,700,000 army men were compared by Stoddard, and found wanting. However, Lippmann points out that the army test used a scoring method different from Binet's. And in fact, the Army's average score did not agree with Terman's adult version of the Binet scale. Which average is more representative, Lippmann asks, the one derived from 400 Californians or the one derived from 1,700,000 men? Lippmann points out that the army intelligence testers themselves said that their results were the most representative.

Lippmann's conclusion is that Stoddard is a propagandist, more interested in his existing beliefs and prejudices than in the facts. For Lewis Terman's response to Lippmann's articles, see entry #125.

91.   Lippmann, Walter. "The Mystery of the 'A' Men." *The IQ Controversy: Critical Readings.* Edited by N. J. Block and Gerald Dworkin. New York, Pantheon, 1976. pp. 8-13.

Lippmann says we should not assume that intelligence tests are measuring something real simply because their results are expressed in numbers. In fact, intelligence testers don't really know what intelligence is. They assume that it is a general ability to "deal successfully with the problems that confront human beings" (p. 9). But how does one measure this? Which problems? How does one define "success?" Because of these difficulties, testers try to measure the abilities that they believe underlie intelligent behavior (i.e. ingenuity, memory, etc.). But the testers can only guess at the questions that will tap these abilities. Furthermore, when is a test an appropriate test for an age group? When 60% can complete it successfully? 70%? These are arbitrary decisions made by the testers. According to Lippmann, then, two major problems with intelligence tests remain: 1) are the tests really testing intelligence?; and 2) were the tests developed using a large enough number of subjects? Because of these problems, an intelligence test cannot be considered an objective standard of intelligence. At best, says Lippmann, it is a ranking of individuals according to an arbitrary standard.

Given this understanding, Lippmann criticizes some interpretations of the results of the WWI army intelligence tests. Because the army test classified only 4.5% of recruits as "A" men (of "very superior intelligence"), some observers concluded that this was the case for the American population as a whole.   Lippmann points out, however, that the tests were constructed so that only 4 to 5% of recruits would score at the top. This was because the army only needed that percentage as officers. The test was just an arbitrary ranking of recruits, not a test of intelligence. For other articles by Lippmann, and responses by Terman, see entries #87-90, #92-93, and #125.

92.   Lippmann, Walter. "The Reliability of Intelligence Tests." *The IQ Controversy: Critical Readings.* Edited by N. J.

Block and Gerald Dworkin. New York, Pantheon, 1976. pp. 13-18.

According to Lippmann, although results of intelligence test correspond to the normal curve and correlate with one another, and the tests seem to be measuring the same thing, one cannot be sure they are measuring intelligence. For Lippmann, a crucial test of the validity of intelligence tests is their correlation with an individual's long-term success at dealing with life. However, he said there was no evidence on this point (as of the article's writing in the 1920s), so the question was unanswerable. Another test of the intelligence test's validity might be its correlation with school results and teacher evaluations. But in fact the correlation is poor. And in any event, there is no assurance that school success is a valid indication of one's mental capacity. A student's poor performance could mean poor teaching, not an inherently limited ability. Lippmann does contend that IQ tests may be better at ranking and grading students than existing methods. However, we cannot draw the conclusion from this that the test is also a valid measure of intelligence. For other articles by Lippmann, and responses by Lewis Terman, see entries #87-91, #93, and #125.

93. Lippmann, Walter. "Tests of Hereditary Intelligence." *The IQ Controversy: Critical Readings*. Edited by N. J. Block and Gerald Dworkin. New York, Pantheon, 1976. pp. 21-25.

In this article, written in the 1920s, Lippmann attacks some of the evidence supposedly proving that intelligence tests measure hereditary intelligence. He accepts the evidence that students from prosperous social backgrounds have median IQs higher than students from less prosperous backgrounds. Lippmann believes that this clearly supports an environmental explanation for intelligence; favorable environments generate higher scores than unfavorable ones. Lewis Terman, however, draws a different conclusion. He points out that as students get older, the correlation of their social status with their IQ score decreases. This, he says, supports the argument that inherent abilities determine a family's class standing.

Lippmann interprets this correlation differently. As a child gets older and goes to school, one should expect the influence of the home environment to diminish. Correspondingly, the equalizing influence of the school and non-home environment should increase. So, it is no surprise that the class/IQ correlation decreases. Furthermore, if one believes the testers' argument that intelligence stops growing around age 16, then later social influences should have a reduced effect. Terman's inability to see these points, according to Lippmann, shows that "he is obeying the will to believe, not the methods of science" (p. 25).

94.   Liungman, Carl G. *What is IQ?: Intelligence, Heredity and Environment.* London, Gordon Cremonesi, 1975. 234p.

"The purpose of this book is to describe what intelligence tests are and what results have been achieved by research on intelligence" (p. 1). Liungman reviews many of the fundamental issues that comprise the IQ debate. Chapters address such topics as the definition of intelligence, tests and test items, environmental factors, social class and racial differences in IQ, family position and IQ, the test taking situation, intelligence and the brain, heredity and intelligence, and cross-cultural comparisons of intelligence. Liungman consistently takes an environmental position in explaining racial, class, and cultural differences in intelligence test performance; he sees family and school experiences, as well as other environmental factors, as being crucial in explaining IQ differences.

95.   Loehlin, John C., Gardner Lindzey, and J. N. Spuhler. *Race Differences in Intelligence.* San Francisco, W. H. Freeman, 1975. 380p.

This overview of research on race differences in intelligence is divided into three parts. The first part sets the historical, political, social, and scientific context of the debate. It also clarifies the issues of race as a biological concept, heritability, and the measurement of intelligence. Part two reviews research on genetic and environmental contributions to race differences in intelligence. Specifically, this includes the findings of various genetic research designs (e.g. twin studies, adoption studies, studies of racial admixture); research on temporal changes in IQ; research on racial, social class, and ethnic group differences in intellectual abilities; and research on the effect of nutrition on intellectual performance. In their summary, the authors suggest that previous research does not justify definitive conclusions regarding genetic and environmental explanations of race differences. The authors also discuss potential policy implications, as well as directions for future research.

96.   Marks, Russell. *The Idea of IQ*. Lanham, New York, University Press of America, 1981. 309p.

According to Marks, the "idea of IQ" assumes the existence of innate and unmalleable differences between individuals; Marks refers to this as the construct of individual differences. This assumption is reflected in many of the institutions, reforms, and social policies of the early 20th century. Marks traces its impact through the professionalization of psychology, the legitimation of industrial capitalism, the reform of schooling, the eugenics movement, and the restriction of immigration. Policy and practice in each of these areas was based on the assumption of innate differences between and inherent limitations on individuals' abilities. This assumption promoted a meritocratic world view, where inequality was seen as unavoidable and a consequence of differences in innate ability and effort. Marks also discusses the IQ debate of the 1920s, the Brown vs. Board of Education case of 1954, and the revival of the IQ debate by Arthur Jensen.

97.   Matthews, Michael R. "The IQ Controversy." *The Marxist Theory of Schooling: A Study of Epistemology and Education*. Atlantic Highlands, New Jersey, Humanities Press, 1980. 214p.

After a brief examination of the historical origins of the IQ and eugenics movement, Matthews criticizes some of the premises of the hereditarian position. The first premise is that intelligence tests measure intelligence. Matthews argues, however, that there is no real entity to which the concept "intelligence" corresponds. Intelligence testers have substituted a preoccupation with the test's concurrent validity (i.e. whether its results correspond to those of other such tests) for the more basic problem of its construct validity (i.e. does the test really measure intelligence). Matthews further argues that the tests measure learned knowledge and class-based values, not innate ability. The second premise is that intelligence determines success in life. Here, Matthews cites research by Samuel Bowles and Herbert Gintis showing that parents' income and years in school, not IQ, are most determinative of success. Finally, Matthews disputes the third premise that intelligence is heritable, arguing that it reflects a misunderstanding of the concept of heritability.

98.   McClelland, David C. "Testing for Competence Rather Than for 'Intelligence.'" *The IQ Controversy: Critical Readings.* Edited by N. J. Block and Gerald Dworkin. New York, Pantheon, 1976. pp. 45-71.

McClelland argues that the testing movement's power and influence in the United States is unwarranted because the tests are not valid. Specifically, he attacks the poor correlation between aptitude or intelligence test scores and success in life. Where such correlations do exist, such as between level of grade completed and later success, usual explanations ignore the influence of one's social class background. It is this background that generates opportunities for success. Those with the money and contacts that accompany high social standing are more likely to succeed; innate intelligence is not the determining factor.

As an alternative to intelligence tests, McClelland suggests that we test for specific abilities and skills that will be needed to perform competently in a particular job or activity. This is called criterion sampling. Furthermore, the criterion to be tested should be made explicit, so that students and their teachers could prepare accordingly. McClelland also recommends that tests reflect and measure one's learning and development; this runs counter to most intelligence tests, which attempt to measure an intelligence that is fixed and innate. Competencies that have more general applicability, such as communication skills, could be tested as well; the same holds true for testing thought patterns, from which testers might generalize about one's potential behaviors. Finally, McClelland also recommends that tests be less structured and allow for the more creative responses that one might find in real life.

99.   Mercer, Jane R. "Latent Functions of Intelligence Testing in the Public Schools." *The Testing of Black Students: A Symposium.* Edited by Lamar P. Miller. Englewood Cliffs, N. J., Prentice-Hall, 1974. pp. 77-94.

According to Mercer, the manifest function (i.e. intended consequence) of intelligence tests is to identify innate ability and, therefore, to provide a means of measuring the success of appropriate educational programs. However, intelligence tests also have latent functions (i.e. unintended consequences). First, they help to maintain the differential status of subgroups within the population. This is brought about by the disproportionately high percentage of blacks, American Indians, and Spanish surname students who are placed in classes for the educable mentally retarded or trainable mentally retarded. Such placement serves to limit opportunities for higher education and economic success. Second, the tests are based on an Anglocentric cultural tradition, and thus serve to legitimate the dominance of that tradition over other cultural traditions. Third, intelligence tests "cool out" those with low scores by blaming their lack of success on their innate, intellectual deficiencies. As an alternative, Mercer argues for assessment based on multiculturalism.

100. Mercer, Jane R., and Wayne Curtis Brown. "Racial Differences in I.Q.: Fact or Artifact?" *The Fallacy of I.Q.* Edited by Carl Senna. New York, Third Press, 1973. pp. 56-113.

The first part of this article clarifies the concepts of genotype and phenotype and discusses the logic of IQ testing and the circumstances under which one could draw inferences about the innate intelligence of those tested. The rest of the discussion criticizes IQ tests for being biased because 1) they have been standardized only on whites, 2) they assume that IQ scores are distributed along the lines of the normal curve, and 3) they are Anglocentric, emphasizing the "core values" and knowledge of a white, middle-class culture. The second part of the article reviews the results of a study on white, black, and Mexican-American students in Riverside, California. This study tested the relative contribution of genes and environment in explaining IQ differences between these groups of students. The results showed that genes did explain 80% of the difference between IQ scores within a specific ethnic/racial group, but that environmental factors explained differences in average scores between such groups.

101. Milofsky, Carl. *Testers and Testing: The Sociology of School Psychology.* New Brunswick, Rutgers University Press, 1989. 266p.

In this Illinois study, Milofsky analyzes the day-to-day, professional activity of school psychologists involved in testing students and making recommendations for placement in EMR (educable mentally retarded) classes. Milofsky found a difference between the orientation and practice of urban school psychologists, serving a disproportionately minority population, and nonurban school psychologists. The urban school psychologists, many of whom were former teachers, were school administration-oriented and generally saw themselves as passive functionaries in a bureaucratic system. Their daily practice, including the speedy administration of large numbers of intelligence and other tests, was detrimental to the educational opportunities of the minority and low-income students they served. The nonurban school psychologists were more profession-oriented (i.e. toward school psychology). While they too violated strict testing norms in practice, they did so in a more creative, activist and, consequently, educationally constructive manner. Milofsky speculates about some of the organizational and structural factors that may have contributed to the different orientations of these two groups of school psychologists.

102. Modgil, Sohan, and Celia Modgil, eds. *Arthur Jensen: Consensus and Controversy.* New York, Falmer Press, 1987. 420p.

This is a collection of articles on various aspects of the work of Arthur Jensen. The articles are arranged into chapters covering such topics as the genetics of intelligence, level I/II theory, test bias, class and racial differences in intelligence, Jensen's reaction time studies, and the educational and social implications of Jensen's work. Most chapters include one article that is "predominately positive" toward Jensen and another that is "predominately critical"; the articles are followed by rejoinders from each of the authors to the other's article. Contributing authors include James Flynn, Hans Eysenck, Robert Sternberg, Carl Bereiter, Philip Vernon, and others; there is a concluding chapter by Arthur Jensen. The editors chose not to include authors whose positions they considered to be polemical rather than scientifically objective.

103. Montagu, Ashley. "Introduction." *Race and IQ.* Edited by Ashley Montagu. New York, Oxford University Press, 1975. pp. 1-18.

Montagu explains that, according to a social conception of race, physical differences between the races reflect inherent intellectual differences. These differences are supposed to account for social inequalities between the races. However, Montagu contends that these arguments are racist and un-scientific. Racial inequalities are better understood as the result of unequal opportunities for social, cultural, and economic development. Intelligence tests reflect these inequalities, not the alleged inequalities of a genetically determined intelligence.

The original intelligence test, as developed by Binet and Simon, was not a measure of innate, fixed ability. In fact, Binet considered such an assertion to be brutally pessimistic. Nonetheless, Lewis Terman, in adapting the test to the United States, argued that it was such a measure. Montagu suggests that Terman did this to satisfy his prior racist and eugenic beliefs.

Montagu considers Arthur Jensen's arguments to be just as error-prone and unscientific as Terman's. His main criticism centers on Jensen's proposition that if isolated groups can evolve differently physiologically, why not also mentally? This, argues Montagu, incorrectly equates the physical brain with "mind" or our thinking, reasoning processes. What has been selected out by evolution is not the brain itself, but rather the ability to use it to adapt flexibly to one's environment; in this ability, there is no difference between the races. The major part of human history has been marked by hunting and gathering, which has placed similar demands on all groups. As a result, their intellectual development and capabilities should be comparable.

Finally, Montagu cites research demonstrating that improving the human environment of poor children had a significant effect on their IQ scores and their personal-social adjustment. The implication is that equalizing social environments will allow the fulfillment of human potential. And while genes and environment do interact in producing intelligence, the relationship is far too complex and intricate to be understood at this time, Arthur Jensen notwithstanding.

104. Newman, Horatio H., Frank N. Freeman, and Karl J. Holzinger. *Twins: A Study of Heredity and Environment.* Chicago, University of Chicago Press, 1937. 369p.

The authors' purpose is to suggest some rough estimates of the relative contributions of heredity and environment to human ability and behavior. In part one, they compare 50 pairs of monozygotic (identical) twins reared together with 50 pairs of dizygotic (fraternal) twins reared together; the twins are compared on a variety of physical measurements, mental tests, and personality tests. Overall, the authors conclude that monozygotic twins are "much more alike" than dizygotic twins, suggesting that heredity is a "large factor" in most of the traits measured. However, the influence of heredity does vary by trait, and there seems to be relatively less genetic difference in personality. In part two, nineteen pairs of monozygotic twins reared apart are also measured, tested, and compared on the same characteristics. The authors conclude that the relative roles of heredity and environment are a function of both the "kind of trait and grade of environmental difference" (p. 349).

105. Plotkin, Lawrence. "Research, Education, and Public Policy: Heredity v. Environment in Negro Intelligence." *The Testing of Black Students: A Symposium.* Edited by Lamar P. Miller. Englewood Cliffs, N. J., Prentice-Hall, 1974. pp. 67-76.

Plotkin demonstrates how scientific theories are sometimes seized upon by policy makers to justify regressive social policy. Historically, both the Immigration Restriction Act of 1924 and the opposition to integration after Brown vs. Board of Education received "scientific" support from many psychologists. More recently, the work of Arthur Jensen (intelligence), Christopher Jencks (inequality), and D. J. Armor (busing) served to legitimate existing racial inequality. In fact, Plotkin labels their work "scientism" (i.e. having only the appearance of science) because of its methodological flaws. Despite the flaws, their ideas were "congenial" to existing preferences in public policy and, consequently, were circulated widely in the media. Plotkin recommends that psychological testing be regulated so as to eliminate its misuse with black children.

106. *Racism, Intelligence, and the Working Class.* New York, Progressive Labor Party, 1973. 68p. (A Progressive Labor Party Pamphlet).

This pamphlet attacks what it identifies as the four major lies of the hereditarian position on IQ. The first lie is that one's

IQ score reflects one's intelligence. Sample IQ test questions, drawn primarily from the Stanford-Binet test and the Wechsler Intelligence Scale for Children, are shown to be culturally biased. The second lie is that compensatory education has failed to remediate the school achievement of the disadvantaged. This argument is countered with evidence of IQ gains in many compensatory and intervention programs. Lie number three is that IQ is 80% heritable. The evidence in support of this proposition, namely the twin studies, adoption studies, and kinship correlations, is criticized as being deficient. The fourth lie, that blacks are genetically inferior to whites, is wrong because heritability estimates explain only differences within a population (e.g. whites), and not between two different populations (e.g. whites and blacks).

107. Richardson, Ken, and David Spears, eds.; Martin Richards, associate ed. *Race and Intelligence: The Fallacies behind the Race-IQ Controversy*. Baltimore, Penguin, 1972. 205p. index.

This is a collection of nine articles by British authors critical of the hereditarian position on intelligence. The authors were brought together by the Open University in England to write non-technical explanations of the issues. The resulting critiques fall within three broad areas: psychology, biology, and sociology. From the field of psychology, the contributing authors were Joanna Ryan, Peter Watson, John Radford and Andrew Burton, and John Daniels and Vincent Houghton. The biologically-oriented critiques were written by W. F. Bodmer, John Hambley, and Steven Rose. The contributing sociologists were John Rex and Donald Swift. This book is also available under the title *Race, Culture and Intelligence* (entry #108).

108. Richardson, Ken, and David Spears, eds.; Martin Richards, associate ed. *Race, Culture and Intelligence*. Harmondsworth, Penguin, 1972. 205p. index.

See entry #107.

109. Robinson, David Z. "If You're So Rich, You Must Be Smart: Some thoughts on status, race, and IQ." *The Fallacy of I.Q.* Edited by Carl Senna. New York, Third Press, 1973. pp. 18-30.

Robinson makes three major criticisms of the hereditarian position on IQ. First, he points out that both one's genes and one's environment contribute, in a wide variety of ways, to the development of human characteristics such as IQ. This makes it difficult to attribute differences in IQ to one cause. Accounting for black/white IQ differences is confounded by the unequal social environments of blacks relative to whites. Robinson cites a research study showing that heavy environmental intervention with children of low IQ mothers produced high IQs in the children four years later. Second, Robinson argues that IQ is a poor and somewhat superficial indicator of intelligence, which is broader and more complex in the real world. Third, IQ, whether inherited or not, contributes only a small amount to social success. This diminishes the importance of IQ as an explanation for social inequality.

110. Rose, Hilary, and Steven Rose. "The IQ Myth." *Education & Equality*. Edited by David Rubinstein. Harmondsworth, Penguin, 1979. pp. 79-93.

The authors argue that Arthur Jensen's 1969 *Harvard Educational Review* article reflects a resurgence of broader theories of biological determinism, of which sociobiology is the latest example. These theories, they contend, attempt to reduce explanations of social phenomena to biological causes; all are forms of scientific racism.

The historical and social roots of IQ theory are traced back to the eugenic theories of Sir Francis Galton, the mental testing movements in the U.S. and England, and Hitler's Germany. Such theories have resurfaced because they provide convenient explanations for the social upheavals of Britain and the U.S. in the 1960s.

Finally, the authors criticize a number of assumptions of IQ theory. First, intelligence is not a biological property, but simply an abstraction created by the intelligence testers. Second, the differences in IQ scores reflect the way the tests are arbitrarily constructed to correspond both to the bell-shaped curve and to school results. Third, it is meaningless to partition an IQ score into a "'genetic' and 'environmental' component" (p. 90) since genes and environments are inextricably linked.

111. Samuda, Ronald J. "Nature versus Nurture." Ronald J. Samuda, et al. *Assessment and Placement of Minority Students*. Toronto, C. J. Hogrefe and Intercultural Social Sciences Publications, 1989. pp. 41-68.

Samuda presents the hereditarian and environmentalist positions on the IQ debate, and he points out some fallacies of those positions. The hereditarians use research with adopted children and identical twins to arrive at estimates that IQ differences are 60% to 88% heritable. Environmentalists argue that blacks suffer from inequalities of class and caste, and that this accounts for the racial differences in IQ test performance. Some environmentalists have suggested that blacks are culturally deprived, and that this contributes to their cognitive deficiencies. Samuda criticizes the hereditarians for assuming that blacks are a distinct, biological race. He also points out that hereditarians have not controlled for or equalized environmental inequalities between blacks and whites, thus making interracial comparisons meaningless. Regarding the environmentalist position, Samuda argues that poor blacks are culturally different, not culturally deprived. The concept of cultural deprivation reflects class bias, ethnocentrism, and an inadequate understanding of cultural variation.

112. Scarr, Sandra. *Race, Social Class, and Individual Differences in I. Q.*. Hillsdale, New Jersey, Lawrence Erlbaum Associates, 1981. 545p.

This volume is primarily a collection of reprinted articles or book chapters that were authored or coauthored by Scarr. They are arranged into four major sections: "Genetics and Intelligence," "Race and IQ," "Social Class and Individual Variation," and "Conclusions and Implications." Many of the articles are accompanied by comments and replies which were written in response to the original journal article. The final section includes commentaries on the book written by Leon Kamin and Arthur Jensen, as well as a reply and "last word" by Scarr.

113. Schiff, Michel, and Richard Lewontin. *Education and Class: The Irrelevance of IQ Genetic Studies*. Oxford, Clarendon Press, 1986. 243p.

Schiff and Lewontin reassert the significance of social class as a variable explaining differences in IQ and school achievement. Previous research, they say, has fairly systematically ignored social class, choosing to focus instead on the deficient genes or family environments of the subjects. The authors present data from a French adoption study in which children from poor backgrounds were adopted by upper-middle-class families. The research "results demonstrate the importance of the social contribution to the school and psychometric failures of working-class children" (p. 223). Using other research, the authors show that social class is also a critical variable in explaining differential access to university study. In the last section, Schiff and Lewontin discuss many of the methodological flaws and ambiguities in genetic studies of IQ; these relate to the areas of individual variability, family transmission, and social heredity.

114. Senna, Carl, ed. *The Fallacy of I.Q.* New York, Third Press, 1973. 184p.

   This is a collection of seven articles on the IQ debate, all critical of the hereditarian position. The contributing authors include Richard Lewontin (entry #85), David Robinson (entry #109), Christopher Jencks, David Layzer (entry #82), Stephen Strickland (entry #122), Carl Senna, and Jane Mercer and Wayne Brown (entry #100). Articles vary in focus, with two reflecting perspectives of critical physical scientists (Layzer and Lewontin), two reflecting the results of specific research studies (Strickland, and Mercer and Brown), and the remaining three providing more general critiques. A selected bibliography is provided.

115. Shields, James. *Monozygotic Twins Brought Up Apart and Brought Up Together*. London, Oxford University Press, 1962. 264p.

   This is one of the most frequently cited twin studies. Shields reports the findings of a study of 88 pairs of monozygotic twins; 44 of these pairs were raised together and constituted the control group, while the other 44 pairs were raised apart and comprised the separated group. Shields also collected some data on dizygotic twins. After reviewing other twin studies, Shields discusses the identification and selection of the twins, the areas on which data were collected, the testing instruments used, and the findings. The twins were compared on physical measurements, intelligence, and personality.

Shields found that monozygotic twins, both separated and control, were significantly alike on intelligence and other characteristics. He suggests that genetic or hereditary factors are implicated. By contrast, early family environments are not very important. The case histories and test results of the 44 separated pairs are appended.

116. Shockley, William. "Dysgenics--A Social-Problem Reality Evaded by the Illusion of Infinite Plasticity of Human Intelligence?" *Shaping the American Educational State: 1900 to the Present*. Edited by Clarence J. Karier. New York, Free Press, 1975. pp. 409-417.

In this symposium paper, Shockley asks whether the "disproportionate reproduction of the genetically disadvantaged" (p. 409) causes social problems. He believes that this proposition is true, at least with regard to the genetic disadvantage of low IQ. In defense of his position, he responds to what he says are the four major objections to his calls for further research.

The first objection is that it is too complex a problem to quantify the contribution of genetics to intelligence, given all of the ways IQ can be affected by culture. Shockley reviews the results of some twin studies done by Jensen and by Newman, Freeman and Holzinger. He argues that these data support the interpretation that 80% of the difference between two people's IQ scores are attributable to genetic differences. Shockley disagrees with the second objection, that IQ is not relevant "to successful living," by alluding to the writings of Jensen, H. J. Eysenck, and Richard Herrnstein. Their work demonstrates that IQ correlates "with many socially-accepted measures of human quality" (p. 413).

As for the objection that race is a meaningless distinction, Shockely asserts to the contrary that it is significant. He refers to a study showing that, at least up to a certain point, increases in percentage of Caucasian ancestry lead to corresponding increases in IQ.

Shockley responds to the final objection, that his ideas would lead to a repugnant eugenic control of the population, with a speculative recommendation that cash bonuses be given to those with below average IQs who undergo sterilization. This, he argues, would be a constitutionally permissible and humane eugenic measure, and it would save taxpayers money heretofore spent on the care of the mentally retarded.

117. Shuey, Audrey M. *The Testing of Negro Intelligence.* 2nd ed. New York, Social Science Press, 1966. 578p.

Shuey reviews the findings of some "380 original investigations of Negro intelligence" (p. 3), and almost 200 related sources, published over a 50 year period. The research studies are grouped into chapters according to the specific subject population that was studied. These chapters include "Young Children," "School Children--Individual Tests," "School Children--Non-Verbal Group Tests," "School Children--Verbal Group Tests," "High School Students," College Students," "Armed Forces," "Veterans and Other Civilians," "The Gifted," "The Retarded," "Delinquents," "Criminals," "Racial Hybrids," and "Selective Migration." For each study there is information on the date and location of the study, the number of subjects, their age or rank, method of selection, results, and the comments of the study's author. According to Shuey, all of the studies together "point to the presence of native differences between Negroes and whites as determined by intelligence tests" (p. 521).

118. Smith, G., and T. James. "The Effects of Preschool Education: Some American and British Evidence." *Heredity & Environment.* Edited by A. H. Halsey. New York, Free Press, 1977. pp. 288-311.

Smith and James review British and American research on the effectiveness of preschool education programs such as Head Start. Many of the initial programs were not particularly effective because they assumed that a single, early intervention would be sufficient to alter a child's long-term, educational outcome. This approach ignored the real and ongoing effects of environmental deprivation. It was replaced by an approach referred to as "ecological intervention," which assumed that intervention would have to involve more areas of the child's environment for an extended period of time. The authors argue that preschool intervention is still important, although not sufficient; resources should also be spent on "the main transitional points in schooling, and certain forms of adult education" (p. 310). It is also important to understand the social context in which the intervention is undertaken.

119. Snyderman, Mark, and Stanley Rothman. *The IQ Controversy, the Media and Public Policy.* New Brunswick, Transaction Books, 1988. 310p.

    Snyderman and Rothman argue that there is a disjuncture between expert opinion on and media portrayal of the issues in the IQ debate. Their support comes from a survey of experts on intelligence testing and a content analysis of the media. The experts were questioned about their opinions on four key areas in the debate: 1) "The Nature of Intelligence," 2) "The Heritability of IQ," 3) "Race and Class Differences in IQ," and 4) "The Impact of Intelligence Testing." The extent and nature of media coverage was determined from an analysis of the *New York Times, Washington Post, Wall Street Journal,* news magazines, and network television. The authors conclude that the media have misrepresented the facts of the IQ debate; this is due in part to the liberal bias of many members of the media. The authors' position is that the political aspects of the controversy have overwhelmed the scientific consideration of the technical issues.

120. Sternberg, Robert J. *The Triarchic Mind: A New Theory of Human Intelligence.* New York, Viking, 1988. 354p.

    While most of this work explains Sternberg's triarchic theory of intelligence, the first part provides a brief review and critique of "Traditional Views of Human Intelligence." Among his criticisms, Sternberg argues that the technique of intelligence testing has advanced without a clear understanding of what intelligence is. He is also critical of the assumptions that intelligence is a unitary entity and that it is fixed and unchanging. He further criticizes the politicization and misuse of research on intelligence testing, specifically as it relates to racial and ethnic differences on intelligence test performance. Sternberg also identifies some fallacies of intelligence testing; these include the assumptions 1) that being smart means being quick; 2) that intelligent, "high verbal" individuals read everything equally carefully; 3) that intelligence is reflected in a big vocabulary; and 4) that intelligent individuals solve problems the same way as the less intelligent.

121. Storfer, Miles D. "The Black/White IQ Disparity: Myth and Reality." *Intelligence and Giftedness.* San Francisco, Jossey-Bass, 1990. 636p.

Storfer attributes much of the average difference in IQ scores between blacks and whites to differences in their intrauterine environments and to "disadvantageous family configurations" (p. 120). Family configuration refers to such factors as the age of the mother at birth, the number of children, and the spacing between children. Storfer argues that both the intrauterine and family configuration problems are compounded or made worse by social class inequalities between blacks and whites. In all, says Storfer, these differences account for approximately half of the average IQ difference between blacks and whites. He further points out that the historical increase in black IQ scores refutes the contention that the black - white IQ disparity is due to the inherent inferiority of blacks.

122. Strickland, Stephen P. "Can Slum Children Learn?" *The Fallacy of I.Q.* Edited by Carl Senna. New York, Third Press, 1973. pp. 150-172.

Strickland provides an overview and preliminary analysis of an intensive early intervention program aimed at disadvantaged children. Known as the Milwaukee Project, this program targeted young slum children with mothers of 80 I.Q. or less; these children were the most likely to be diagnosed later as mentally retarded. The intent of the program was to see if environmental intervention measures could reduce the likelihood of retardation. After four years of intervention both with the children and their mothers, researchers found significantly better performance by the experimental group on a variety of tests. For example, at the age of 42 months, the IQ scores of the experimental group were 33 points higher than the average score of the control group. Strickland concludes that "the trend of the data...engenders real hope that mental retardation of the kind that occurs in children whose parents are poor and of poor ability can be prevented" (p. 159).

123. Taylor, Howard F. *The IQ Game: A Methodological Inquiry into the Heredity-Environment Controversy.* New Brunswick, N. J., Rutgers University Press, 1980. 276p.

Taylor's main point is that the heritability of IQ is not an estimable quantity. To support this argument, he criticizes many of the methods and statistical techniques used by Jensen and others to estimate IQ heritability. He also criticizes the major twin studies, arguing that there were four major sources of environmental similarity that inflated the twins' IQ correlations: 1) "late separation" of the twins; 2) reunion of the twins "prior to testing"; 3) "relatedness of adoptive families" ; and 4) "similarity in social environment after separation" (p. 77). Finally, Taylor documents many of the "wholly arbitrary and implausible assumptions" (p. 170) made by researchers studying kinship correlations in their efforts to produce IQ heritability estimates.

124. Terman, Lewis M., ed. *Genetic Studies of Genius*. Stanford, California, Stanford University Press, 1925-1959. 5v.

This is Lewis Terman's multi-volume, longitudinal study of geniuses. Four of the five volumes follow children identified as geniuses from childhood to mid-life, with detailed measurement, description, and analysis of their physical, intellectual, and behavioral traits. These four volumes are *Mental and Physical Traits of a Thousand Gifted Children* (Vol. 1), *The Promise of Youth: Follow-Up Studies of a Thousand Gifted Children* (Vol. 3), *The Gifted Child Grows Up: Twenty-Five Years' Follow-Up of a Superior Group* (Vol. 4), and *The Gifted Group at Mid-Life: Thirty-Five Years' Follow-Up of the Superior Child* (Vol. 5). The other volume, Catharine Cox's *The Early Mental Traits of Three Hundred Geniuses* (Vol. 2), is a study of the childhood traits of eminent, deceased authors, philosophers, statesmen, musicians, etc., with IQ scores assigned based upon biographical information.

125. Terman, Lewis M. "The Great Conspiracy: The Impulse Imperious of Intelligence Testers, Psychoanalyzed and Exposed by Mr. Lippmann." *The IQ Controversy: Critical Readings*. Edited by N. J. Block and Gerald Dworkin. New York, Pantheon, 1976. pp. 30-38.

This is Lewis Terman's response to a series of critical articles on intelligence testing written by Walter Lippmann in the early 1920s (see #87-93). Terman's rebuttal consists of a number of major points. First, he reasserts the position that World War I army recruits had an average mental age of fourteen. The verification of this, he argues, is found in the age norms established by many independent intelligence tests other than the Stanford-Binet. Second, Terman says that the average score of the recruits was not a consequence of having only a limited time in which to do the test. Scores for recruits given twice the time were practically identical to the scores of the recruits given the shorter amount of time. Third, in defense of the validity of the test, Terman points out the high correlation between a pupil's intelligence test scores over time. Fourth, Lippmann's concern that the tests "could be" misused is irrelevant; according to Terman, they are not misused. Finally, Terman contradicts Lippmann's claim that the tests do not measure intelligence. While they may not measure "simon-pure intelligence," they do measure "native ability plus other things" (p. 36). Terman says that although the relative contribution of these various factors is unclear, "native ability" dominates.

126.   Thoday, J. M. "Educability and Group Differences." *The IQ Controversy: Critical Readings*. Edited by N. J. Block and Gerald Dworkin. New York, Pantheon, 1976. pp. 146-155.

This is a review and assessment of some of the points raised by Jensen both in his book *Educability and Group Differences* (#69) and in his earlier writings. Thoday is generally supportive of the evidence that there are genetic intelligence differences within the white population, though he finds fault with Jensen's exact figures. However, Thoday finds greater problems in Jensen's explanation of racial differences in IQ. While Jensen dismisses many conventional environmental explanations for these differences, he discounts the possibility of yet unknown environmental factors that might exclusively affect blacks. Thoday also points out that black and white sibling IQ scores can regress to the population mean for either genetic or environmental reasons; evidence of this regression does not support Jensen's argument. Moreover, Jensen was not critical enough of research linking degree of white ancestry to the test scores of Aborigines.

Thoday concludes that there is no definitive evidence concerning the causes of IQ differences between whites and blacks and that we must keep an open mind on the matter. He is also concerned that the controversy over group differences will hurt sound educational and social policies concerning individual differences.

127.   Thoday, J. M. "Limitations to Genetic Comparison of Populations." *The IQ Controversy: Critical Readings*. Edited by

N. J. Block and Gerald Dworkin. New York, Pantheon, 1976. pp. 131-145.

In the debate over the alleged genetic intelligence differences between the races, Thoday addresses which conclusions are and are not scientifically warranted. In studying genetic traits that are discontinuous variables (e.g. blood groups), Thoday says it is straightforward to identify genetic differences between populations or races. However, with continuous variables (e.g. IQ), it is impossible to identify genotypes and to count gene frequencies. And while one may be able to gauge the relative influence of genes and environment within a population, this tells us nothing about differences between groups.

Thoday provides some examples of plant studies in which one can determine the relative contributions of genes and environment to plant height. However, he contrasts this with the study of some human traits, where it is difficult to separate out these influences. Finally, Thoday discusses some of the research questions involved in trying to determine the influence of genes and environment both within and between human populations. He concludes that there is not yet scientific evidence to answer whether racial differences in average intelligence are genetically or environmentally determined.

128. Thorndike, Robert L. "Intelligence and Intelligence Testing." *International Encyclopedia of the Social Sciences.* Vol. 7. Edited by David L. Sills. New York, Macmillan and Free Press, 1968. pp. 421-429.

Thorndike briefly reviews the difficulties in defining intelligence and credits Charles Spearman with identifying the existence of a common factor (g or general intelligence) which explains the "common variance...among tests involving a wide variety of cognitive performances" (p. 422). Tests discussed include the Stanford-Binet Intelligence Scale, the Wechsler Adult Intelligence Scale (WAIS) and Wechsler Intelligence Scale for Children (WISC), group tests, nonverbal and culture-free tests, and tests for infants and preschoolers. Thorndike also discusses intelligence tests as measures of creativity or divergent and convergent thinking, the stability of one's intelligence scores, their correlation with school success, and explanations for age, sex, and social class differences in scores. Finally, Thorndike reviews the heredity vs. environment debate concerning the causes of differences in intelligence. While supporting the environmental explanation, he also points out some of the reasons why the issue is so difficult to resolve.

129. Thorndike, Robert M., and David F. Lohman. *A Century of Ability Testing.* Chicago, Riverside Publishing Co., 1990. 163p.

This is generally a historical overview of the development of mental testing. While the authors avoid taking sides on the issue of the heritability of intelligence, there are a number of sections that describe key issues and events in the history of the IQ debate. These include the Walter Lippmann v. Lewis Terman debate in the 1920s, the World War I army mental tests, and immigration policy. From more recent history, the book recounts the controversies surrounding the work of Arthur Jensen and Richard Herrnstein, as well as legislative attempts to restrict psychological testing. The authors conclude with a review of more recent theories and research on the nature of intelligence.

130. Tobach, Ethel, and Harold M. Prohansky, eds. *Genetic Destiny: Race as a Scientific and Social Controversy.* New York, AMS Press, 1976. 163p.

In 1972, 50 psychologists and other scientists published a "Comment" in the *American Psychologist* that made a plea for freedom of inquiry in the IQ debate (entry #160). Specifically, they complained that those researching IQ differences from a hereditarian perspective were being harassed, sometimes threatened, and generally constrained in their efforts to research the topic. This collection of articles grew out of the ensuing debate over the "Comment." Some authors (e.g. Robert Cancro; Harold Prohansky) address the specific chain of events surrounding the "Comment" and reactions to it; other authors (e.g. Abraham Edel; Ernest Drucker and Victor Sidel) treat more general issues of freedom in inquiry and the scientific and social responsibilities of researchers. Still other authors (e.g. David Layzer; Gerard Piel) level criticism at the research of Jensen, Herrnstein, and other hereditarians.

131. Tobias, Phillip V. "IQ and the nature-nurture controversy." *Heredity & Environment.* Edited by A. H. Halsey. New York, Free Press, 1977. pp. 263-287.

Tobias presents a broad range of criticisms of Jensen's hereditarian position. He is particularly critical of Jensen's inadequate understanding of the variety of subtle ways that environment can influence behavior. This can include such factors as early environmental stimulation of the child, parental stress during pregnancy, malnutrition, and the intra-uterine and early childhood development of the parent. Tobias also raises questions concerning the effect of the IQ tester's race, age, sex, and class on the performance of the test taker. Other questions raised concern the culture fairness of the tests, and the adequacy of environmental controls in the twin studies.

132. Vernon, P. E. "Intelligence: Heredity-Environment Determinants." *The International Encyclopedia of Education: Research and Studies.* Volume 5. Torsten Husen and T. Neville Postlethwaite, Editors-In-Chief. New York, Pergamon, 1985. pp. 2605-2611.

Vernon reviews a wide range of evidence and research relating to hereditary versus environmental determinants of intelligence. He groups this research into a number of broad categories: kinship studies; adoption studies and other biological indicators of intelligence (i.e. reaction time, inspection time, evoked potentials); ethnic and racial group differences; constitutional factors (i.e. physiological, non-genetic factors that can affect development and learning); early stimulation and deprivation; intervention studies (e.g. Head Start); effects of schooling and socioeconomic status; and criticisms of intelligence tests.

133. Vernon, Philip E. *Intelligence: Heredity and Environment.* San Francisco, W. H. Freeman, 1979. 390p.

The book is divided into four parts addressing broad subject areas; within each part, the chapters focus on more specific issues and research. Part 1, "The Nature of Intelligence," addresses theories, definitions, and conceptions of intelligence, as well as many of the criticisms of the tests. Part 2, "Child Development and Environmental Effects on Intelligence," reviews not only developmental aspects of intelligence, but also research on some major environmental influences, such as prenatal environment, socioeconomic background, and education. Part 3, "Genetic Influences on Individual Differences in Intelligence," reviews the research on the heritability of intelligence, specifically the major twin studies, kinship studies, and foster-child studies. Part 4, "Genetic Influences on Group Differences," not only reviews research on group differences in intelligence, but also examines the issues of cultural bias, racism, and the social responsibilities of scientists.

134. Wechsler, David. "Intelligence: Definition, Theory, and the IQ." *Intelligence: Genetic and Environmental Influences.* Edited by Robert Cancro. New York, Grune and Stratton, 1971. pp. 50-55.

Wechsler points out that despite varying definitions of intelligence, there are common, underlying abilities that the tests identify. These include abstract reasoning, adapting, learning from experience, and solving problems. Tests of intelligence are considered valid measures of these abilities if they "correlate with variously esteemed and otherwise desirable capacities commonly accepted as indicators of intelligence" (p. 53). They must also have been standardized on a representative population and have test items that are fair to all tested groups. According to Wechsler, opposition to the tests is probably a result of a misunderstanding. The tests are simply indicators of relative brightness or ability. A low IQ score should not be seen as an "inadequacy" of the test, but rather as an indicator of "social causes" that may have helped to create that score.

135. Wiseman, Stephen, ed. *Intelligence and Ability: Selected Readings.* Harmondsworth, Penguin, 1973. 2nd ed. 384pp.

This edited collection includes 17 articles or excerpts of articles written by some of the most influential early British and American researchers on intelligence. Contributors include Sir Cyril Burt, R. B. Cattell, Charles Spearman, Sir Francis Galton, Arthur Jensen, Hans Eysenck, P. E. Vernon, J. McV. Hunt, and others. These articles are arranged into six broad subject categories reflecting their focus or significance: "The Pioneers," "Structure of the Mind," "Nature v. Nurture," "Theory v. Practice," "Cross-Cultural Studies," and "Wider Implications." Arthur Jensen's *Harvard Educational Review* article (1969) is the most recent contribution included, so the collection predates the subsequent IQ debate. However, the introduction to the "Cross-Cultural Studies" section does refer to the post-Jensen debate, and the articles in that section do suggest "inter-group, inter-class and inter-race differences on important educational variables" (p. 271).

136. Yoakum, Clarence S., and Robert M. Yerkes, comps. and eds. *Army Mental Tests.* New York, Henry Holt, 1920. 303p.

Yoakum and Yerkes provide an overview of the development and use of the World War I army mental tests. Chapter one briefly discusses some of the principles involved in developing the tests. Chapter two discusses the types of tests used, the methods used in administering and scoring them, and some of the results. Both group and individual tests were administered; there were tests for literates (alpha tests), illiterates (beta tests), and non-English speakers. An examiner's guide to giving the tests is included, as are the test blanks and forms. The authors also discuss the social, educational, and industrial applications to which the tests might be put.

6 Professional Journal Articles

137. Adams, Phillip. "False Gods of a New Religion." *Australian Journal of Mental Retardation* 4 (8): 13-15, December 1977.

Adams expresses contempt for the reaction of radical activists to the Australian visit of Arthur Jensen and Hans Eysenck. He argues that the strident protests of the activists dignified Jensen's and Eysenck's ideas; sound criticism would have been more useful and effective. However, despite finding fault with the activists, Adams is even more critical of Jensen and Eysenck, whose ideas, he says, serve to rationalize inequality. Furthermore, Adams considers it inappropriate to reduce something as complex as intelligence to statistics, as Eysenck and others do. For Adams, the understanding of intelligence must "encompass both genetics and environmental factors" (p. 15).

138. Anastasiow, Nicholas. "Educational Relevance and Jensen's Conclusions." *Phi Delta Kappan* 51 (1): 32-35, September 1969.

According to Anastasiow, many of Jensen's critics object both to his attributing black/white IQ differences to genetic factors and to his suggestion that compensatory education has been a failure. Anastasiow also argues that Jensen ignores research showing that even highly heritable traits can be significantly affected by environment. Furthermore, he believes that Jensen is "naive" about the growth and development of intelligence and about the importance of early socialization and deprivation. Anastasiow suggests further that poor/black students often do not come to school prepared for the verbal orientation of instruction, and thus, are at a disadvantage. While Anastasiow accepts Jensen's suggestion that different modes or styles of teaching be used with poor children, he rejects the suggestion that such students cannot learn abstract reasoning or cognitive skills. Anastasiow argues for better models of compensatory education and for better teacher training. Educators should be "discovering what kind of environmental stimulations are necessary to reach the potential of what is inherited" (p. 35).

139. Andrews, Greg. "Testing for Order and Control: IQ and Social Class." *Radical Education Dossier* 4: 11-13, October 1977.

Andrews argues that schools necessarily reproduce inequality because they serve the manpower needs of an unequal economy. In this process, schools favor middle-class students, and IQ tests provide seemingly objective evidence for the poorer performance of poor and minority children. However, these tests are unfair to non middle-class children, and thus, help to perpetuate inequality.

Andrews points out that vocabulary sections of intelligence tests measure what one has learned, not some innate intellectual ability. Similarly, comprehension questions test whether one has middle-class values and attitudes. Minor quantitative differences in scores are inappropriately considered to reflect qualitative differences in intelligence. Also, IQ scores correlate (.50) with school success because both measure the same thing--mastery of school skills.

Finally, Andrews asserts that the tests are constructed by middle-class psychologists, thus introducing bias, and are validated against both teachers' evaluations of students and students' class rankings. Furthermore, while tests are standardized to remove differences in average scores between the sexes, they are not standardized to remove differences between the races.

140. Beck, Clive. "Why General Intelligence Assessment Should Be Abandoned." *Interchange* 7 (3): 29-35, 1976-77.

Beck contends that general intelligence assessment can lead to "distortions and harmful human consequences" (p. 29). His primary criticism is that general ability assessment minimizes the variety of more specific abilities that people possess. Furthermore, it ignores the fact that intelligence is relative; different social and cultural contexts demand different intellectual skills and abilities. In addition, general assessments of ability connote a judgement of one's human worth, and they also devalue acquired intelligence at the expense of innate intelligence. Politically, intelligence assessment serves to oppress the poor by defining and stereotyping their potential abilities. "People are judged not on what they may reasonably be expected to be able to do and what needs to be done for them and their community, but on the extent to which they possess a mysterious quality of intelligence" (p. 33). For the above reasons, Beck recommends abandoning general intelligence assessment and replacing it with assessment of students' specific needs and abilities. This knowledge, in turn, would aid in the attainment of the students' and society's educational objectives.

141. Bereiter, Carl. "The Future of Individual Differences." *Harvard Educational Review* 39 (2): 310-318, Spring 1969.

In response to Jensen's 1969 article, Bereiter agrees that the reduction of social and educational inequities will not reduce inequality. However, he goes farther than Jensen in arguing that inequalities will increase and become more entrenched. This is because the elimination of unequal opportunities will result in innate intelligence being the only cause of differential success. Furthermore, the use of intellectual tools that aid our problem-solving abilities will differentially favor those intelligent enough to use them. As a result, social inequalities will become entrenched in a meritocratic caste system, with the most intelligent occupying the higher social positions. Assortative mating among the intelligent will only solidify the inequalities based on innate intelligence. The goal of remedial education, argues Bereiter, should be to attempt to find ways to teach the less intelligent cognitive and thinking skills.

142. Bereiter, Carl. "IQ and Elitism." *Interchange* 7 (3): 36-44, 1976-77.

Bereiter attempts to explain why many Canadian students deny the "self-evident truth" of intelligence differences and why they identify IQ tests with elitism. He speculates that their radical egalitarianism, their fear of evaluation, their equating of intelligence differences with differences in human worth, and their "devaluing of formal education" are possible explanations, among others. However, as Bereiter sees it, IQ is a measure of intelligence, which is essential for any society's elites to govern and for the society to survive. As he put it, "a modern society run by low-IQ elites is bound to collapse" (p. 38). If the students' anti-IQ ideology wins out, and if the more intelligent and competent individuals are not responsible for the more demanding jobs, work quality will decline and society will function poorly. Furthermore, Bereiter argues that IQ is not elitist; it is a fairer basis for social mobility than many other criteria.

143.   Biggs, J. B. "Genetics and Education: An Alternative to Jensenism." *Educational Researcher* 7 (4):   11-17, April 1978.

Biggs suggests that Jensen's arguments on the inheritance of intellectual abilities provide an overly pessimistic view of the possibilities for teaching and learning. Specifically, Biggs reviews research on the processes by which people learn; these processes are identified as either simultaneous or successive. Evidence indicates that students were able to achieve equally high results using either process, as long as it was appropriate for them. He reports further that these processes overlap Jensen's Level I (rote) and Level II (abstract reasoning) learning abilities. This suggests that within the broad genetic limits on ability, there are equally powerful ways of learning. The role of the teacher, then, is to create an instructional strategy that matches the appropriate learning process or processes with the desired learning outcome.

144.   Blum, Jeffrey M. "Was Michelangelo's IQ 180?" *New York University Education Quarterly* 10 (3):   30-32, Spring 1979.

This is primarily a critique of Lewis Terman's five-volume *Genetic Studies of Genius* and its role in legitimizing the hereditarian view of intelligence. Blum is particularly critical of Terman's longitudinal study of some 1,500 gifted students. While Terman showed that these students ultimately were more successful than the population as a whole, he provided no scientific explanation for why this was the case. Blum also criticizes Terman's estimation of the IQs of 300 deceased geniuses. The estimation process was not objective, according to Blum, and it virtually ensured that the IQs would be high. In criticizing Terman's work, Blum's intent is to correct the mistaken belief in the scientific basis of Terman's findings. Blum argues further that focusing on IQ scores "has led us to view differences in academic achievement as an individual rather than a social problem" (p. 32).

145. Bodmer, Walter F., and Luigi Cavalli-Sforza. "Intelligence and Race." *Scientific American* 223 (4): 19-29, October 1970.

The authors contend that current scientific evidence does not allow one to attribute racial differences in intelligence to genes. They point out that intelligence is a polygenic trait, and that any of the contributing genes could be affected by non-genetic factors. Furthermore, different genotypes can be affected differently by various environments, making this genotype-environment interaction difficult to predict and control. Even adoption and twin studies, which attempt to separate genetic and environmental factors, do not fully control genotype-environment interaction or the "environmental variation among families" (p. 25). Furthermore, such studies are typically done within an environmentally homogeneous population, making generalizations to other environments difficult. The authors also argue that it is questionable whether natural selection could have produced a 15 IQ point deficit among blacks in only seven generations (since slavery). They also point to such environmental effects on blacks' IQ as the race of the tester, protein deficiency, early childhood sensory deprivation, and expectancy of failure. Since this is not, in their opinion, a useful scientific inquiry, the authors suggest that public research funds would be better spent elsewhere.

146. Boone, James A. "Racial Differences in Standard I.Q. = Cultural Bias." *The Negro Educational Review* 28 (3 & 4): 183-188, July-October 1977.

According to Boone, research contending that blacks are innately inferior to whites has a negative affect on black self-esteem and achievement. Even environmental explanations of the black/white difference do not fully control for environmental differences or cultural bias. To demonstrate this cultural bias, Boone administered a standard intelligence test, the Shipley Institute of Living Scale, and a black-oriented intelligence measure, the Black Environmental Adjustment Test (BEAT), to a group of black and white college students. He found that while black students did worse on the Shipley scale, white students did worse on the BEAT. Furthermore, he found that socioeconomic status (SES) did not "contribute significantly to the differences in scores earned by the two groups" (p. 187). This finding implicated cultural bias as the source of the differential performance of the two groups.

147. Boone, James A., and Vincent J. Adesso. "Racial Differences on a Black Intelligence Test." *Journal of Negro Education* 63 (4): 429-436, February 1974.

The authors argue that most research into racial differences in intelligence does not adequately control for environment. While these studies control for SES (socioeconomic status), they ignore other sources of environmental influence such as "cultural biases inherent in the tests" (p. 430). These biases favor high-status groups, say the authors, and could account for the observed racial differences in IQ. To demonstrate this cultural bias, the authors administered a traditional intelligence test (the Shipley Institute of Living Scale) and the Black Intelligence test (BIT) to white and black subjects from low- and high-status backgrounds. Their findings support the hypothesis that cultural bias in the tests accounts for differences in group performance.

148. Boozer, Bernard. "An Alternative to Intelligence Testing for Minority Children." *The Journal of Negro Education* 47 (4): 414-418, Fall 1978.

Boozer proposes cognitive style mapping as an alternative to the use of intelligence tests with minority children. Cognitive style mapping identifies a particular student's learning style or styles; this information can be used to individualize instruction in order "to capitalize on the minority child's strengths...and to strengthen weaknesses" (p. 418). Boozer considers the information derived from cognitive style mapping to be more useful for instructional purposes than the information gained from an intelligence test. As the author points out, one's cognitive style is "augmentable and modifiable," and therefore provides some direction for the teacher in improving the student's learning.

149. Borkowski, John G., and Audrey Krause. "Racial Differences in Intelligence: The Importance of the Executive System." *Intelligence* 7 (4): 379-395, October-December 1983.

Borkowski and Krause hypothesize that IQ differences between blacks and whites are attributable to differences in the executive system. This executive system includes our knowledge base, metacognitive processes, and control processes or strategies; it affects how an individual processes information. In research on black and white children, the authors found racial differences in these components of the executive system. They suggest that these differences "may be, in large part, responsible for differences in intelligence and problem solving" (p. 391) between blacks and whites. According to the authors, deficiencies in the executive system are environmentally caused, and can therefore be remediated.

150. Bouchard, Thomas J., Jr. "Do Environmental Similarities Explain the Similarity in Intelligence of Identical Twins Reared Apart?" *Intelligence* 7 (2): 175-184, April-June 1983.

The similarity of IQ scores of identical twins reared apart is considered by hereditarians to be support for the view that intelligence differences are mostly innate in origin. However, critics such as Howard Taylor (entry #123) and Susan Farber (entry #53) have argued that the major twin studies (Shields, #115; Newman, Freeman, and Holzinger, #104; and Juel-Nielsen, #77) are invalid because the twins were not reared in significantly different environments. Bouchard defends these twin studies by reanalyzing Taylor's data using different measures of intelligence. Contrary to Taylor, he finds that environmental similarities do not explain the similar IQs of identical twins reared apart.

151. Brown, A. E. "Intelligence Tests and the Politics of School Psychology." *Interchange* 7 (3): 17-20, 1976-77.

According to Brown, intelligence tests have become controversial because schools have relied upon them too much in tracking students into special programs. This has resulted from both the misunderstanding of the tests by non-experts and their "administrative usefulness." While the test is useful as a "warning light" for students in need of help, it has inappropriately been seen as an indication of innate ability.

Consequently, the role of the school psychologist has been limited to that of psychometrician or clinician. As an alternative, Brown argues for a broader role in which the school psychologist would not just administer tests, but would make other contributions to the educational process. Under such circumstances, intelligence tests would be just one assessment option and would therefore be less likely to be misused. Furthermore, other aspects of the learning environment, not just the alleged deficiencies of the student, could be focused upon.

152. Burt, Cyril. "The Genetic Determination of Differences in Intelligence: A Study of Monozygotic Twins Reared Together and Apart." *The British Journal of Psychology* 57 (1 & 2): 137-153, 1966.

Burt presents a range of data to support his argument that differences in intelligence are largely genetic in origin. His main support comes from his study of 53 pairs of genetically identical (monozygotic) twins reared apart. Despite being reared in different environments, their IQ scores showed a correlation of 0.87; this is not appreciably different from the IQ correlation (0.92) of identical twins reared together. Burt also presents data on the IQ correlations of various relatives; these data show higher correlations for closer relatives and smaller correlations for more distant relatives. According to Burt, all of these data support his position that intelligence differences are affected far more by genetic differences than by differences in environments.

153. Burt, Cyril. "Inheritance of General Intelligence." *American Psychologist* 27 (3): 175-190, March 1972.

After reviewing different theoretical positions on the existence of inherited general and special intellectual abilities, Burt presents support for a hierarchical theory. In this theory there is a general intelligence, g, that is broader than, but common to, the more specific, group abilities. Burt then describes a theoretical model of multifactorial inheritance that is intended to explain how intelligence is inherited. Based upon the model, he presents equations for estimating intelligence correlations among various categories of relatives. Burt tests this model by comparing the expected correlations with actual observed correlations; he finds the model satisfactory.

154. Burt, Cyril. "The Inheritance of Mental Ability." *The American Psychologist* 13 (1): 1-15, January 1958.

This is the text of a Burt lecture given in London at the invitation of the American Psychological Association. Burt begins by reviewing some of the theories concerning the existence and nature of general intellectual ability and special abilities. He then provides an overview of the evidence that supports arguments for the heritability of intelligence. This evidence include studies of children in orphanages, studies of identical (monozygotic) twins reared apart, and knowledge of Mendelian genetics. He concludes from this evidence that approximately 80% of the variance in intelligence is due to genetic differences. Burt also suggests that other cognitive and temperamental traits "are influenced both by unifactor and by multifactor modes of inheritance" (p. 11). He ends with a call for further research into the inheritance of these various abilities and traits.

155. Burt, Cyril. "Intelligence and Social Mobility." *The British Journal of Statistical Psychology* 14 (Part 1): 3-24, May 1961.

Burt argues that because the IQs of children within each occupational class vary more widely than those of their fathers, intergenerational social mobility will result. Within each occupational class there is a spread of IQ scores. Among the children, however, there is an even wider spread or variance in IQ scores; the correlation between fathers and sons scores is only 0.50. This is due in large part to biological regression, whereby parents whose IQ scores are farther from the mean are more likely to have children whose scores regress toward the mean. Consequently, children may have IQs that would place them in an occupational class that is either higher or lower than that of their parents, resulting in social mobility. In a related study, Burt shows that one's intelligence and motivation, in that order, are the two most important factors in determining one's social mobility.

156. Capron, Christiane, and Michel Duyme. "Assessment of Effects of Socio-economic Status on IQ in a Full Cross-fostering Study." *Nature* 340 (6234): 552-554, August 17, 1989.

In this French adoption study, Capron and Duyme measure the effect of parental SES (socio-economic status) on the IQ of the children. This is measured by comparing children from high- and low-SES biological families who have been placed into both high- and low-SES adoptive families. The authors found that children reared in high-SES adoptive homes had "significantly higher IQs than those reared by low-SES parents....independent of the SES of the biological parents" (p. 553). This indicates the influence of the postnatal environment. Capron and Duyme also found that children with high-SES biological parents had higher IQ scores than children with low-SES biological parents, independent "of the SES of the adoptive parents" (p. 553). While this fact indicates the influence of genetic differences on intelligence, it does not distinguish between prenatal environmental factors and genetic factors.

157. Cinzio, Steve. "Labels that Stick." *New Horizons in Education*: 27-28, June 1984.

To illustrate the dangers of labeling students, Cinzio recounts a college professor's classroom experiment with intelligence testing. College students taking a course on testing were given an intelligence test so they could experience it first hand. While their scores ranged from 87 to 143, the professor returned to each student a folder with an IQ score of 87. Though he cautioned the class against seeing an IQ score as an inherent limitation, he acknowledged that many teachers place students in ability groups based upon their scores. The professor wanted the class to experience an ability group, and thus tried to divide them by IQ score. However, none of the students acknowledged their 87 score and some pretended to have scored higher. When informed that they had been tricked, the class became quite emotional. The professor pointed out that what they had been feeling illustrated the danger of labeling; students see themselves as they believe others see them.

158. (Clark), Cedric X. "The Shockley-Jensen Thesis: A Contextual Appraisal." *The Black Scholar* 6 (10): 2-11, July/August 1975.

According to the author, there are three possible explanations for why whites are preoccupied with the theory of black inferiority. One hypothesis argues that the need among whites for racial superiority is inherent in the Judeo-Christian tradition. Another hypothesis says this need stems from jealousy of blacks' ability to produce offspring of color and fear that whites "may eventually be destroyed by the darker races" (p. 6). The third hypothesis suggests that the need for superiority reflects the subconscious belief by whites that blacks are actually superior. The author also criticizes IQ theorists for assuming that blacks must opt for integration or segregation. Both options presume white control and ignore the desire by many blacks for separation and self-determination. The author also points out that the dominant environment vs. heredity paradigm incorrectly assumes a false dichotomy between these factors, which are unavoidably interrelated. The author suggests that General Systems Theory provides a better perspective for analyzing the issues in the debate.

159. Colman, Andrew M. "'Scientific' Racism and the Evidence on Race and Intelligence." *Race* 14 (2): 137-153, October 1972.

Colman disagrees with the assertion that the average IQ difference between blacks and whites is primarily genetic in origin. There is no evidence, he says, that the brains of blacks and whites differ; nor do different brain sizes necessitate different IQs. Colman also points out that "race" is a social, not genetic category, and is therefore invalid for genetic comparisons. Furthermore, correlations of black IQ with degree of white ancestry show no relationship. Colman disputes Jensen's contention that compensatory education has failed, pointing to successes in Rick Heber's Milwaukee Project and in the Israeli kibbutz. Also, the important intrauterine and early childhood environments are not addressed by most Head Start-like programs. Finally, Colman suggests a number of possible environmental explanations for the fact that Mexican Americans, despite their worse socio-economic status, surpass blacks on culture-fair IQ tests.

160. "Comment." *American Psychologist* 27 (7): 660-661, July 1972.

Fifty scientists signed this resolution protesting the "suppression, censure, punishment, and defamation...applied against scientists who emphasize the role of heredity in human behavior" (p. 660). They said they believe that heredity has a strong influence on ability and behavior and that research into this should be encouraged as a complement to environmental research. They support the right of teachers to discuss the hereditarian perspective, and they "deplore" the "evasion of hereditary reasoning in current textbooks" (p. 660) and in the social science disciplines. Finally, they urge liberal academics to support openness to biobehavioral reasoning. Signees include Arthur Jensen, Richard Herrnstein, Hans Eysenck, Raymond Cattell, Robert Thorndike, Philip Vernon, and David Wechsler.

161.   Conwill, William L.   "The Inheritance of IQ and Scholastic Achievement: Further Comments on the Jensen Article." *Journal of Negro Education* 49 (1): 97-104, Winter 1980.

In reviewing Jensen's 1969 article, Conwill finds questionable assumptions and data that should make policymakers wary. Historically, the early IQ tests were used to justify the ethnic bias of the 1920's immigration restriction. Conwill is also critical of the capacity metaphor, an hereditarian assumption that there are innate limits on one's ability to learn. This assumption limits efforts to find treatable causes of differential learning. Conwill criticizes the generalizability of heritability studies, arguing that they were done on white populations from average environments. He further points out the criticisms of Sir Cyril Burt's twin studies, which have been suspected of fraud. Finally, Conwill considers Jensen unfair in criticizing the results of Head Start, a program which was not intended to raise IQ.

162.   Cronbach, Lee J.   "Five Decades of Public Controversy Over Mental Testing." *American Psychologist* 30 (1): 1-14, January 1975.

Cronbach's intent is to illustrate some of "the difficulties that arise when the scholar enters the arena of policy" (p. 1). To illustrate his point, he reviews some of the historical controversies surrounding mental testing. Specifically, he discusses the publication of Arthur Jensen's *Harvard Educational Review* article, Richard Herrnstein's *Atlantic Monthly* article, R. Rosenthal and L. Jacobsen's *Pygmalion in the Classroom*, the World War I Army intelligence tests and their aftermath, and a few other incidents. Cronbach suggests that the controversies are a result of both the scholars' inabilities to deal with the popular media and the media's eagerness to generate, exploit, or inflame potential controversies.

163. Crow, James F. "Genetic Theories and Influences: Comments on the Value of Diversity." *Harvard Educational Review* 39 (2): 301-309, Spring 1969.

Crow focuses on the "genetic aspects" of Jensen's analysis and is cautiously supportive of Jensen's conclusions. He concurs that the heritability of intelligence must be large, but he also discusses reasons for lack of precision on this point. The evidence exists, says Crow, for the effectiveness of eugenic efforts to improve IQ. However, heritability estimates do not tell us the effect that different environmental influences might have on intelligence. Even if intelligence is highly heritable, innovative changes in the environment could still produce large gains. This may be especially true for those individuals "at the end of the scale" (p. 307). Consequently, Crow supports continued efforts at compensatory education. Crow also argues that high heritability of intelligence within white and black populations tells us nothing definitive about the causes of average differences between the two groups. Environmental variables, he believes, are not yet fully understood. Finally, Crow agrees with Jensen that a diversity of educational opportunities should be provided for individuals.

164. Delgado, Richard, et al. "Can Science Be Inopportune?: Constitutional Validity of Governmental Restrictions on Race-IQ Research." *UCLA Law Review* 31 (1): 128-225, October 1983.

This article explores the competing individual rights and social interests involved in government and other institutional attempts to regulate or prohibit race-IQ research. After reviewing the historical development of the debate, the authors discuss ways in which race-IQ research has been or could be restricted. These include guidelines imposed by professional associations and journals; employment, promotion, and tenure decisions within institutions; and restrictions on publicly funded research. The "individual and social interests at stake" (p. 131) in these regulatory efforts are then evaluated in light of relevant court decisions. Finally, the article discusses ways in which the state might regulate race-IQ research while not infringing on legitimate rights of free inquiry as guaranteed in the first amendment.

165. Dent, Harold E. "The San Francisco Public Schools Experience with Alternatives to I.Q. Testing: A Model for Non-

Biased Assessment." *Negro Educational Review* 38 (2-3): 146-162, April-July 1987.

In 1979, IQ testing was legally banned in California schools for being culturally biased; that bias had led to the over-representation of minorities in classes for the mentally retarded. This article reviews the six stages of a non-discriminatory assessment program used by the San Francisco Unified School District as an alternative to IQ testing. The stages are sequenced to provide safeguards against bias and to move to more intrusive interventions only as the evidence dictates. Stage one provides for monitoring special education referrals by various categories (e.g. ethnicity) in order to spot potential patterns of bias. Stage two assesses each student's referral in light of their educational history and record. If there is a learning problem, stage three provides for modification of the student's instructional program in the regular classroom. Stage four specifies an evaluation of the student's "present instructional program," as well as its relationship to and impact upon the rest of the class. Stage five assesses the student's learning environment and abilities at home. Stage six provides for a clinical/cognitive assessment of the student's learning abilities; this may lead to special education placement.

166. Dent, H. E., et al. "Court Bans Use of I.Q. Tests For Blacks For Any Purpose In California State Schools: Press Release by Law Offices of Public Advocates, Inc., San Francisco, California." *Negro Educational Review* 38 (2-3): 190-199, April-July 1987.

This is a chronology and fact sheet reviewing the court decision banning the use of IQ tests in the California public schools. It tracks the sequence of events from the beginning of the Larry P. case in 1971 to the final appeal decision in 1986. The fact sheet also briefly summarizes some of the evidence used by the plaintiffs to demonstrate that IQ tests were biased and led to disproportionate placement of blacks in classes for the educable mentally retarded (EMR). Finally, there is the text of a 1986 court order requiring that data on minority and ethnic group EMR placements be kept and monitored and that IQ tests be replaced by alternative forms of assessment.

167. Deutsch, Martin. "Happenings on the Way Back to the Forum: Social Science, IQ, and Race Differences Revisited." *Harvard Educational Review* 39 (3): 523- 557, Summer 1969.

Deutsch finds Jensen's 1969 article to be full of errors and misinterpretations, all of which help to reinforce Jensen's hereditarian position. As a result of Jensen's findings, Deutsch argues, many blacks will be stigmatized as having only Level I (associative/rote) learning abilities; their opportunities for more advanced learning will be restricted. According to Deutsch, Jensen either ignores or does not fully understand the effects of environment, let alone the complexity of the interaction of environmental and hereditary factors. For example, Jensen ignores successful intervention or compensatory programs and their implications for constructing successful future programs. Also, Jensen does not seem to understand the complex environmental differences between middle-class blacks and whites and between American Indians and blacks.

168. Dorfman, D. D. "The Cyril Burt Question: New Findings." *Science* 201 (4362): 1177-1186, September 29, 1978.

In this detailed statistical review of Sir Cyril Burt's "Intelligence and Social Mobility" (entry #155), Dorfman demonstrates that Burt's data were fabricated. Burt's study attempted to prove the stability of "IQ differences between social classes" (p. 1179); his explanation for this agreed "with a genetic theory of IQ and social class" (p. 1177). Those data also helped Burt to refute some of his critics. However, Dorfman shows that the data in Burt's tables were systematically constructed by Burt, who presented these constructions "as if they were actual data" (p. 1184).

169. Doris, John L., and Stephen J. Ceci. "Varieties of Mind." *National Forum* 68: 18-22, Spring 1988.

Doris and Ceci provide a historical review of various models of the human mind. While the earliest theorists simply distinguished humans from other animals, Francis Galton studied human differences in ability and intelligence. Alfred Binet, who was less optimistic about the ability to "assess the nature of mind" (p. 20), focused more on measuring practical intelligence. Subsequent theorists, such as Spearman, Thurstone, and Burt, argued for various models of intelligence focusing on a general intelligence and a number of more specific ability factors. More recently, models of the mind have focused on assessing intelligence directly through tests of reaction time, inspection time, and measures of averaged evoked potentials (AEP). Performance on such tests is said to correlate highly with intelligence. Other recent studies of intelligence suggest that psychological measures of intelligence do not necessarily assess cognitive competence as demonstrated in everyday problem solving. The authors suggest that the variety of the human mind has yet to be fully captured by existing theories.

170. Douglas, John H. "Intelligence: The Hundred Years' War." *Science News* 114 (22): 370-371, November 25, 1978.

Douglas reports on new research by Arthur Jensen that goes beyond the study of intelligence test results. By studying the reaction times of individuals to stimuli, Jensen is attempting to measure "the neurological processes underlying intelligence" (p. 370). Presumably, quicker reactions reflect not only reaction time but also thinking speed, both of which are hereditary in origin, says Jensen. However, other researchers, disputing Jensen's hereditarian position, argue that the Milwaukee Project and research on the Israeli kibbutz demonstrate how susceptible IQ is to environmental manipulation. In both studies, intensive improvements in environment led to large gains in IQ. Others argue that "cognitive therapy" can actually teach intelligence and that motivation and the elimination of poverty are key to improvements in intelligence.

171. Ebel, Robert L. "Intelligence: A Skeptical View." *Journal of Research and Development in Education* 12 (2): 14-21, Winter 1979.

Ebel raises questions about the concept of intelligence, its inheritance, its relation to achievement and culture, and its use in schools. First, he is skeptical of the assumption that intelligence is a fixed capacity to learn. It is not even possible to identify physical differences that cause differences in intelligence among normal individuals. Second, proving the heritability of intelligence is difficult both because of limitations in the twin studies and because genes and environment interact in ways that are difficult to separate out. Third, it is difficult separating intelligence from achievement since the measurement of intelligence entails using learned knowledge. Even test items not based on school knowledge presume similar "learning opportunities and motivations" (p. 17). Fourth, Ebel argues that it is impossible to make culture-free or culture-fair intelligence tests. Fifth, Ebel contends that intelligence tests should not be used in schools, since they may inhibit teachers' efforts to help students learn.

172. Eckland, Bruce K. "Genetic Variance in the SES-IQ Correlation." *Sociology of Education* 52 (3): 191-196, July 1979.

Eckland raises and explores many of the questions involved in explaining the correlation between SES (socioeconomic status) and IQ. Does this correlation exist because low SES children come from a deprived environment or because their parents pass on to them an inadequate genetic endowment for intelligence? If it is environmental, what is different about middle class home environments? Is there evidence that IQ differences are inherited? Why do children's IQs often differ from their parents' scores? Is IQ an important causal factor in one's status attainment, or are both factors the result of one's social class background? Do years in school reflect ability or simply the expectations of the teacher? Eckland also discusses possible implications of genetic variance in fertility and the value of knowing more about the genetic basis of the IQ-SES correlation.

173. Elkind, David. "Piagetian and Psychometric Conceptions of Intelligence." *Harvard Educational Review* 39 (2): 319-337, Spring 1969.

Elkind initially discusses the similarities between intelligence as understood by Piaget and by psychometricians. First, both perspectives agree that intelligence is partially genetic in origin. Second, both perspectives do not rely on the experimental method, though for different reasons. Finally, both perspectives agree that intelligence is essentially the ability to reason or to think rationally.

Elkind also points out differences between the perspectives. In the study of how genes determine intelligence, psychometricians focus on chance and the random combining of parental genes. Piagetians, however, are concerned with those invariant factors that affect the sequence of acquiring mental abilities. Furthermore, Piagetians study mental growth in terms of the acquisition of new mental abilities at various stages of development; psychometricians are more concerned with correlating measures of intelligence at different ages, focusing less on "the nature of what is developing" (p. 326). Finally, while psychometricians attempt to quantify the contributions of nature and nurture to intelligence, Piagetians focus on those rational processes (intelligence) which are "relatively autonomous from environmental and instinctual influence" (p. 330).

174. Epps, Edgar G. "Race, Intelligence, and Learning: Some Consequences of the Misuse of Test Results." *Phylon* 34 (2): 153-159, June 1973.

According to Epps, Arthur Jensen's 1969 *Harvard Educational Review* article rekindled the "'racial inferiority' thesis" and lent pseudoscientific support to racists. Jensen hypothesized that the average IQ difference between blacks and whites was mostly genetic in origin. Epps is highly critical of this, given that Jensen stated elsewhere that the evidence on such a hypothesis did not exist. Furthermore, Epps accuses Jensen of excluding studies that would have undermined his hypothesis. More importantly, says Epps, Jensen's theory could provide policy makers with an excuse for not pursuing equal educational opportunity and desegregation. Epps argues that it would be more fruitful to study the learning styles of the poor or the factors affecting their ambition and motivation. Tests should be used for diagnostic purposes to enhance learning; they should not be used to justify a dead-end education. Policy makers, with the knowledge generated by social scientists, should make the elimination of unequal educational opportunity their highest priority.

175. Erlenmeyer-Kimling, L., and Lissy F. Jarvik. "Genetics and Intelligence: A Review." *Science* 142 (3598): 1477-1479, December 13, 1963.

In this often-cited review of kinship correlation data, the authors review the correlation coefficients for IQ scores of over 30,000 correlational pairings. These data were drawn from 52 studies conducted over a 50 year period. The correlations are for individuals with various degrees of biological relationship, ranging from unrelated individuals to monozygotic (one egg) twins reared together. Overall, the authors find that "a marked trend is seen toward an increasing degree of intellectual resemblance in direct proportion to an increasing degree of genetic relationship, regardless of environmental communality" (p. 1477). They concede that while there may be some methodological problems with the data, they are nonetheless impressed by the "overall orderliness of the results" (p. 1478). The data, they believe, support a polygenic theory of the inheritance of mental ability.

176. Ertis, B. P. A. "The Raging Battle Over Intelligence." *The Educational Courier* 45: 25-27, 29, February 1975.

Part of this article reviews the history of the development of the concept of intelligence and of the intelligence test itself. Ertis touches upon the various contributions of Galton, Binet, Terman, Spearman, and Thurstone, among others. The other focus of the article is the current IQ debate. Here, the author discusses how the ideas of Arthur Jensen, William Shockley, and Richard Herrnstein figured in the controversy. Ertis also addresses the larger question of the debate's impact on the equality theory. This is the theory that "people are born equal and that they become unequal through environmental influences" (p. 25). He suggests that the validity of the theory be determined by scientific investigation, not by our wishes or desires. Furthermore, Ertis doubts whether IQ tests measure intelligence as it is "commonly understood." He also argues that the imperfect correlation between IQ and scholastic/career achievement suggests the need for more equalized opportunities.

177. Eysenck, H. J. "Equality and Education: Fact and Fiction." *Oxford Review of Education* 1 (1): 51-58, 1975.

Eysenck is critical of the blurred distinction between equality of opportunity and equality of endowment or outcome. Genetics has proven, he argues, that all children are not born equal; genetic differences contribute heavily to differences in IQ scores, for example. To believe that all children are equally capable intellectually and to try to equalize learning experiences and school outcomes, is to do a disservice both to the brighter and the less able students. Real equality of opportunity, he believes, is rooted in maximizing the differing potentials and learning abilities that children are born with. Inevitably, such an educational policy will not lead to equal outcomes. It will, he argues, result in a truly meritocratic society.

178. Eysenck, H. J. "The Inheritance of Intelligence, and Its Critics: Some Myths Reconsidered." *New Education* 4 (1): 1-8, 1982.

Eysenck identifies and refutes a number of myths concerning the inheritance of intelligence, many of which result from a misunderstanding of behavioral genetics. For example, heritability estimates do not apply to individuals, but to particular populations. Also, high heritability does not mean that a trait is unalterable. Nor does the heritability of intelligence necessarily lead to permanent castes; regression to the mean will ensure some intergenerational changes in intelligence levels and, consequently, social status. In fact, this pattern of change is predicted by the genetic hypothesis and runs counter to the predictions of the environmentalist position. Similarly, both twins studies and adoption studies support the genetic hypothesis on the causes of intelligence differences; this is true even if one excludes Sir Cyril Burt's questionable twin data. According to Eysenck, the greatest myth is that there is substantial disagreement over the role of heredity in intelligence differences.

179. Eysenck, H. J. "The Sociology of Psychological Knowledge, the Genetic Interpretation of the IQ, and Marxist-Leninist Ideology." *Bulletin of The British Psychological Society* 35: 449-451, 1982.

Eysenck briefly acknowledges the growing interest in the sociology of knowledge and its extension to the field of psychology. However, he is critical of A. R. Buss' analysis of the social basis of differential psychology and of his rendering of the Marxist and capitalist/liberal positions on the origins of differences in mental abilities. According to Eysenck, Buss incorrectly argues that Marxists are environmentalists and capitalists/liberals are hereditarians. In fact, Marx, Engels, and Lenin, as well as contemporary researchers in the Soviet Union and Poland, have acknowledged the important role of genetics in individual differences.

180. Fehr, F. S. "Critique of Hereditarian Accounts of 'Intelligence' and Contrary Findings: A Reply to Jensen." *Harvard Educational Review* 39 (3): 571–580, Summer 1969.

Fehr argues that Jensen confounds the effects of environment and heredity in estimating the heritability of IQ. Fehr reviews the various twin studies, as well as the different statistical formulas for estimating the contributions of heredity and environment. He finds that the 1937 study by Newman, Freeman, and Holzinger suggests additional methods of separating out the effects of heredity and environment. When applied to available data, one of these methods suggests that Jensen has considerably overestimated the heritability of intelligence. More appropriate data would probably reduce the heritability estimate even more.

181. Fischbein, Siv. "IQ and Social Class." *Intelligence* 4 (1): 51–63, January/March 1980.

Fischbein uses Swedish data on twins to test two different hypotheses about social class differences in IQ. One hypothesis attributes the differences to genes, while the other attributes them to the environment. The results confirm the environmental hypothesis and correspond to earlier findings by Sandra Scarr-Salapatek. The research shows that genetic variance, which should be similar in all classes, is greater among environmentally advantaged than disadvantaged groups. This, according to Fischbein, shows how unstimulating environments can "inhibit the full expression of genetic endowment" (p. 60).

182. Florissant, Belle Gibson. "I.Q. Panic." *School and Community* 56 (3): 9, November 1969.

Florissant appeals to fellow educators to fight against "I.Q. Panic," which is parental worry over their children's intelligence as it is measured by I.Q. tests. She points out that parents often misunderstand I.Q. test results and put too much stock in the I.Q. score. Parents must realize that the real indicators of their children's success are qualities such as drive, motivation, persistence, and imagination--qualities that cannot be measured adequately on I.Q. tests. These qualities, along with thinking and problem solving skills, can be taught in the home.

183.   Friedrichs, Robert W.   "The Impact of Social Factors Upon Scientific Judgement: The 'Jensen Thesis' as Appraised by Members of the American Psychological Association."   *The Journal of Negro Education* 42:   429-438, Fall 1973.

Friedrichs sampled the opinions of members of the American Psychological Association regarding Jensen's thesis that black-white intelligence differences were primarily genetic in origin.   Friedrichs hypothesized 1) that most psychologists would reject the thesis, 2) that those rejecting it would be younger, 3) that southern psychologists would be more likely to support the thesis, 4) that "ethnically Jewish" psychologists would be disproportionately at the extremes of support and opposition, 5) that quantitatively oriented psychologists would be more supportive than clinically trained psychologists, and 6) that there would be no difference in opinion by sex. Friedrichs confirmed hypotheses one, two, three, and six, while hypothesis number four was only modestly supported. Hypothesis five was disproved.   Overall, the study shows that demographic and social factors affect scientific judgements.

184.   Furby, Lita.   "Implications of Within-Group Heritabilities for Sources of Between-Group Differences: IQ and Racial Differences." *Developmental Psychology* 9 (1):   28-37, July 1973.

A major argument within the IQ debate is whether the alleged high heritability of intelligence among whites, and its suspected high heritability among blacks, means that black/white IQ differences are mostly due to heredity.   Furby explores this argument by constructing various models in which a trait has high, low, intermediate, and unequal heritability for two groups.   She also discusses how environmental variation would work within these models.   After discussing all of the possible ways that heredity and environment can contribute to within- and between-group differences, Furby concludes that high heritability within two groups tells us nothing about the source of difference between the groups. She also argues that equating blacks and whites on socioeconomic status is not a sufficient control for environmental differences.

185.   Gage, N. L.   "I.Q. Heritability, Race Differences, and Educational Research." *Phi Delta Kappan* 53 (5):   308-312, January 1972.

Gage contends that the best way to counter Jensen's theory is to show how improved environments can "reduce race difference." In fact, Gage finds that a major flaw in the twin studies is that they did not adequately control for the twins' environments; it was their similar environments, not their genes, that accounted for the high correlation of their IQs. He reinterprets some data to demonstrate that improved en vironments for the disadvantaged could lead to significant improvements in school attainment. Though lacking research on environmental effects among blacks, Gage speculates that the environmental differences between blacks and whites are large enough to account for the average 15 point difference in IQ. The IQ difference could be the result of the systematic harm caused by slavery and discrimination and their negative effect on cognitive development. Disagreeing with Jensen's pessimistic view of compensatory education, Gage contends that such programs need to be systematically planned, supported, and researched.

186. Gardner, Howard. "Beyond the IQ: Education and Human Development." *National Forum* 68: 4-7, Spring 1988.

Gardner contends that the traditional view that there is a single, unitary intelligence is inadequate. His research with special populations (e.g. prodigies, idiot savants, the learning disabled) demonstrates that people have "jagged cognitive profiles--profiles that are extremely difficult to explain in terms of a unitary view of intelligence" (p. 5). As an alternative, Gardner suggests there are multiple intelligences which individuals possess in varying degrees: linguistic, logical-mathematical, spatial, musical, bodily-kinesthetic, interpersonal, and intrapersonal. Traditional schooling focuses upon primarily the linguistic and logical-mathematical intelligences. Gardner suggests making schools more individual-centered so that students with different intelligences could have these identified and developed.

187. Gill, C. E., R. Jardine, and N. G. Martin. "Further Evidence For Genetic Influences on Educational Achievement." *British Journal of Educational Psychology* 55 (3): 240-250, November 1985.

The authors attempt to demonstrate that performance on achievement tests is as heritable as performance on IQ tests.

To test this hypothesis, they analyzed the results of 246 pairs of Australian twins on both the Tertiary Admission Examination and the Australian Scholastic Aptitude Test. Statistical analysis "of the causes of variation in examination performance demonstrates that a significant proportion of this variation in each subject (except perhaps Mathematics in females and Biology) must be due to genetic factors" (p. 248). The genetic variance is similar to that found on IQ tests. Furthermore, the authors suggest that the effect of the environment is through the channeling of one's ability into different subject areas.

188. Gillie, Oliver. "Did Sir Cyril Burt Fake His Research on Heritability of Intelligence? Part I." *Phi Delta Kappan* 58 (6): 469-471, February 1977.

Gillie reviews and supports the charges that Sir Cyril Burt "published false data and invented crucial facts to support his controversial theory that intelligence is largely inherited" (p. 469). Burt is accused of having "guessed at" parental intelligence scores, which were crucial in showing parent-child correlations in intelligence. Also, his correlations for twins' IQs remained the same to three decimal points even after increased numbers of twins were added to the study. Leon Kamin (entry #79) pointed out the statistical impossibility of such consistency, and Gillie concludes that Burt "worked backwards" from the correlations to the scores for the twins. Burt is also accused of having fraudulently published articles under the names of two nonexistent colleagues (Margaret Howard; J. Conway). Gillie suspects that Burt did this to increase his contributions to his own journal, while lending further credence to his arguments. Overall, the suspicion is that Burt's obsession with proving his theory led to his faking the data. See also Jensen's rebuttal (entry #206).

189. Golden, Mark, and Wagner Bridger. "A Refutation of Jensen's Position on Intelligence, Race, Social Class, and Heredity." *Mental Hygiene* 53 (4): 648-653, October 1969.

Golden and Bridger dispute Jensen's claim that social class and racial differences on intelligence test scores reflect hereditary differences. Jensen makes this claim because he finds that the IQ scores of relatives (i.e. in twin studies, adoption studies) are highly correlated; if differences between individuals are mostly genetic, then differences between groups must also be genetic. However, Golden and Bridger demonstrate that even if individual differences in intelligence within a group are the result of heredity, the differences between groups are not necessarily hereditary in origin. As the authors state, "correlations and mean differences between two sets of measures vary completely independently of one another" (p. 652). They suggest that while heredity may explain differences within a group, the differences between groups are probably environmental in origin.

190. Gordon, Edmund W., with Derek Green. "An Affluent Society's Excuses for Inequality: Developmental, Economic, and Educational." *American Journal of Orthopsychiatry* 44 (1): 4-18, January 1974.

The authors identify and criticize two arguments that are used to justify persistent social inequality: 1) certain racial and ethnic groups are not intelligent enough to profit from schooling; and 2) "schools make little difference...in changing the life chances of the pupils who pass through them" (p. 74). On the first point, Gordon and Green review the arguments of Arthur Jensen, Hans Eysenck, William Shockley, and Richard Herrnstein, among others, and specifically point out deficiencies with the twin studies and with the use of the concept of heritability. On the second point - that schools make little difference - the authors examine the work of Christopher Jencks. Jencks is criticized for overlooking the importance of process variables in schools (e.g. teacher-pupil, pupil-pupil interaction) and for ignoring evidence that schools make a difference for the very poor and black. Gordon and Green conclude that to equalize educational outcomes we must better understand 1) the different developmental patterns and learning styles of students, 2) the effect that poor health and nutrition can have on the learning of poor children, and 3) the "cultural, ethnic, and political incongruencies" (p. 97) between schools and students from diverse ethnic, cultural, and social class backgrounds.

191. Gordon, Edmund W., and Tresmaine J. Rubain. "Bias and Alternatives in Psychological Testing." *The Journal of Negro Education* 49 (3): 350-360, Summer 1980.

Gordon and Rubain argue that mental tests are unbiased only if one accepts the narrow assumptions on which the tests are constructed and evaluated. Evaluation of test bias ignores the ways in which one's culture influences the "manifestations" and "expression" of intelligence; if one does not match the "culturally encapsulated" standard of intelligence, one is considered unintelligent. The authors are also critical of the fact that mental tests are used primarily to sort and select students, rather than to inform educational intervention. They review the major strengths and weaknesses of some alternatives to culturally biased tests, such as culture-fair, culture-specific, and criterion-referenced tests. Finally, there is a discussion of future trends in testing, including moratoriums on and legal challenges to standardized tests.

192. Gordon, Robert A., and Eileen E. Rudert. "Bad News Concerning IQ Tests." *Sociology of Education* 52 (3): 174-190, July 1979.

According to the authors, existing research demonstrates that IQ tests are not culturally biased against blacks. This conclusion is supported by studies of the tests' external and internal validity. First, regarding external validity, the tests predict the achievement of blacks as well as they do of whites. Second, the internal validity of the tests is indicated by the comparable rank order of difficulty of the test items for whites and blacks. This fact contradicts the "cultural diffusion" argument of many IQ test critics, who argue that race differences in scores reflect differential access to knowledge. According to Gordon and Rudert, it is highly unlikely that one could have unequal diffusion of knowledge across races yet a comparable rank order of test item difficulty. Finally, the authors show that IQ is equally significant in the status attainment of blacks and whites.

193. Gray, J. "Why Should Society Reward Intelligence?" *Education News* 13 (12): 18-20, December 1972.

Referring to data from Sir Cyril Burt, Gray argues that there is substantial proof of social class differences in intelligence. Furthermore, these differences have remained stable because of equal opportunity and the resulting mobility between classes; individuals rise and fall between the classes based, in large part, upon their inherited intelligence. Consequently, Gray sees little hope of eliminating social class differences through equal opportunity. Given these facts, the goal of equality can only be achieved by three different means. Two of these, social engineering and genetic engineering, are politically and ethically unacceptable. The third option, which Gray prefers, is to equalize pay, regardless of the difference in jobs and their required ability. While critics of this proposal argue that unequal pay is a necessary incentive to get intelligent people to undertake socially important jobs, this remains to be proven.

194. Green, Robert L., Robert J. Griffore, and Cassandra Simmons. "A Restatement of the IQ/Culture Issue." *Phi Delta Kappan* 57 (10): 674-676, June 1976.

The authors disagree with Allan Ornstein's contention (entry #244) that IQ tests are fair measures of the abilities needed for educational and social success. In fact, they argue that IQ tests help to create inequality. The poorer performance of the disadvantaged on such tests reflects environmental disadvantage, not hereditary deficiencies. Furthermore, the testing helps to perpetuate these environmental disadvantages through the mechanism of ability grouping. Those placed in low-ability groups, as a result of their test scores, receive worse instruction; this creates a self-fulfilling prophecy that perpetuates lower performance. Contrary to Ornstein, the authors argue that IQ tests are biased in their content, norming, and testing situations. While they agree that IQ tests can be valuable as diagnostic tools, they emphasize that it is essential for bias to be eliminated. Only unbiased tests can be helpful in eliminating educational and social inequalities.

195. Grubb, Henry J. "A Tripartite Taxonomy of Theories Explaining the Black-White Group Difference on Standardized IQ Tests, Based on the Models of Development." *Negro Educational Review* 36 (2): 66-71, April 1985.

The three theories that Grubb identifies are the racial-genetics theory, the sociological or interactional theory, and the cultural distance theory. The racial-genetic theory considers black vs. white IQ differences to be primarily genetic in origin; it concedes little impact to environmental differences. Grubb refers to this theory as a main effect model and criticizes its lack of explanatory power for individuals. The sociological theory does identify environmental factors that affect performance, but it does not explain how the process works. The cultural distance theory explains black vs. white IQ differences in terms of how distant the individual's subculture is from the culture on which the IQ tests were developed.

196. Grubb, Henry Jefferson. "Intelligence at the Low End of the Curve: Where Are the Racial Differences?" *The Journal of Black Psychology* 14 (1): 25-34, August 1987.

Grubb argues that if the genetic explanation of racial differences in intelligence is correct, then one would expect to see a disproportionately higher percentage of blacks identified as mentally retarded. This would be predicted because blacks score one standard deviation below whites on IQ tests, and because intelligence is said to be distributed unequally along the lines of the normal curve. Grubb tests this genetic hypothesis by comparing the numbers and percentages of blacks, whites, and others identified as retarded in three Western states (California, Colorado, and Nevada). Contrary to what would be predicted by the genetic hypothesis, the data show that the percentage of blacks identifed as retarded is comparable to that for whites.

197. Gutterman, Stanley S. "IQ Tests in Research on Social Stratification: The Cross-Class Validity of the Tests as Measures of Scholastic Aptitude." *Sociology of Education* 52 (3): 163-173, July 1979.

Gutterman attempts to prove that IQ tests are not biased against any particular social class. He tests this hypothesis by giving a sample of students an intelligence test, the Quick Test, and by correlating the results with measures of scholastic abilities, grades, and general knowledge. Gutterman found that regardless of a student's social class background, the Quick Test was an equally good predictor of the various measures of scholastic aptitude. Therefore, he concludes that IQ is a valid variable to be used in social stratification research. However, Gutterman does not "take a position on whether IQ is mainly genetic or environmental in origin" (p. 164).

198. Hilliard, Asa G., III. "The Ideology of Intelligence and I.Q. Magic in Education." *Negro Educational Review* 38 (2-3): 136-145, April-July 1987.

While he points out that intelligence is a poorly defined and scientifically inadequate concept, Hilliard's primary criticism of IQ tests is that they do not advance teaching or student learning. In fact, the main functions of the tests in schools, diagnosis and prediction of achievement, are not accompanied by appropriate or standard instructional strategies to improve student achievement. The only tangible outcome from using IQ tests is the sorting of students for an unequal and unspecified educational treatment. Therefore, IQ tests have no valid pedagogical purpose. Hilliard suggests clarification of and increased sensitivity to such issues as cultural and language bias, among others.

199. Hilliard, Asa G., III. "IQ and the Courts: Larry P. vs Wilson Riles and PASE vs Hannon." *The Journal of Black Psychology* 10 (1): 1-18, August 1983.

Hilliard reviews two of the major court challenges to IQ testing in the 1970s, Larry P. vs. Wilson Riles and PASE vs. Hannon. These cases challenged the use of IQ tests for the placement of minority children in classes for the educable mentally retarded (EMR). Though the courts ruled differently in each case, both decisions challenged the credibility of psychometric experts. Beyond this, Hilliard argues that IQ tests were challenged only on the narrow grounds of cultural bias. The more basic issues relating to the tests' validity and usefulness were ignored. Hilliard argues, for example, that there are no definitive scientific data on the effects of school, instruction, language, and culture, among other factors, on group IQ differences. Furthermore, IQ psychometry is preoccupied with the ranking of individuals and the predicting of performance, rather than with the more important goals of improving pedagogy and affecting educational outcomes.

200. Hirsch, Jerry. "Jensenism: The Bankruptcy of 'Science' Without Scholarship." *Educational Theory* 25 (1): 3-27, 102, Winter 1975.

Hirsch is critical of what he finds to be misrepresentations and faulty scholarship in the work of Arthur Jensen and some other Jensenists. The first part of the article is an overview of the extent of the uncritical acceptance of Jensen's work by other academicians. In the remainder of the article, Hirsch traces many of Jensen's references, showing that Jensen had misrepresented the evidence he was citing. Throughout, Hirsch questions Jensen's integrity and scholarly competence.

201. Horn, Joseph M. "The Texas Adoption Project: Adopted Children and Their Intellectual Resemblance to Biological and Adoptive Parents." *Child Development* 54 (2): 268-275, April 1983.

Horn reports the initial findings from a study of 300 adopted children. Their IQs were compared to those of their biological and adoptive families, with the goal of assessing the relative influences of genes and environment on intelligence. The study generally found that the adopted children were more like their biological mothers than their adoptive parents; this, along with related evidence, indicates "the influence of genes...in the creation of individual differences for intelligence" (p. 273). Furthermore, the study controlled for variables that can contaminate adoption studies: delayed separation of the adoptees from their biological parents and selective placement of adoptees. While supporting the importance of genes in individual differences in intelligence, the study also recognizes the value of radical environmental intervention in raising adoptees' IQs.

202. Hunt, J. McVicker. "Black Genes--White Environment." *Trans-Action* 6 (7): 12-22, June 1969.

Hunt fears that the failure of ill-conceived and poorly supported compensatory education programs might lead to their reduced support by policymakers and the public. Furthermore, their failure might appear to support the proposition that the poor are innately less intelligent, thus the failure of the programs. Hunt believes, to the contrary, that good programs can promote cognitive development. He argues that IQ tests are not measures of innate ability. His main criticisms concern fallacies about the concept of development. It is not true, he argues, that one's developmental rate and maturation process are predetermined. In both instances, research shows the significant effect of environment. And while developmental order may be based in biological factors, interaction with the environment is inherent in the process. To promote the cognitive development of the poor, Hunt says we must remediate and counter the environmental deprivations to which they are subjected. He makes some suggestions based upon model nursery school and compensatory programs.

203. Hunt, J. McV. "Has Compensatory Education Failed? Has It Been Attempted?" *Harvard Educational Review* 39 (2): 278-300, Spring 1969.

Hunt agrees with Jensen that genetic factors influence human behavior, and that education should be individualized as a result of the genetic and experiential differences between individuals. However, he disagrees that intelligence is "essentially a static function of growth, largely predetermined in rate" (p. 284). For Hunt, the growth of intelligence is the result of the cumulative interaction of children with their social and physical environment. Environmental deprivations at earlier stages of development can have cumulative negative effects on later stages. He also shows that Jensen underestimates both environmental influences (e.g. class differences in child rearing) and the interaction of social and biological factors. Furthermore, he argues that the norm or range of reaction of human intelligence may be quite large and that we have not yet developed educational experiences to maximize this genetic potential. Hunt denies that the existing distribution of intelligence is biologically fixed and that racial and class differences are inevitable. Finally, he argues, contrary to Jensen, that compensatory education has not yet really been tried.

204. Jensen, Arthur R. "Compensatory Education and the Theory of Intelligence." *Phi Delta Kappan* 66 (8): 554-58, April 1985.

Jensen argues that 20 years of compensatory education has shown that such programs have very little long-term impact on intelligence scores or scholastic achievement. He suggests that this is because differences in IQ and achievement are reflections of biological differences in ability. In support of this point, Jensen cites recent research on speed of cognitive processing. Since performance on these tests is not dependent on knowledge, differences in peformance must be a reflection of biological differences. Scores on these tests explain 70% of the variance in IQ scores. This, says Jensen, indicates that IQ tests are measuring innate differences that are independent of the knowledge or content of the tests. Furthermore, the ranking of IQ test items by difficulty shows that items rank the same across social class and ethnic categories; this, says Jensen, refutes the idea that differential test performance is a function of the cultural bias of the test items.

205.   Jensen, Arthur R.   "The Current Status of the IQ Con-
       troversy." *Australian Psychologist* 13 (1): 7-27, March 1978.

       Jensen notes the persistence of the IQ controversy and argues
       that the ability of "normal science" to resolve the issues has
       become hindered by ideological concerns. Specifically, many
       are ideologically opposed to the genetic explanation for race
       differences in intelligence. Jensen also suggests that the con-
       troversy is really four separate controversies, two of which
       have been resolved by the data. The nature and measurement
       of general intelligence, as well as heritability of intelligence
       within groups, have been established by research and are
       generally agreed upon. The explanation of between-group
       differences in intelligence is not resolved, but various lines of
       evidence make a genetic explanation probable. Finally, the
       social and educational implications of this research are not
       clear cut; they are dependent upon societal goals and values.
       Jensen makes a plea for allowing normal science to resolve the
       facts of the controversy through the creation of theories and
       the generation and testing of hypotheses.

206.   Jensen, Arthur R.   "Did Sir Cyril Burt Fake His Research on
       Heritability of Intelligence?   Part II."   *Phi Delta Kappan* 58
       (6):   471+, February 1977.

       Jensen argues that the attacks on Sir Cyril Burt's research are
       ideologically motivated and that the accusations of fraud are
       libelous.   In reviewing all of Burt's research on the
       heritability of IQ, Jensen found some 20 errors. Most of
       these were trivial in nature, and they revealed carelessness
       rather than fraud or intent to deceive. None of the errors
       was large enough to change or undermine Burt's conclusions.
       Furthermore, Jensen points out the consistency of Burt's find-
       ings with those of other researchers in the field; this further
       supports the validity of Burt's research. Jensen maintains that
       even if Burt's data were dismissed, the remaining evidence on
       the heritability of inelligence would lead to the same conclu-
       sion: "genetic factors considerably outweigh the existing en-
       vironmental factors" (p. 492). See also entry #188.

207.   Jensen, Arthur R.   "How Much Can We Boost IQ and
       Scholastic Achievement?" *Harvard Educational Review* 39 (1):
       1-123, Winter 1969.

According to Jensen, compensatory education has failed to improve the IQ and educational achievement of the disadvantaged because it assumes that the causes of differential achievement are all environmental. Jensen reviews evidence on the genetic and environmental contributions to intelligence differences. He concludes that intelligence is approximately 80% heritable; that is, 80% of the difference in scores is attributable to genetic differences. Environmental improvement demonstrates a threshold effect; it can significantly improve IQs only for the most severely disadvantaged. Jensen also reviews evidence on racial differences in IQ and suggests that it is not an "unreasonable" hypothesis that these differences, too, are primarily genetic in origin. He further points out that while the disadvantaged are not equal to higher classes in conceptual ability (Level II), they are comparable in associative learning ability (Level I). Consequently, teaching of the disadvantaged would be more effective if, rather than assuming all students had the same learning abilities, it took advantage of their different patterns of ability.

208. Jensen, Arthur R. "Interaction of Level I and Level II Abilities with Race and Socioeconomic Status." *Journal of Educational Psychology* 66 (1): 99-111, February 1974.

Jensen tests the extent to which Level I (rote) and Level II (general intelligence) mental abilities interact with race and socioeconomic status (SES). He hypothesized that SES differences were greater for Level II than for Level I. In fact this was proven true, and Jensen suggests this is due to the fact that high SES standing is more dependent on Level II ability. While the white-black differences were larger than the SES differences, the implications of this fact are ambiguous due to the small percentage of blacks in the middle- and upper-SES categories in this study (p. 110). Jensen also verified his hypothesis that Level I and Level II abilities were more correlated within the middle- and upper-SES groups than in the lower-SES group. Finally, Jensen hypothesized that acquiring Level II ability was dependent, somewhat, on having Level I ability; "but the reverse is not true" (p. 101). This, too, was demonstrated by the data, although only for the non-verbal, not the verbal part of the intelligence test.

209. Jensen, Arthur R. "IQ Tests Are Not Culturally Biased For Blacks and Whites." *Phi Delta Kappan* 57 (10): 676, June 1976.

In this companion piece to a longer article on test bias and construct validity, Jensen argues that IQ tests are not culturally biased against blacks. He tested potential sources of bias in a number of standardized tests of intelligence (e.g. Stanford-Binet, Wechsler Intelligence Scale for Children) and found no evidence that they were biased toward blacks. Jensen critizes those who repeatedly claim that intelligence tests are culturally biased, yet who refuse to acknowledge or refute the "objective evidence."

210.   Jensen, Arthur R. "IQ's of Identical Twins Reared Apart." *Behavior Genetics* 1 (2): 133-148, May 1970.

Jensen reviews the four major twin studies by Burt; Juel-Nielsen; Shields; and Newman, Freeman, and Holzinger. He finds that the twin samples are similar, allowing him to pool the data and draw stronger inferences from them. Jensen concludes that, at least for the populations sampled, the values for the IQ's (phenotypes), genes (genotypes), and environmental effects are all normally distributed. Moreover, there is no "evidence of asymmetry or of threshold conditions for the effects of environment on IQ" (p. 146). Jensen also finds that there is no relationship between the intelligence of a twin pair and the effect of the environment; this is called genotype X environment interaction. The small effect on twins' IQ differences that he does acknowledge relates to "prenatal intrauterine factors."

211.   Jensen, Arthur R. "Kinship Correlations Reported by Sir Cyril Burt." *Behavior Genetics* 4 (1): 1-28, 1974.

Jensen reproduces and comments upon all of the tables of kinship data reported by Sir Cyril Burt, including data on identical twins. Jensen notes possible misprints, ambiguities, and inconsistencies in the data that may affect their usability. In particular, he points out some 20 instances where there were varying numbers of subjects (Ns) studied, yet where the correlations did not vary. The loss of much of Burt's original data makes these problems virtually impossible to resolve or clarify. As a result, Jensen suggests that Burt's kinship data are not usable for hypothesis testing. He concludes with suggestions for standard ways of collecting and reporting future kinship data.

212. Jensen, Arthur R. "The Nature of the Black-White Difference on Various Psychometric Tests: Spearman's Hypothesis." *The Behavioral and Brain Sciences* 8 (2): 193-263, June 1985.

Jensen attempts to account for the fact that black vs. white differences in IQ vary depending upon the test used. Drawing upon the work of Charles Spearman, Jensen suggests that this variation reflects the different "g" loadings of the tests; that is, success on the tests requires different amounts of general intelligence. Jensen rejects the argument that the variation reflects the cultural or language bias of the tests. His test of Spearman's hypothesis confirms that the variations are a result of the different "g" loadings of the tests. Jensen suggests further that black vs. white differences in "g" may be related to differences in the speed and efficiency of one's information processing. However, we do not yet know how susceptible these abilities are to training. Jensen's article is accompanied by a number of brief commentaries by others in the field.

213. Jensen, Arthur R. "The Nonmanipulable and Effectively Manipulable Variables of Education." *Education and Society* 1 (1): 51-62, 1983.

Jensen argues that efforts to improve education and to reduce inequalities in academic achievement have often failed because they were based on an incorrect assumption. He labels this assumption the "specificity doctrine," which is the idea that educational inequalities result from differences in learned knowledge and cognitive skills. However, various lines of evidence contradict this assumption. For example, even diverse mental tests "share some common source of variance" (p. 55), which is the general intelligence factor "g." Also, genetic studies indicate that intelligence is about 70% heritable. Furthermore, reaction time and other content-free tests correlate with intelligence and also demonstrate that mental growth develops "autonomously just as do the physical features of the organism" (p. 57). Jensen identifies pupil/teacher ratios, school expenditures, and related variables as being weak in improving academic achievement. On the other hand, spending time on task, instructing efficiently, matching instruction to maturational readiness, and offering a diverse curricula are effective in improving achievement.

214.   Jensen, Arthur R. "The Price of Inequality." *Oxford Review of Education* 1 (1): 59-71, 1975.

According to Jensen, the egalitarian emphasis on equality of performance or outcomes, and not just on equality of opportunity, has its social price. First, it has made research into genetic causes of IQ or achievement differences a taboo subject. Second, it promotes an environmental explanation of individual and group differences, despite data to the contrary. While Jensen is for the removal of all barriers to equal opportunity, he is against quotas or "compensatory discrimination" to achieve equal outcomes. Such a policy exacts a price from 1) the marginally qualified, who might otherwise have been selected; 2) the qualified members of the group favored by the quota, whose qualifications now become suspect; and 3) the general public, who do not benefit from the full development of talented individuals. Furthermore, attempts to equalize school attainment and occupational rewards inevitably lead to a waste of talent.

215.   Jensen, Arthur R. "Reducing the Heredity Environment Uncertainty: A Reply." *Harvard Educational Review* 39 (3): 449-483, Summer 1969.

Following the publication of Jensen's initial *Harvard Educational Review* article, the journal solicited responses from others in the field. This is Jensen's response to those articles. He first notes the subjects on which he believes there is some agreement. These include the heritability of intelligence, race differences in intelligence, dysgenic trends in current public policies, and the limited success of compensatory education programs. Jensen then defends his interpretation of the evidence on rat breeding studies (which suggest that intelligence can be bred), twin studies, and the normal distribution of intelligence. Finally, Jensen discusses some points on which there is confusion or misunderstanding. First, he says that some critics do not understand that the environment can affect the population average on a certain trait, but that hereditary differences can explain differences between individuals on that same trait. Second, he argues that evidence on the effect of sensory deprivation does not explain the IQ deficits of the culturally disadvantaged. Third, he defends his catagories of Level I and Level II learning abilities. Fourth, he reasserts that social class differences in intelligence have a "genetic component."

216. Jensen, Arthur R., and Ella Munro. "Reaction Time, Movement Time, and Intelligence." *Intelligence* 3 (2): 121-126, April-June 1979.

Jensen and Munro test the hypothesis that the speed with which one processes information, one's reaction time, is significantly correlated with general intelligence. The authors tested ninth grade students on their reaction time, movement time, and intelligence (using Raven's Standard Progessive Matrices). They found that both reaction time and movement time were significantly correlated with Raven's, comparable to the correlation of other intelligence tests with that measure. They also found that one's reaction time increased as the number of choices increased; movement time showed no such effect. Finally, Jensen and Munro thought that reaction time was a better measure of general intelligence than movement time and would therefore have a higher correlation with intelligence. This was not the case.

217. "Jensen: Environment is a factor in IQ." *Science News* 111 (25): 390, June 18, 1977.

In a study of 653 rural black children in Georgia, Arthur Jensen found a "steady decline" in their IQ scores. According to this news report, the decline amounted to approximately one IQ point each year from the age of 5 to 16. Jensen attributed this decline to environmental factors. Though he could not specify which aspects of the environment were causing the decline, he speculated that they could include such factors as "nutrition, general health and a disadvantaged home environment" (p. 390). While he did not get similar results in a comparable study in Berkeley, California, Jensen felt that the Georgia results reflected the impact of living "in a rural, depressed community" (p. 390).

218. Jones, F. L. "Obsession Plus Pseudo-Science Equals Fraud: Sir Cyril Burt, Intelligence, and Social Mobility." *The Australian and New Zealand Journal of Sociology* 16 (1): 48-55, March 1980.

Sir Cyril Burt was a key figure in the history of both British psychology and the IQ debate. He purported to have research data proving the hypotheses that intelligence was inherited, that it was distributed along the lines of the normal curve, and that occupational inequalities were a reflection of these differences in intelligence.

Jones reviews a vast amount of evidence demonstrating that much of Burt's research on these points was, at best, highly misleading, and probably fraudulent. For example, Burt penned articles under the names of fictitious academics so as to increase his contributions to the journal he edited. He also used data that were not scientifically valid; these data, on the IQs of parents, were crucial in Burt's attempts to prove the hypotheses mentioned above. Upon examination by other scholars, Burt's data appear to have been either fabricated or, at the very least, collected in so unscientific a manner as to be unusable. In either event, Jones argues that Burt should have been open about the shortcomings of the data and, therefore, the speculative nature of his arguments. Finally, Jones also reviews the chronology of critical writing that uncovered the fraud surrounding Burt's data on the IQs of identical twins raised in different environments. Jones suggests that requiring open data, limiting the tenure of journal editors, and adhering to policies of peer review of articles would help reduce cases of blatant fraud.

219.   Kagan, Jerome S. "Inadequate Evidence and Illogical Conclusions." *Harvard Educational Review* 39 (2): 274-277, Spring 1969.

Kagan argues that Jensen's *Harvard Educational Review* article contains mistakes of logic and gaps in its supporting evidence. First, even if IQ differences within a group (e.g. whites) are genetically determined, one cannot argue that the differences between groups (e.g. blacks and whites) are also genetically determined. Second, genetically identical twins raised in different environments can have IQ scores as different as that between average white and black scores. Therefore, average differences between white and black scores do not prove genetic intellectual inferiority. Third, some research shows that poorer IQ test performance among those from poor backgrounds could be the result of social class differences in mother-child interaction. Fourth, the IQ test-taking environment could be alien to poorer scoring black children, thus hurting their performance. Fifth, Jensen's negative evaluation of Head Start programs is premature since little assessment of them has been undertaken. Sixth, genetic factors only pro-

vide for a broad range of ability, which should not constrain
the achievement of relatively easy school tasks (e.g. reading).

220. Kagan, Jerome. "The IQ Puzzle: What Are We Measuring?"
Social Education 38 (3): 260-266, March 1974.

Kagan questions the widespread belief in our culture that intellectual differences between people are caused by biological
factors. Using the Wechsler Scale as an example, he argues
that intelligence tests are a culturally biased measure of what
one has learned; they do not measure innate ability. The bias
inheres in the narrowness of acceptable answers, the "familiarity with the grammar or vocabulary" of the question, and
the "examiner's pronunciation" (p. 263). These factors work
against poor, minority children. Kagan also argues that
studies of the IQs of related individuals overestimate the contribution of genetic similarity and underestimate environmental similarities. He also points out that the interaction or correlation of heredity and environment is mostly ignored in research on the heritability of intelligence. The belief in innate
intelligence persists, he believes, because of the need to explain and rationalize differences in status and power.

221. Kamin, Leon. "The Politics of IQ." *National Elementary
Principal* 54 (4): 15-22, March/April 1975.

According to Kamin, the pioneers of intelligence testing in
the U. S. (Lewis Terman, Henry Goddard, and Robert
Yerkes) reinterpreted the work of Alfred Binet to correspond
to their eugenic beliefs. While Binet's original intelligence
test was only a diagnostic test, these individuals interpreted
and used it as a test of innate ability; this grew out of their
belief that races and ethnic groups had different amounts of
innate intelligence. Some of their research on intelligence,
such as Goddard's work on immigrants and Yerkes' data on
World War I draftees, was used to support the racist and
restrictive Immigration Act of 1924. Kamin sees a parallel
between that early eugenic position on immigration and the
contemporary hereditarian explanation of the black/white
average IQ difference. In the face of "overwhelming cultural-
environmental differences between the races" (p. 22), says
Kamin, the IQ test serves to oppress the poor.

222. Kamin, Leon J. "Selective Migration--Again." *Intelligence* 4
(2): 161-164, April-June 1980.

Research data by E. S. Lee have shown that blacks migrating to the north show improvements in IQ, lending support to an environmentalist explanation of black-white IQ differences. Joseph Wolff argues that these higher IQs run counter to an assumed cumulative deficit or decrease in the IQs of southern blacks. Consequently, the scores reflect a selective migration to the north of more intelligent blacks. According to Kamin, however, Wolff is mistaken in assuming that the IQs of southern blacks show a cumulative deficit. Longitudinal research findings show that the IQ scores of migrant blacks are stable; this contradicts the cumulative deficit theory.

223.   Kamin, Leon J. "Social and Legal Consequences of I.Q. Tests as Classification Instruments: Some Warnings From Our Past." *Journal of School Psychology* 13 (4): 317-323, 1975.

Kamin argues that scientific theories and instruments frame how scientists view reality and can have tangible social and political consequences. If this is so, he suggests that school psychologists be wary of IQ tests. The early intelligence testing movement was rooted in eugenics societies, which believed in the inherent inferiority of certain races and nationalities. The movement gained influence after testing army recruits in World War I. Ultimately, the eugenicists' views influenced Congress and helped in the passage of the Immigration Restriction Act in 1924. This act set quotas on immigrants from certain countries whose populations were considered inferior. Kamin warns that school psychologists "would be remiss, in light of warnings from our past, not to question the assumptions and predictable consequences of current classification and placement practices" (p. 322). Furthermore, there is an increased risk of law suits for discriminatory or inequitable placements.

224.   Karier, Clarence. "Testing for Order and Control in the Corporate Liberal State." *Educational Theory* 22 (2): 154-80, Spring 1972.

Karier criticizes the historical role of corporate foundations in rationalizing and supporting the development of a more efficiently managed corporate capitalist society. He focuses on one aspect of this corporate liberal agenda: the meeting of the manpower needs of a corporate economy while protecting existing class inequalities. The school system plays a crucial role in this, and the testing movement provides a mechanism to allocate students to the different slots in the school and economy. Ultimately, the school system and the economy are seen as a meritocracy, with the best students succeeding in school and life. However, Karier shows how those involved in the early testing movement held the racist beliefs and social class biases of the eugenics movement of the period. The early IQ tests reflected these class and ethnic biases and served to justify the existing class inequalities.

225. Kilgore, William J., and Barbara Sullivan. "Academic Values and the Jensen-Shockley Controversy." *JGE: The Journal of General Education* 27 (3): 177-187, Fall 1975.

Kilgore and Sullivan oppose the suggestion that some ideas, such as William Shockley's, be considered nondebatable because some groups find them objectionable. The authors argue that freedom of inquiry is essential for both academic freedom and the common good of the society; it allows all ideas to be accepted or rejected on their merits. In the second half of the article, Kilgore and Sullivan raise questions about the internal and external validity of the twin studies. They suggest that the internal validity may be confounded by the twins' prenatal environmental similarities and by their age at separation. The external validity, or generalizability, of the studies is doubted because 1) the separated twins are a "nonrandom selection of subjects" (p. 183), and 2) the twins' adoptive homes are nonramdom. On the latter criticism, the authors point out that the socioeconomic status, family size, birth order, and family stability of adoptive homes is nonrandom.

226. Light, Richard J., and Paul V. Smith. "Social Allocation Models of Intelligence: A Methodological Inquiry." *Harvard Educational Review* 39 (3): 484-510, Summer 1969.

Using what they refer to as a social allocation model, Light and Smith argue that blacks are differentially and nonrandomly assigned to social environments. They show that the effect of these different environments, in combination with a small effect for genetic/environment interaction, fully accounts for the average racial differences in IQ. Therefore, they reject Jensen's genetic hypothesis, even while using his parameters for the relative contributions of genes, environment, and genetic/environment interaction. However, the authors also criticize Jensen's parameter estimates, particularly the estimate for genetic/environment interaction. They show that even "a small amount of interaction between genetic endowment and environment can easily explain how two races with identical genetic endowments can have large differences in mean IQs" (p. 508).

227. Lindsey, Richard A. "Negro Intelligence and Educational Theory." *The Clearing House* 45 (2): 67-71, October 1970.

This article reviews evidence from Audrey Shuey and Arthur Jensen to the effect that black/white differences in intelligence may be due to heredity. Shuey found that blacks scored worse than whites even when they were matched for socioeconomic status. She also found that blacks of mixed racial ancestry did better than those without mixed ancestry. These findings suggested a genetic explanation for the difference. Jensen, pointing to the failure of compensatory programs and to the lower IQ scores for blacks on even culture fair tests, also suggested "that a genetic factor may be at work" (p. 69). Lindsey sympathizes with both the hereditarians' concern for free inquiry and the environmentalists' concern to stop "social recidivism." Ultimately, however, he suggests that the scientific search for truth should allow for further research and the fair consideration of all evidence.

228. Lowe, Roy A. "Eugenics and Education: a note on the origins of the intelligence testing movement in England." *Educational Studies* 6 (1): 1-8, March 1980.

Lowe traces the role of the Eugenics Education Society in the establishment of intelligence testing in England in the early 20th century. The society believed that mental deficiency was inherited and that it posed a growing threat of racial deterioration. Early mental tests were used to help diagnose mental deficiencies. However, the society moved beyond the identification of the mentally defective to the identification of all ability levels, especially the talented. Lowe points out that these efforts foreshadowed the subsequent full development of England's 11+ exams and its tripartite system of education. In short, the society played an important role in establishing a hereditary view of intelligence and, ultimately, in influencing educational policy after 1944.

229. Mackenzie, Brian. "Explaining Race Differences in IQ: The Logic, the Methodology, and the Evidence." *American Psychologist* 39 (11): 1214-1233, November 1984.

The genetic explanation of racial differences in IQ suffers from what Mackenzie calls the "hereditarian fallacy"; this is the assumption that the high heritability of intelligence within groups, plus the inability to find environmental variables explaining between-group differences, makes the genetic racial difference explanation likely. Similarly, many environmental explanations suffer from the "sociologist's fallacy"; environmentalists overlook the fact that social differences between groups may have genetic origins. Mackenzie argues that given the current state of the research, neither the genetic nor environmental models can resolve the IQ debate. He does find promise in some joint genetic/environmental models of research, such as studies of racial admixture or racial crossing. However, rather than trying to explain between-group differences, these studies would be more appropriate for analyzing environmental factors in the development of intelligence within groups.

230. Mackintosh, N. J. "The Biology of Intelligence?" *British Journal of Psychology* 77 (1): 1-18, February 1986.

Mackintosh examines research on both ethnic group differences in intelligence and the biological basis of intelligence. In Great Britain, he finds that "differences in IQ between white, West Indian, Indian or Pakistani children are closely correlated with differences in their social circumstances" (p. 1). Studies of inspection time, evoked potentials, and reaction time attempt to correlate these measures of various properties of the nervous system with IQ; high correlations might suggest that IQ is genetically determined. According to Mackintosh, however, this research does not offer unambiguous evidence that IQ is reducible to some simple, biological property.

231. Marks, Russell. "Providing for Individual Differences: A History of the Intelligence Testing Movement in North America." *Interchange* 7 (3): 3-16, 1976-77.

According to Marks, the intelligence testing movement gave legitimacy to the measurement of individual differences and furthered the interests of both the field of psychology and in-

dustrial capitalism. Psychologists demonstrated the capabilities of intelligence testing with the World War I army mental
tests. This effort helped the field of psychology attain
scientific status. Beyond this, however, the measurement of
individual differences also met the growing needs of industrial capitalism for social control and an appropriately differen-
tiated workforce. This process was aided by philanthropic
foundations (e.g. Rockefeller, Carnegie), which helped fund
the development of tests and their expansion into industry
and education. Thus, intelligence testing and the measurement of individual differences rationalized educational and
social inequality. While ostensibly catering to individual
needs, this movement helped fit "individuals into educational,
economic, military, and social institutions" (p. 3) whose inequality was in need of justification.

232. McGue, Matt. "Nature-Nuture and Intelligence." *Nature* 340
(6234): 507-508, August 17, 1989.

McGue reports on the findings and implications of a recent
French adoption study by C. Capron and M. Duyme (#156).
They found that children adopted to high-SES (socioeconomic
status) homes averaged 12 IQ points higher than children
adopted into low-SES homes. This, they concluded, indicated
the significant influence of environment. However, they also
found that adoptees with high-SES biological parents averaged
15 IQ points higher than adoptees with low-SES biological
parents. This indicates the influence of genetic differences.
McGue contends, however, that behavior genetic research
does not adequately explain the mechanisms by which the environment or genes influence intelligence or other behaviors.
As a result, the policy implications are ambiguous.

233. McNeil, Nathaniel D. "IQ Tests and the Black Culture." *Phi
Delta Kappan* 57 (3): 209-210, November 1975.

McNeil argues that IQ tests reflect white, middle-class culture
and are therefore culturally biased against blacks. He argues
that a test specific to the urban, black subculture, such as the
Black Intelligence Test of Cultural Homogeneity (BITCH), is
better for juding the abilities of those within that subculture.
McNeil hypothesized that whites would do as poorly on the
BITCH test as blacks would do on a standard intelligence test,
such as the Lorge-Thorndike. McNeil's test of this hypothesis

proved that he was correct. He concluded that black and white cultures are signficantly dissimilar and that the difference is not reducible to social class differences. Consequently, it is inappropriate and harmful for individuals from a distinct culture to be given an intelligence test constructed for a different culture.

234. Miller, Douglas R. "An Analysis of the Treatment of 'Jensenism' in Introductory Psychology Textbooks." *Teaching of Psychology* 7 (3): 137-139, October 1980.

After analyzing 21 introductory psychology textbooks published after 1976, Miller found little outright support for Arthur Jensen's position on the heritability of intelligence. Almost half of the textbooks disagreed with Jensen or the hereditarian position associated with him. Of the remaining texts, four mentioned the debate, five said that it was an open question, and two did not mention the debate. According to Miller, "all the books utilize an interactionist position with regard to the general relationship between heredity and environment, stating that both factors are important contributors to development" (p. 137). Miller also found that most of the discussions of Jensenism were well-supported, citing more than five relevant pieces of research. Only eight of the textbooks mentioned critiques of the twin studies.

235. Miller, M. Sammy. "Black Intelligence Still on Trial." *Journal of Negro Education* 45 (3): 329-333, Summer 1976.

Miller reviews some of the scholarly reactions to Arthur Jensen's 1969 *Harvard Educational Review* article. Among the critics, Jerome Kagan (entry #219) argued that Jensen ignored "evidence of environmental influence" (p. 330) and prematurely decided that compensatory education was unsuccessful. J. McVicker Hunt (entry #203) questioned whether compensatory education had yet been fully tried, while William Brazziel talked of the racist uses to which Jensen's thesis would be put. David Elkind (entry #173) compared and contrasted Piaget's conception of intelligence and development with that of the psychometricians; he particularly questioned the ability of school methods and materials to stir the child's "intrinsic motivation." Finally, among Jensen's defenders, William Shockley (entry #116) suggested that low intelligence blacks be offered cash incentives for voluntary sterilization.

Miller draws parallels between this idea and the positions of Adolf Hitler and Sir Thomas More.

236. Moore, Clifford L., and Paul M. Retish. "Effect of the Examiner's Race on Black Children's Wechsler Preschool and Primary Scale of Intelligence IQ." *Developmental Psychology* 10 (5): 672-676, September 1974.

The authors attempted to test experimentally the effect of the examiner's race on the IQ test performance of black children. They had white and black female examiners administer the Wechsler Preschool and Primary Scale of Intelligence (WPPSI) to 42 preschool black children. Their findings, which ran counter to earlier research on the effect of the examiner's race, showed that the black children performed significantly better with black examiners. Citing other research, the authors suggest that blacks' negative attitudes about white professionals, as well as their "fear of displaying inadequacies" (p. 675), might explain the test results.

237. Moore, Elsie G. J. "Ethnic Social Milieu and Black Children's Intelligence Test Achievement." *Journal of Negro Education* 56 (1): 44-52, Winter 1987.

According to Moore, differences in the IQs and scholastic achievement of blacks and whites may be partly attributable to differences in the social milieus in which they are raised. This milieu is made up of the environment outside of the family, and some milieus may be more conducive to learning the "mainstream cultural orientations" needed for success on IQ tests and in school. To test this hypothesis, Moore compares the social milieus of black adoptees adopted by either white parents (transracial adoptees) or black parents (traditional adoptees); both groups of adoptive parents are middle-class. Social milieu is measured by the parents' educational attainments, the child's "number of white friends," "number of white neighbors," and "average reading level of the adoptive child's grade peers" (p. 47). The data suggest that the white social milieu has a more favorable affect on IQ and scholastic achievement.

238. Moore, Elsie G. J. "Family Socialization and the IQ Test Performance of Traditionally and Transracially Adopted Black Children." *Developmental Psychology* 22 (3): 317-326, May 1986.

Moore conducted a study to determine if and how family socialization differences between blacks and whites might contribute to differences in performance on IQ tests. She studied black children who had been adopted by either middle-class black (traditionally adopted) or middle-class white (transracially adopted) families. Moore found a significant difference in the IQ performance of the two groups of adoptees. Furthermore, she found a significant difference in "their styles of responding to test demands" (p. 322); this difference favored adoptees of white families. By contrast, the response style of adoptees of black families could lead to the underestimation of their competence. According to Moore, the black adoptive homes did not cultivate the same problem-solving strategies as the white adoptive homes, nor did the mother's affective behavior toward the child help the child's response style. These differences contributed to poorer test performance, which Moore attributed to cultural differences in these socialization processes.

239. Morgan, Harry. "Myth and Reality of I.Q. Scores." *The Black Scholar* 4 (8-9): 28-31, May-June 1973.

There are similarities, says Morgan, between Arthur Jensen's argument that Head Start was a failure and Henry Garrett's opposition to integration in the South. Both based their arguments on the alleged inferiority of blacks in innate intelligence. Morgan argues, however, that hereditarians overlook examples of intervention programs that have led to significant improvements in cognitive development, as measured by IQ. After reviewing the findings of a few such studies, Morgan discusses the negative effect that a student's low IQ score can have on the teacher's expectations for that student. Morgan also questions whether the 15 point average IQ difference between blacks and whites is all that significant; most classrooms, he points out, have spreads of 25 points or more. Still, Morgan says that the IQ test may have utility as a diagnostic tool. However, the tests should not be used to arrange students in a hierarchy; this leads to a devaluing of the lower-ranked students and, consequently, unequal educational treatment.

240. Muir, Sharon Pray. "Intelligence Tests Reconsidered." *Social Education* 48 (1): 66+, January 1984.

Muir argues that intelligence tests are not biased and that they should not be discarded. She points out that the tests are accurate predictors of academic success, regardless of one's race or ethnic background. Contrary to popular belief, the tests do not contribute to the unfair labeling of students; research suggests that test results often contradict the teacher's assessment. The test, then, ensures fairness and objectivity in diagnosing those students needing educational intervention. Muir suggests that educational inequities may result from the misuse or misinterpretation of the tests, not from the tests themselves. Also, the educational system may be failing "to adjust to a culturally pluralistic society" (p. 78).

241. Murphy, Claudia M., and Benjamin D. Stickney. "Nature - Nurture Re-Examined: Compensatory Education and Scholastic Achievement." *Journal of Intergroup Relations* 13 (2): 22-33, Summer 1985.

The authors review the original rationale for compensatory education, as well as Arthur Jensen's criticisms of that program's effectiveness. They conclude that both the hereditarian and environmentalist positions share two "conceptual misunderstandings." First, both theories have a narrow conception of the environmental influences on scholastic achievement; they overestimate the impact of school and underestimate the impact of other environmental factors. Second, both theories tend to see the contributions of nature and nurture as mutually exclusive. Murphy and Stickney argue for an interactionist view of the relationship between heredity and environment. Finally, the authors reassert the value of compensatory education and discuss four key factors in its success: supplemental instruction, testing or monitoring, coordination of efforts, and parental involvement.

242. Ogbu, John U. "Human Intelligence Testing: A Cultural-Ecological Perspective." *National Forum* 68: 23-29, Spring 1988.

Ogbu argues that one's IQ score does not measure genetically-determined intelligence, but rather the cognitive skills defined as important by one's culture. American IQ tests are biased against other cultures in that they sample the skills deemed important by Western, middle-class culture. Other cultures, facing different ecological and environmental demands, might define intelligent behavior differently, and would cultivate those cognitive skills. According to Ogbu, immigrant cultures have been motivated to acculturate to the cognitive skills valued in our society. However, blacks and other involuntary minorities, in response to their oppression and denial of opportunity, have adopted their own oppositional cultural identity and cultural frame of reference. According to this oppositional culture, involuntary minorities "interpret IQ tests as detrimental to their cultural and personal well-being" (p. 29). As a result, they do not perform as well as they could.

243. Olneck, Michael R., and James Crouse. "The IQ Meritocracy Reconsidered: Cognitive Skill and Adult Success in the United States." *American Journal of Education* 88 (1): 1-31, November 1979.

Olneck and Crouse attempt to test the IQ meritocracy theory, which argues that socioeconomic success in our society is based largely on one's intelligence. Testing hypotheses with data from Project Talent and the Kalamazoo Brothers study, the authors' findings are mixed. One's cognitive ability does seem to contribute increasingly to getting a college education and to achieving occupational success. However, the authors also find the continuing influence of socioeconomic background, father's educational attainment, and other noncognitive, family-related factors in the explanation of inequality. They point out that, "in many respects, the IQ model does not characterize the process of socioeconomic achievement in the United States", and that the "vast preponderance of inequality in schooling, occupational status, and earnings has no relationship to differences in measured cognitive ability" (p. 24).

244. Ornstein, Allan. "IQ Tests and the Culture Issue." *Phi Delta Kappan* 57 (6): 403-404, February 1976.

Rather than defend IQ tests as being culture-fair, Ornstein argues that they are necessarily culture-laden. That is, the tests measure the presence of the knowledge, skills, and abilities that the society has deemed important and necessary for success in school and work. Culture-fair tests, on the other hand, are misguided because they attempt to equalize the performance of different cultural groups, and thus eliminate the test items that are most predictive of success.

Consequently, the culture-fair tests are "irrelevant to the larger society" (p. 403). Ornstein suggests that the remedy for the poor IQ test performance of the disadvantaged is not "the elimination of test," but rather "the elimination of learning inequalities and social inequalities" (p. 404).

245. Padilla, Amado M., and Blas M. Garza. "IQ Tests: A Case of Cultural Myopia." *National Elementary Principal* 54 (4): 53-58, March/April 1975.

The authors argue that IQ tests are unfair to "Spanish-surnamed children because they do not sample from their particular cultural and linguistic life experiences" (p. 53). Consequently, these students do poorly on such tests and too often end up either being treated as slow learners or dropping out. Specifically, the authors question testing such children in English, or at least testing them before they have had a chance to master English. They also doubt that the tests measure more than a narrow range of abilities. For the above reasons, the tests are imperfect and result in the mislabeling of these children. Among the alternatives to testing, the authors believe that culture-free and translated tests are unachievable and inadequate, respectively. While the development of culturally sensitive tests is considered preferable, the expense makes this alternative unlikely. Until such tests are implemented, the authors favor a ban on testing.

246. Peers, John. "Is That You Behind That IQ Score?" *The Western Teacher* 3 (12): 15, November 21, 1974.

Peers challenges the belief that IQ test scores reveal some immutable trait. In fact, intelligence is not a thing, says Peers, but an abstraction inferred from behavior. Moreover, it only indicates one's behavior at one point in time; the behavior could change in the future. Furthermore, the tests do not explain the causes for the behavior. Also, behaving intelligently depends on the circumstances and on who is doing the defining. Peers cites some research findings suggesting that intelligence depends as much on what one has learned as on what one is born with. He also argues that intelligence tests are just achievement tests, which explains their correlation with school achievement. Peers concludes that IQ tests should be phased out, or at least used only as information-gathering or diagnostic tools.

247. Perney, Lawrence R., Elizabeth M. Hyde, and Bernadine J. Machock. "Black Intelligence - A Re-Evaluation." *The Journal of Negro Education* 46 (4): 450-455, Fall 1977.

This article presents data challenging the assumption that blacks perform worse on IQ tests than whites. The authors administered the Kuhlman-Anderson Test of Intelligence to predominantly black first graders in the impoverished community of East Cleveland, Ohio. After two years of testing, the authors found that the children scored slightly, but significantly, above the national norm. The students' scores were also "more closely clustered around the school system mean" (p. 453) than the national norm. In the discussion of these data, the authors discount the idea that these students were somehow exceptional; the students lived in a community characterized by high unemployment, with 50% of the students on ADC (Aid to Dependent Children) and 25% living below the poverty level. Rather, the authors see these data as undermining the assumption of black students' intellectual inferiority.

248. Persell, Caroline Hodges. "Genetic and Cultural Deficit Theories: Two Sides of the Same Racist Coin." *Journal of Black Studies* 12 (1): 19-37, September 1981.

Persell finds fault with both inherited IQ and cultural deprivation as "explanations for differential school achievement" (p. 19). While these theories are often posed as opposites, Persell argues that they both place blame on the individual, not on society. IQ theory blames the poor for their genetic deficiencies, while cultural deprivation theory blames them for their deficient family environment. Both theories also share the meritocratic assumption of the importance of IQ in achieving success. However, Persell disputes this assumption, showing the importance of socioeconomic status and other social, cultural factors in achievement. In fact, Persell argues that these theories function as self-fulfilling prophecies, perpetuating unequal school achievement and obscuring the influence of inequalities of power and wealth.

249. Pezzullo, Thomas R., Eric E. Thorsen, and George F. Madaus. "The Heritability of Jensen's Level I and Level II and Divergent Thinking." *American Educational Research Journal* 9 (4): 539-546, Fall 1972.

The authors tested a sample of monozygotic and dizygotic twins to determine the heritability of Level I (associative or rote) learning abilities, Level II (abstract reasoning) learning abilities, and divergent thinking. They found that Level II abilities were 85% heritable; this figure is consistent with Arthur Jensen's 80% heritability figure for Level II abilities. Level I abilities were only moderately heritable (54%), while divergent thinking showed no heritability at all. The authors conclude that the "mental capacities that have only low or moderate heritability are identified as candidates for [IQ] facilitation efforts" (p. 545). Consequently, the authors disagree somewhat with Jensen's conclusion that IQ is not susceptible to improvement through compensatory education.

250. Pine, Patricia. "What's the IQ of the IQ Test?" *Education Digest* 35 (6): 13-16, February 1970.

According to Pine, abuses of IQ or aptitude tests stem from misconceptions about them. One of these misconceptions is that the tests measure innate ability. As a result, school personnel sometimes mistakenly assume that low-scoring students are less educable. While IQ and aptitude tests can predict school success and indicate educational needs, they are subject to the same cultural biases as measures of school performance. To try to avoid abuse, Pine suggests that we improve both teacher training and the evaluation of students. Also, future tests should attempt to identify students' needs, the causes of their difficulties, and potentially effective instructional techniques.

251. Plomin, Robert, and J. C. DeFries. "Genetics and Intelligence: Recent Data." *Intelligence* 4 (1): 15-24, January-March 1980.

In a review of recent research, Plomin and DeFries find that estimates for the heritability of intelligence are closer to 50% than to 70%. The authors reach this conclusion after examining three types of related research: twin studies, studies of non-twin siblings, and parent-offspring studies. They hypothesize that the lower estimate for the heritability of intelligence is attributable to either "environmental or genetic changes in the population" or "differences in sample size and methodological differences" (p. 21). Despite this reduced heritability estimate, they point out that genes are still a major factor in explaining IQ differences.

252. Plotkin, Lawrence. "Negro Intelligence and the Jensen Hypothesis." *The New York Statistician* 22: 3-7, 1971.

Plotkin reviews some of the changing beliefs in psychology regarding Negro intelligence. He points out that early mental testers believed in both the heritability of intelligence and the inferiority of certain nationalities and races. By contrast, the work of Otto Klineberg demonstrated environmental influences in IQ differences; these included such factors as socioeconomic status, language, schooling, and speed of work. Although some environmentalists have since tried to develop "culture free" IQ tests, Plotkin believes their efforts to be misguided. He prefers a developmental or Piagetian approach to understanding intelligence. Within such an approach, racial or ethnic differences are viewed as differences in one's stage of development, not in one's genetically determined ability. Plotkin suggests there is a need for more research to provide better understanding of environmental influences on intelligence. He also notes some improvement in attitudes of whites toward the intelligence of blacks, but wonders if the Jensen hypothesis will reverse that progress.

253. Purvin, George. "The Hidden Agendas of IQ." *National Elementary Principal* 54 (4): 44-48, March/April 1975.

In the court of "scholarly inquiry," says Purvin, the hereditarian position on the IQ debate would have a difficult time of it. Experts like Henry Dyer argue that IQ tests are not culture fair, nor are they measures of inborn intelligence. Other critics point out that the tests were standardized on white, middle-class students, to the disadvantage of poor and minority students. Furthermore, Purvin believes that the radical critics of IQ testing may have a point: IQ tests may be used to stifle the aspirations of minority groups. Historically, the argument for inherent inequalities helped justify both slavery and the mistreatment of immigrants. Purvin ends by talking about the importance of early developmental environments and experiences in the intellectual development of children. While the cost of equalizing the provision of such experiences may be high, the cost of not providing them may be higher. Purvin suggests that if we do not equalize these experiences, we should stop using IQ tests.

254. Ramey, Craig T., and Ron Haskins. "The Modification of Intelligence Through Early Experience." *Intelligence* 5 (1): 5-19, January-March 1981.

Ramey and Haskins report the findings from an experimental intervention program for infants who were considered "at risk for subnormal intellectual growth" (p. 5). The experimental group of children participated for almost three years in a daycare program intended to aid their intellectual development; the control group received no such treatment. The authors found that the daycare program helped the children in the experimental group maintain normal intellectual growth, as reflected in their IQ and developmental test scores. The control group, by contrast, had significantly lower IQ scores. Furthermore, the control group's IQ scores correlated .5 with those of their mothers; this would be predicted by a polygenic theory of intelligence. However, there was no correlation between the IQs of the experimental children and their mothers. According to the authors, this indicates the importance of early experiences and environments in intellectual development.

255. Richards, Graham. "Getting the Intelligence Controversy Knotted." *Bulletin of The British Psychological Society* 37: 77-79, March 1984.

Richards identifies some "conceptual riddles" in the IQ debate that have yet to be clearly addressed. For example, if one's genes set a limit on how much the environment can increase IQ, then it is difficult to separate the influence of genes and environment; people with a high genetic intelligence would be more susceptible to environmental influence than those with a low genetic intelligence. Richards also argues that the concept of environment is too broad and incoherent to be "lumped together as a single supposed" intervening variable (p. 78). Furthermore, environmental factors can determine heredity (e.g. intentional selective breeding for low intelligence). Thus, a changed environment could lead to a change in heredity.

256. Samuda, Ronald J. "From Ethnocentrism to a Multi-Cultural Perspective in Educational Testing." *Journal of Afro-American Issues* 3 (1): 4-18, Winter 1975.

Samuda describes three models used to account for black/white differences on intelligence tests. The first model, genetic deficiency, says that blacks are genetically less intelligent than whites. Research on identical twins reared apart and on unrelated foster children reared together purportedly supports this position. The second model, cultural disadvantage, blames poor nutrition, poor and unstimulating home environment, poor motivation, poor values and other factors for causing the poor test performance of blacks. Intervening to make their environments more like those of middle-class whites is considered an appropriate remedy. The last model, cultural difference, argues that minority cultures are different from white culture, not worse. A fair and effective educational system would create bi-cultural students. Existing intelligence tests ignore this third model, and thus serve a gatekeeping function by unfairly labelling minorities as less intelligent.

257. Sanday, Peggy R. "On the Causes of IQ Differences between Groups and Implications for Social Policy." *Human Organization* 31 (4): 411-424, Winter 1972.

Sanday disagrees with Jensen's suggestion that the IQ differences between blacks and whites are mostly genetic in origin. She is specifically critical of the methods and formulae used by Jensen to estimate the heritability of IQ, which she says "cannot be estimated with the methods currently available to geneticists" (p. 413). Sanday disputes Jensen's argument that no environmental factors have been found that can reduce group differences in IQ. In fact, she cites studies by Jane Mercer, G. W. Mayeske, and others where environmental factors have reduced or eliminated the average IQ difference between blacks and whites. As a research alternative, Sanday proposes a diffusion hypothesis in which group differences in IQ reflect different biological environments and unequal exposure to mainstream culture.

258. Sanders, James T. "Marxist Criticisms of IQ: A Defence of Jensen." *Canadian Journal of Education* 10 (4): 402-414, Fall 1985.

Sanders is critical of the Marxist accusations, represented by the work of Michael Matthews (entry #97), that IQ theory is racist and pseudoscientific. Sanders argues that early IQ theorists were not racist, nor did their theories necessarily support or have any impact on the passage of the racist Immigration Act of 1924. Furthermore, Sanders suggests that even if these theorists were racists, that fact is irrelevant to the evaluation of current research. On the charge of pseudoscience, Sanders contends that Jensen did not reify the concept of intelligence (i.e. treat it as if it were a real entity). Also, Sanders defends Jensen's statistical support for the existence of "g" or general intelligence. Finally, Sanders argues that Jensen understood and correctly used the concept of heritability. Sanders suggests that the Marxist criticisms are themselves "ideologically inspired" and pseudoscientific.

259. Scarr, Sandra. "From Evolution to Larry P., or What Shall We Do About IQ Tests?" *Intelligence* 2 (4): 325-342, October 1978.

In recent court cases, IQ tests have been accused both of being biased and of restricting the equitable division of social and economic rewards. In addressing some of the underlying issues, Scarr provides an evolutionary perspective on human intelligence and reviews the research on individual, social class, and racial differences in intelligence. She argues that there is evidence for significant genetic variability of intelligence between individuals and social classes. However, sociocultural or environmental differences, not genetic ones, are the major source of variance between races. Scarr views IQ tests not as tests of innate ability, but as tests of the knowledge and skills defined as important by that culture. Eliminating IQ tests, as was done in California, will not address inequality, since that problem originates in the broader society, not in schools.

260. Scarr, Sandra, and Richard A. Weinberg. "The Influence of 'Family Background' On Intellectual Attainment." *American Sociological Review* 43 (5): 674-692, October 1978.

Scarr and Weinberg point out that one's family background is correlated with measures of intellectual and social achievement or success. The dominant assumption has been that favorable family environments create this higher likelihood for success. However, the authors tested this assumption in a study of adoptive and biologically-related families. They found "that intellectual differences among children at the end of the child-rearing period have little to do with environmental differences among families that range from solid working class to upper middle class" (p. 691). In other words, family environments within this range are "functionally equivalent." The authors argue that genetic differences between families account for the differential success of the parents and of the children.

261. Scarr, Sandra, and Richard A. Weinberg. "Intellectual Similarities within Families of Both Adopted and Biological Children." *Intelligence* 1 (2): 170-191, April 1977.

In this study of 101 Minnesota families with both biological and adopted children, the authors attempted to determine the relative contributions of genes and environment to intellectual (IQ) differences. When comparing the IQ scores of parents and children, Scarr and Weinberg found that the correlations indicated "moderate heritability" of intelligence. However, when comparing siblings, both biological and adopted, the authors found "negligible heritability values" (p. 170). Their explanation for this was that "the unusually high correlations between unrelated sibs lies in their common rearing environments" (p. 189).

262. Scarr, Sandra, and Richard A. Weinberg. "IQ Test Performance of Black Children Adopted by White Families." *American Psychologist* 31 (10): 726-739, October 1976.

In this Transracial Adoption Study, the authors analyze the IQ scores and school performance of 130 black children adopted by upper-middle-class white families. Furthermore, they compare these scores to those of other adoptees, and to the scores of the biological children of these adoptive families. The first major finding was that black adoptees had average IQ scores of 106; the average was higher for those adopted at earlier ages. Second, black adoptees with two black parents averaged 12 points less than those with interracial parents. However, most of this difference was attributable to environmental causes. Third, the average IQ score of black early adoptees (110) compared well with the scores of adoptees in other studies (112.6). The biological children in the adoptive families had higher average scores than the adoptive children; however, this is consistent with the findings of other studies. Fourth, the black/interracial adoptees scored above average on aptitude and achievement tests, although still less than the natural children in the adoptive families. Fifth, if "all black children had environments such as those provided by the adoptive families in this study, we would predict that their IQ scores would be 10-20 points higher than the scores are under current rearing conditions" (p. 738).

The authors conclude that if achieving higher IQ scores is the goal, then both the home and educational environments of black children need to be improved. They further conclude that social factors play a "dominant role" in the average scores of black children, although both genetic and environmental factors are involved in differences between these children.

263. Scarr, Sandra, and Richard A. Weinberg. "The Minnesota Adoption Studies: Genetic Differences and Malleability." *Child Development* 54 (2): 260-267, April 1983.

Scarr and Weinberg report and discuss the results of the Minnesota Adoption Studies, which consisted of the Transracial Adoption Study and the Adolescent Adoption Study. In the former study, the authors found that transracially adopted children scored as well as other adopted children. Their above-average scores were consistent with their adoptive family backgrounds, indicating the influence of environment and the malleability of IQ scores. There was also evidence that IQ differences between adoptees were more attributable to genetic differences. In the latter study, the authors found that the adolescents' IQ scores were more correlated with their biological parents. They were also similar to their biological parents on measures of personality and interests. Overall, the authors conclude that while there is "evidence of genetic sources of variability for all of the psychological characteristics we have studied," there is also "evidence for the malleability of development--the responsiveness of genotypes to differences in their environments" (p. 266).

264. Scarr-Salapatek, Sandra. "Unknowns in the IQ Equation." *Science* 174: 1223-28, December 17, 1971.

Initially, Scarr-Salapatek discusses popularizations of Jensen's theory by Hans Eysenck and Richard Herrnstein. Eysenck's arguments in support of black-white genetic differences in intelligence are considered "inflammatory" and not well supported. However, Scarr-Salapatek does note that Eysenck is optimistic about the ability to modify highly heritable IQs through environmental improvements.

Herrnstein's article is considered more responsible, although not without flaws. His argument is that social class differences in IQ are largely genetic in origin. As environments and opportunities become more and more equalized, social classes will become virtual castes; the intelligent will rise to the top, while the less intelligent will occupy lower social classes. However, Scarr-Salapatek believes that Herrnstein overestimates the heritability of intelligence and its role in social class differences. Also, she argues that we have little evidence with regard to differences between racial groups; within group heritability estimates tell us nothing about differences between groups. Furthermore, environmental sources of IQ differences, both between classes and racial groups, are not fully understood. However, Scarr-Salapatek does support further study of the heritability of intelligence, since it would impact upon intervention measures.

265. Schoenfeld, William N. "Notes on a Bit of Psychological Nonsense: 'Race Differences in Intelligence.'" *The Psychological Record* 24: 17-32, 1974.

Schoenfeld considers the issue of racial differences in intelligence to be nonsense because it is culturally biased and unscientific. Our culture and science predispose us to look for and accept group differences. Furthermore, our preoccupation with black vs. white differences to the exclusion of, for example, Japanese vs. white differences reflects bias. Schoenfeld argues that blacks and whites cannot be fairly compared on all the factors that might affect IQ. In fact, he argues that it is unscientific to talk of hereditary vs. environmental contributions to intelligence; these factors interact and cannot be separated. Schoenfeld says that IQ tests are inevitably bound by culture and experience and could never test only an innate ability.

266. Schwartz, Judah L. "The Illogic of IQ Tests." *National Elementary Principal* 54 (4): 38-41, March/April 1975.

Schwartz is critical of the artificial distinction drawn between ability (IQ) tests and achievement tests. By examining some test questions, Schwartz shows that both tests are dependent upon information that is learned. This, he argues, explains why ability tests are such good predictors of achievement; both types of tests are measuring the same thing. Schwartz is specifically critical of visual, verbal, and numerical analogy questions, which are a staple of many achievement and ability tests. These types of questions are shown to be ambiguous and subject to interpretation; often, says Schwartz, there is no one, correct answer.

267. Schwenn, John, Anthony F. Rotatori, and Herman Green. "Old Problems and New Directions in IQ Testing." *Early Child Development and Care* 36: 173-180, 1988.

The authors review both differential theories and information-processing theories of intelligence. Differential theories are based on underlying factors or constructs that explain individual differences in intelligence. Information-processing theories focus on mental processes, such as the speed of information processing or the procedures used either to solve problems or to decide how to solve problems. As the authors point out, intelligence testing still has not overcome the problem of sociocultural bias. Some of the techniques used to reduce bias include developing culture-fair tests, adapting existing tests to other languages, constructing multiple test norms for different sociocultural groups, using curriculum based assessment, and using computerized assessment programs.

268. Selden, Steven. "Objectivity and Ideology in Educational Research." *Phi Delta Kappan* 66 (4): 281-283, December 1984.

Selden denies the contention, as expressed in Arthur Jensen's "Political Ideologies and Educational Research" (entry #396), that there is a reality that can be studied in an objective and undistorted manner. Objectivity in science is a myth, and values and ideologies can affect both our research methods and the research questions we ask. He illustrates this point with a brief discussion of how values influenced the work of Sir Francis Galton, Cyril Burt, Edward Lee Thorndike, G. Stanley Hall, and Charles Judd. Rather than deny the effect of values on scientific and educational research, Selden pleas for a broader conception of their interaction and cites approvingly Richard Bernstein's statement that "'adequate social and political theory must be empirical, interpretive, and critical'" (p. 283).

269. Shockley, William. "Dysgenics, Geneticity, Raceology: A Challenge to the Intellectual Responsibility of Educators." *Phi Delta Kappan* 53 (5): 297-307, January 1972.

Shockley challenges his readers to discard their environmental bias concerning the origin of individual differences in intelligence. He demonstrates that the assumption of 80% heritability of intelligence allows him to predict one identical twin's score from the other's. This demonstrates that intelligence differences are highly heritable. Shockley disputes some common criticisms of the genetic argument; these include the argument that "identical twins are not absolutely identical" (p. 300), or that the twins were raised in similar environments. He argues that the high rate of reproduction of the genetically least intelligent poses a dysgenic threat by lowering the overall intelligence of our society. Blacks comprise a disproportionate percentage of this group. Shockley recommends positive eugenic measures, such as a voluntary sterilization plan, to address this and related problems of genetic origin. The major obstacle in implementing such proposals, says Shockley, is the dominant equalitarian-environmental bias.

270. Skodak, Marie, and Harold M. Skeels. "A Final Follow-Up Study of One Hundred Adopted Children." *The Pedagogical Seminary and Journal of Genetic Psychology* 75: 85-125, 1949.

In this often-cited adoption study, Skodak and Skeels report the IQ scores of 100 adopted children and correlate these scores with various characteristics of the natural and adoptive families. The tested children were what remained of an initial group of 180 children who had been tested previously in 1936, 1937, and 1940. The results of this follow-up study indicate no decline in the adopted children's above-average IQ scores. The authors find that as the adopted children got older, there developed a significant correlation between the IQs of the adopted children and their natural mothers. This suggested the influence of genes on intelligence. On the other hand, the authors noted that the adoptees' IQ scores were "consistently higher" than those for their true parents; this suggests the influence of adopted family environment on mental development. While the educational and occupational characteristics of the natural and adoptive families did not predict adoptees' mental development, the authors suggest that other factors of the foster home environment may be more significant.

271. Snyderman, Mark, and R. J. Herrnstein. "Intelligence Tests and the Immigration Act of 1924." *American Psychologist* 38 (9): 986-995, September 1983.

One of the criticisms of intelligence testing is that the early intelligence testers were uniformly racist and supportive of immigration restriction and that their racist opinions were reflected in the Immigration Restriction Act of 1924. Snyderman and Herrnstein dispute these assertions. First, they argue that not all early testers were racist; in fact, there was professional disagreement about the assumed inferiority of certain nationalities. This was reflected, among other places, in the criticisms of C. C. Brigham's *A Study of American Intelligence* (entry #36). Second, regarding the proposed immigration act, the authors show that the opinions and data of the racist psychologists had virtually no impact on either the Congressional hearings or the floor debate.

272. Sternberg, Robert J. "Beyond IQ Testing." *National Forum* 68: 8-11, Spring 1988.

Sternberg argues that current theorizing about intelligence has moved "far beyond the present tests" (p. 8) and is leading to vastly improved tests in the near future. He describes three stages in the evolution of these theories: psychometric, information-processing, and systems. Psychometric theorizing focuses on measuring the mind, usually on a single or a few abilities. But, as Sternberg argues, this approach cannot distinguish the different mental processes involved, nor can it distinguish the "measurement of process from the measurement of knowledge" (p. 8) that has been acquired. Information-processing theories attempt to measure underlying mental processes, but are not really better at predicting performance than traditional intelligence tests. Systems theories, such as those by Howard Gardner and Robert Sternberg, attempt to understand intelligence as an "integrated whole" comprised of different intelligences that people possess in varying degrees.

273. Stickney, Benjamin D., and Laurence R. Marcus. "Nature or Nurture: A Decade of Controversy." *Journal of Intergroup Relations* 9 (1): 37-50, Spring 1981.

Stickney and Marcus review ten years' worth of Arthur Jensen's writing on IQ, as well as some of the criticisms of it. They say that Jensen's work since his 1969 article has focused on two areas: the threshold effect of environment, and test bias. On the first point, Jensen contends that environment affects IQ only at the most disadvantaged levels; it does not, in most cases, account for the average black/white differences in IQ. On the second point, Jensen argues that IQ tests are equally good predictors of school achievement for blacks and whites. He also argues that neither language deprivation nor the alleged culture bias of the tests account for "the racial I.Q. difference" (p. 45). Stickney and Marcus dispute Jensen's evidence for the genetic basis of this difference, citing Sandra Scarr's research on both interracial adoptions (entry #261) and degree of African ancestry.

274. Stinchcombe, Arthur L. "Environment: The Cumulation of Effects Is Yet to be Understood." *Harvard Educational Review* 39 (3): 511-522, Summer 1969.

Stinchcombe criticizes Jensen for not appreciating the cumulative effect of environment and for not appropriately measuring the environmental variables that have this cumulative impact. For example, Stinchcombe demonstrates how Jensen mismeasures the effect of blacks' social class. He also argues that if we were to equalize "the amount of fear between races, put Negroes in all-white schools, or schools with the same conditions, improve the standards of Negro families by a standard deviation, then (if the effects are additive) the IQs would be equalized" (pp. 517-518). Stinchcombe argues that developing advanced cognitive structures requires a supporting network of institutions and relationships that foster these structures. Black environments are generally "less rich" in this type of support, says Stinchcombe, thus accounting for disparities in black vs. white IQ.

275. Stoddard, Ann H. "Intelligence Testing Revisited." *The Negro Educational Review* 35 (1): 17-24, January 1984.

Stoddard is critical of both the unfairness of intelligence tests and their misuse. The unfairness stems from the middle-class cultural bias of the questions, the "sex and racial imbalance in item content" (p. 20), the effect of language differences, and subjectivity in the test scoring. There are a number of ways in which the tests are misused. First, they are used to label students, creating a self-fulfilling prophecy in which the "slow" students live down to expectations. Second, the tests lead to "homogeneous ability grouping," which hurts some students' self-image and places them in dead-end courses of study. Third, the tests lead to the resegregation of schools by placing a disproportionate number of minority children into lower academic tracks. Stoddard concludes that IQ tests are prone to misinterpretation and "highly fallible," and implies that we would be better off without them.

276. Stott, D. H. "A Critique of Eysenck and Jensen." *Australian Psychologist* 13 (1): 29-32, March 1978.

Stott believes that Eysenck and Jensen do not take into account the full range of prenatal and postnatal environmental factors that can affect intellectual development. For example, maternal stress during pregnancy, a circumstance more common among the poor, can adversely affect the health and temperament of the child. According to Stott, the postnatal environment of the poor further "deprives them of the experiences and the opportunity to develop the mental skills required in our educational system" (p. 31). This accumulation of environmental damage is difficult to counteract with brief intervention programs such as Head Start. Even middle-class blacks may not be fully equal to their white counterparts. Crudely equating blacks and whites on social class status does not equalize them on crucial cultural traditions and life-styles.

277. "Symposium: The Jensen Controversy." *Measurement and Evaluation Guidance* 3 (1): 7-24, Spring 1970.

This symposium is a collection of three articles written in response to Arthur Jensen's 1969 article in the *Harvard Educational Review.* William F. Brazziel criticizes both the way Jensen's article was published and Jensen's omission of research "showing black-white comparability in IQ scores" (p. 8). Brazziel calls for a moratorium on racial comparisons of test results until there is social equality. Howard K. Cameron argues that there are no good data on racial and ethnic differences in intelligence. He also points out the cultural bias of IQ tests and criticizes the artificial separation of hereditary and environmental contributions to intelligence. He, too, expresses support for a moratorium on minority group intelligence testing. However, Cameron supports diagnostic testing, which can have a positive educational effect. Frederick G. Brown discusses the implications of Jensen's article for those engaged in psychological testing and argues for greater sensitivity to the social implications of testing.

278. Taylor, Howard F. "IQ Heritability: A Checklist of Methodological Fallacies." *Journal of Afro-American Issues* 4 (1): 35-49, Winter 1976.

This is an overview of more than a dozen statistical and methodological flaws in arguments supporting the heritability of intelligence. Taylor criticizes the major twin studies because they did not have significantly different environments for the twins reared apart. He also argues that heritability estimates are inflated because they do not properly consider the covariance of or interaction between genes and environment. Taylor further points out that heritability has no necessary connection to malleability; even highly heritable traits, such as height, can be modified by environment. Also, high heritability estimates within groups (i.e. blacks and whites) do not explain the cause of differences between groups. Taylor also finds fault with the assumptions and empirical validity of Richard Herrnstein's meritocracy thesis. Among his other criticisms, Taylor points out that intelligence is assumed to be unidimensional and that SES (socioeconomic status) is equated with environment.

279. Taylor, Howard F. "Quantitative Racism: A Partial Documentation." *Journal of Afro-American Issues* 3 (1): 19-42, Winter 1975.

Taylor applies the label "quantitative racism" to any argument that misuses statistical techniques to prove the inferiority of racial or ethnic groups. Arthur Jensen, Hans Eysenck, Richard Herrnstein, and Sandra Scarr-Salapatek are singled out for criticism. Taylor argues, among other things, that they treat intelligence, an abstraction, as if it were real; this mistake is known as reification. They also arbitrarily treat intelligence as unidimensional, not multidimensional. The twin studies that they use for support ignore such factors as

common prenatal environment and the similarity of environments of separated twins; these and other considerations could
account for the IQ similarity of identical twins reared apart.
Furthermore, socioeconomic status is not a sufficient measure
of environmental influence. Among other criticisms, Taylor
also questions the possibility of developing a culture-fair and
culture-free test. He concludes that the scientific method
should be used against scientific racism.

280.   Thomas, William B. "Black Intellectuals' Critique of Early
Mental Testing: A Little-Known Saga of the 1920s." *American Journal of Education* 90 (3): 258-292, May 1982.

Thomas discusses some of the ways in which black intellectuals in the 1920s fought hereditarian explanations of
blacks' poorer performance on mental tests. This opposition
followed three different tacts. First, some black scholars offered alternative, environmental explanations of the data collected and reported on by white mental testers. They argued
that hereditarian explanations ignored both the limited opportunities and the unequal social and educational environments of blacks. Second, other blacks challenged the assumptions, methodological procedures, and data analysis of the
hereditarians. Third, still other black scholars developed an
alternative database of research aimed at refuting the
hereditarian claim of black inferiority. Thomas points out
that despite this opposition many of these same black intellectuals adopted mental tests as means of sorting and selecting talented blacks in black colleges and secondary schools.

281.   Thomas, William B. "Black Intellectuals, Intelligence Testing
in the 1930s, and the Sociology of Knowledge." *Teachers
College Record* 85 (3): 477-501, Spring 1984.

Black intellectuals in the 1920s and 1930s opposed the
hereditarianism common among white researchers and instead
argued for environmental explanations of racial differences on
intelligence test performance. Working in conjunction with
like-minded white researchers, they demonstrated the importance of cultural background and testing methodology on test
performance, and they refuted the hereditarian belief that intelligence among blacks was a function of their degree of
white ancestry (the "mulatto hypothesis"). The persuasiveness
of this environmentally-oriented research contributed to a

modification of the hereditarian position, and it gained blacks "a greater power base and social position in the research community" (p. 492). Ironically, however, these black scholars were coopted into accepting the legitimacy of intelligence tests as scientific tools for selecting and sorting worthy black students.

282. Thomas, William B. "Mental Testing and Tracking for the Social Adjustment of an Urban Underclass, 1920-1930." *Journal of Education* 168 (2): 9-30, 1986.

Faced with increasing numbers of poor Polish, Italian, and southern black immigrants in the 1920s, Buffalo created an Opportunity School to adjust many of these students to their marginal place in the society. Mental tests were used to help identify students for this school; the tests were considered objective means of identifying the least intelligent students, who were seen as potentially the most socially disruptive. The tests also confirmed the belief that the maladjusted students were inherently less intelligent, and therefore in need of separate classes. The school taught both industrial work skills and, importantly, values of respect for the existing social order. As Thomas demonstrates, the school functioned as a mechanism of social control "to mitigate the social problems stemming from [industrialism, urbanization, and inequality]" (p. 27).

283. Trotman, Frances Keith. "Race, IQ, and the Middle Class." *Journal of Educational Psychology* 69 (3): 266-273, June 1977.

Trotman studied whether there were home environment variables, other than socioeconomic status, that could account for black vs. white differences in academic achievement and IQ test performance. Samples of black and white children from middle-class families were compared on variables tapping the intellectuality of their home environments. Trotman found that the black and white families differed on these home environment variables. Also, there was a positive relationship between these variables and the child's IQ. Finally, among black families, "the degree to which the family exhibited an intellectual home environment was at least as good a predictor of the child's academic achievement as was the child's intelligence test score (pp. 269-270). Trotman argues, therefore, that socioeconomic status does not sufficiently measure all of the environmental variables relevant to IQ test performance; this finding undermines the genetic explanation of black vs. white IQ and achievement differences.

284. Vernon, P. E. "Intelligence Testing and the Nature/Nurture Debate, 1928-1978: What Next?" *British Journal of Educational Psychology* 49 (pt. 1): 1-14, February 1979.

In this historical review of intelligence testing, Vernon focuses particular attention on the classic twin studies and adoption studies, as well as on the research on environmental intervention. Overall, Vernon supports data from other researchers suggesting that genetic factors are dominant (65%) in determining intelligence, with the environment and genetic-environment covariance accounting for much smaller percentages (23% and 12%, respectively). Vernon also favorably reviews some of the more thoroughgoing intervention efforts, such as the one by H. Garber and F. R. Heber in Milwaukee, which produced substantial IQ gains. For the future, Vernon sees the continued need for intelligence tests as diagnostic tools, as long as they are used with other evidence. However, he does suggest that group tests, which are prone to misuse, could be eliminated.

285. Vetta, Atam. "Concepts and Issues in the IQ Debate." *Bulletin of The British Psychological Society* 33: 241-243, June 1980.

Research has shown that the IQ scores of children of very bright or very "dull" fathers are, on the average, halfway between the parents' scores and the population mean. This is known as regression to the mean. Although many researchers consider this evidence for the genetic determination of intelligence, Vetta disputes this conclusion. Regression to the mean indicates only that the trait, in the parents and children, is "influenced by the same causes" (p. 241). One cannot conclude whether these causes are genetic or environmental. Furthermore, the unacceptability of conducting breeding experiments on human populations prevents researchers from separating genetic from environmental influences. Vetta concludes that the evidence is inconclusive on the genetic determination of intelligence.

286. Wallace, Bruce. "Genetics and the Great IQ Controversy."
      The American Biology Teacher 37 (1):   12-18, 50, January
      1975.

      After a brief critique of William Shockley, Wallace examines
      the arguments of Arthur Jensen, with particular attention to
      how they conform to the science of genetics. Wallace con-
      cedes that IQ tests do have predictive ability, but he suggests
      that the lower scores of blacks are an understandable result of
      discrimination. Furthermore, such tests reward speed and
      penalize reflection, thereby raising doubts that they really
      measure intelligence. Wallace finds fault with Jensen's
      heritability estimates, pointing out that high heritability
      within groups does not explain between group differences.
      Also, the complete randomization of environments, which is a
      requirement in heritability studies, has not been implemented
      in IQ research. Additionally, Wallace doubts that black and
      white environments could be fully equalized. He also argues
      that genetic studies of Jensen's theory are unavoidably in-
      fluenced by human culture, therefore preventing the success
      of the experiment. Wallace says that IQ research comparing
      groups should cease, since it ignores the educational needs of
      individuals.

287. Wallen, Norman E. "The Case Against IQ Tests." *Social Ed-
      ucation* 48 (1): 67+, January 1984.

      Wallen discusses some theoretical, technical, and practical
      criticisms of IQ tests. The major theoretical problem is that
      IQ tests are not based upon a theory of intelligence. Among
      their technical problems, the tests are imprecise, sometimes
      showing changes over time as well as variations between sub-
      tests. They are also standardized on a norm group that is
      "under-representative of cultural minorities" (p. 70). Further-
      more, the tests allow only the most tentative conclusions about
      one's intellectual abilities or potential; changes in the "content,
      method, or cognitive objectives" (p. 70) of instruction could
      lead to different outcomes. Finally, IQ tests are practical be-
      cause of their predictive ability. However, there are many
      contingencies and limitations on their appropriate use, espe-
      cially with cultural minorities or those for whom English is a
      second language.

288. White, Sheldon H. "Social Implications of IQ." *National
      Elementary Principal* 54 (4): 4-14, March/April 1975.

White argues that the whole concept of intelligence as a single entity has been unexamined since its inception. This, he suggests, is because the intelligence testing movement took hold at the turn of the century, when the country was trying to place education on a scientific basis. Intelligence testing seemed to provide a rational and fair means of categorizing people and allocating social rewards; however, it also preserved existing social hierarchies or inequalities. Because of its social utility, the idea of a single intelligence was taken for granted. However, White says that we need to reconceptualize intelligence as multidimensional, acknowledging that human intellectual abilities are diverse.

289. Zach, Lillian. "The IQ Debate." *Today's Education* 61 (6): 40+, September 1972.

According to Zach, intelligence tests are generally useful for clearly defined and practical applications. For example, they were effectively used during World War I to identify and sort out recruits for different positions in the military. More recently, they have been used to identify students who possess the knowledge and abilities to do well in school. However, she suggests that supporters of the tests go astray when they claim that the tests measure an immutable intelligence that limits achievement. Rather than be preoccupied with how much genes and environment contribute to intelligence, we should focus on how they contribute. Once we understand that, we can better create "the educational environment necessary to raise the child to the next developmental level" (p. 68).

290. Zach, Lillian. "The IQ Test: Does It Make Black Children Unequal?" *School Review* 78 (2): 249-258, February 1970.

Zach credits Jensen with making a few good points concerning the relevance of biology to development and the failure of compensatory education programs. However, she criticizes Jensen for not making clear the distinction between one's biological structure and one's genetic structure. In contrast to the genetic structure, a person's biological structure can be influenced by environmental conditions. Zach says that Jensen cannot separate out these genetic and biological inequalities between blacks and whites. She suggests that blacks are clearly unequal on conditions that affect biological structures, which in turn affect learning, growth, and development. Zach also argues that compensatory programs failed not because of the cognitive limitations of blacks, as Jensen suggests, but because they were hastily developed and poorly planned. The emphasis for the future, she says, should be on "developing educational programs to suit the needs of these children" (p. 258) and on providing blacks with economic security.

291.   Zoref, Leslie, and Paul Williams.   "A Look at Content Bias in IQ Tests."   *Journal of Educational Measurement* 17 (4):   313-322, Winter 1980.

The authors studied the degree to which the content of IQ test questions reflected biases and stereotypes about women and minorities. Five major IQ tests, reputed to be unbiased, were examined and scored on how frequently women, men, whites and nonwhites were represented in the questions. The tests were also scored on the extent and type of stereotyping. The results of the study demonstrated an imbalance, favoring white males, in the frequency of representation in test questions. Furthermore, the role stereotypes were favorable to white males, while disproportionately reflecting unfavorable stereotypes of women and minorities. The authors conclude that the tests' content is biased, and thus reflect the white, male dominance of our society.

7   Magazine Articles

292. Bane, Mary Jo, and Christopher Jencks. "Five Myths About Your IQ." *Harper's Magazine* 246 (1473): 28+, February 1973.

The first myth is that "IQ tests are the best measure of human intelligence" (p. 28). However, the tests primarily measure school abilities, not other aspects of intelligence, such as success in adult work or life. The second myth is that "the poor are poor because they have low IQs" (p. 32). In fact, differences in IQ account for only 12% of the black/white difference in income. The third myth is that a person's genes determine most of their IQ. Bane and Jencks, however, believe that the twin studies have overestimated the influence of genes and that the negative learning consequences of being labelled less intelligent have not been appreciated. The fourth myth is that poor whites and blacks do badly on IQ tests because of their genes. However, "genetic differences between social classes explain no more than 6 percent of the variation in IQ scores" (p. 38). And cultural differences could account for the 15 point difference between white and black IQs. The fifth myth is that better schools can eliminate IQ and achievement differences. However, statistical evidence suggests that school differences account for a very small percentage of differences in test scores.

293. Berger, Brigitte. "A New Interpretation of the I.Q. Controversy." *The Public Interest* no. 50: 29-44, Winter 1978.

Berger argues that IQ tests measure neither innate intelligence nor exposure to middle-class culture, but rather whether a person has acquired the structures of modern consciousness. This consciousness involves the ability to function in our rational, technological society; it includes such specific abilities as dealing with abstractions, breaking "down reality into isolatable components" (componentiality) (p. 42), dealing with numerous relationships simultaneously (multi-relationality), and being oriented toward the future. According to Berger, this new interpretation of the IQ controversy explains many previously puzzling findings of the research. For example, changes of IQ with age and social experience can be better understood, as can IQ variations related to family size and birth order. Furthermore, racial and social class differences in IQ can be attributed to variations in exposure to modern consciousness.

294. Berube, Maurice R. "Jensen's Complaint." *Commonweal* 91 (2): 42-44, October 10, 1969.

According to Berube, Jensen's *Harvard Educational Review* article provides conservatives with a convenient justification for not improving the education of the poor. That is, since many of the poor will not benefit by efforts to raise their intelligence, why spend the money on the effort? Jensen suggests that the educational focus for such children be on improving scholastic performance, not intelligence. However, according to Berube, this could lead to an educational caste system. Berube is also critical of Jensen's use of twin studies for support and of his ignoring the confounding effect of teachers' self-fulfilling prophecies. Berube's primary evidence against Jensen, and for the effect of environment, is the Kibbutz in Israel. Research here showed significant improvements of 10 to 30 points in IQ scores of European and Oriental Jewish children. Berube suggests that more political power, to counter "the psychological effects of poverty" (p. 44), could help the poor learn.

295. Bowles, Samuel, and Herbert Gintis. "IQ in the U.S. class structure." *Social Policy* 3 (3 & 4): 65-96, November/December 1972 and January/February 1973.

Bowles and Gintis dispute one of the basic assumptions of the IQ debate, namely that IQ is crucial to economic success.

Through statistical analysis, they demonstrate that economic success is more dependent on one's level of schooling and one's social class background than on IQ. Furthermore, while economic success is correlated with level of schooling attained, differences in cognitive abilities between students explain very little of this correlation. The authors also demonstrate that the alleged inheritance of IQ does not explain why economic success runs in families. The implication of this evidence is that IQ contributes little to economic success either directly or indirectly. Bowles and Gintis argue that IQ tests serve an ideological or political function by legitimating the inequalities found in society, schools, and the workplace. See also entries #33 and #34.

296. Buchanan, Patrick. "'The IQ Myth': Second Showing Still Leaves Skeptics." *TV Guide* 23: A3+, August 2, 1975.

Buchanan is critical of the CBS News special report, hosted by Dan Rather, called "The IQ Myth" (entry #404). Rather argues, among other things, that IQ is not innate, that it is not a measure of intelligence, and that races do not differ in their innate intellectual abilities. According to Buchanan, these are assertions that are contrary to the evidence but consistent with the political views of liberals. He also points out that Arthur Jensen, Richard Herrnstein, and William Shockley are all under attack, probably because their hereditarian position is true. Buchanan concedes that the special report makes a few good points: IQ does not ensure success, and the tests have been misused by some people in the past. However, this is no reason to discard a clearly useful test. Buchanan argues that liberal educational reforms have done more harm to blacks and the poor than IQ tests.

297. Buckley, William F., Jr. "On Negro 'Inferiority.'" *National Review* 21 (13): 350, April 8, 1969.

Buckley is critical of the liberals' overemphasis on the value of intelligence and their seeming despair at the findings of Arthur Jensen. He agrees with the opinion of Ernest van den Haag, who argues that intelligence is an arbitrary criterion for selecting superior individuals. Even if blacks are proven to be less intelligent on the average than whites, says van den Haag, there are still many blacks and whites both above and below average. Furthermore, whites do not judge each other solely upon intelligence; other qualities enter into judgments of superiority. Consequently, van den Haag concludes that the findings on black intelligence would "not entail any judgment about general inferiority" (p. 350).

298.   Burnham, Dorothy. "Jensenism: The New Pseudoscience of Racism." *Freedomways* 11 (2): 150-157, Spring 1971.

Burnham argues that historically the ruling classes have used whatever respected authority was available to justify their rule. Currently, the oppression of black people is justified by Arthur Jensen's argument that blacks are intellectually inferior to whites. Jensen's theory helps justify policies that reduce budgetary support for social programs for the disadvantaged. However, Jensen's argument has been criticized for overlooking the culture bias of the tests, the effect of test results on teacher expectations, and the array of environmental disadvantages to which blacks are subjected. Furthermore, since he does not know what genes contribute to intelligence, nor how they interact "with the organism and the environment" (p. 153), it is not possible to establish the genetic contribution to intelligence. Also, since blacks are not a race in the scientific sense, and because slaves from the same family and tribe were outbred, Jensen cannot assume the level of inbreeding necessary to support his theory. Burnham calls for the repudiation of Jensen and his racist ideology.

299.   "Can Negroes Learn the Way Whites Do?" *U.S. News and World Report* 66 (10): 48-51, March 10, 1969.

This article summarizes some of the major findings of Arthur Jensen's 1969 *Harvard Educational Review* article. Jensen found that blacks scored, on the average, 15 points less than whites on IQ tests. Jensen attributed 80% of this difference to genetic factors and only 20% to environmental factors. This finding was supported, in part, by research on identical twins and on adopted children. Furthermore, Jensen found that while blacks did worse on tests requiring cognitive skills, they did well on tasks requiring associative or rote learning skills. According to Jensen, this fact helps to account for the failure of compensatory education programs, which stressed teaching cognitive skills. It also indicates that future compensatory programs might take better advantage of the associative learning styles of low achieving students with low cognitive abilities.

300. Chomsky, Noam. "IQ Tests: Building Blocks for the New Class System." *Ramparts* 11 (2): 24-30, July 1972.

Chomsky is responding critically to Richard Herrnstein's 1971 *Atlantic* magazine article entitled "IQ" (entry #316). Herrnstein's basic argument is that the United States is gradually becoming a "stable hereditary meritocracy," with the innately intelligent occupying the most important and well-paid positions in society.

Chomsky takes issue with a number of Herrnstein's assumptions. For example, Chomsky disputes the idea that the only way to motivate the intelligent to undertake important jobs is by the lure of material gain. Furthermore, he denies the assumption that the most socially important positions receive the highest rewards. Chomsky also questions whether those attaining "social success" do so primarily because of their intelligence; other traits may be equally or more important.

Finally, Chomsky addresses the social consequences and scientific usefulness of research into the correlation between race and IQ. In a racist society, such research would surely lend support to racists, even if that were not the researcher's intent. Therefore, it is incumbent upon researchers to weigh such factors against the scientific significance of the research. In fact, Chomsky does not find research into the race/IQ correlation inherently interesting, certainly not any more so than the relationship of height and IQ. It is only the existence of racism, and the mistreatment of individuals according to their racial category, that makes the subject interesting.

301. Cohen, David K. "Does IQ Matter?" *Commentary* 53 (4): 51-59, April 1972.

Cohen argues that the more interesting, and taken-for-granted, question in the IQ debate is "what is IQ good for?" In areas that are pivotal in a person's life chances, such as choosing a high school program, getting into college, and adult occupational status, measured ability is only a minor contributor. In fact, ability and inherited social status combined account for less than half of the variation in outcome in these three important areas. Consequently, because IQ makes only a moderate contribution to adult status, Cohen argues that our society is not a meritocracy in which ability determines success. Furthermore, our society has not become more meritocratic in this century; many factors beyond ability still affect success. Overall, says Cohen, lower intellectual ability is not a very important factor in explaining poverty.

302. Cottle, Thomas J. "The Edge of the I.Q. Storm." *Saturday Review* 55: 50-53, April 15, 1972.

Cottle's article explores how scientific research can have a profound and devastating impact on the everyday lives of people. As a case in point, he reports a conversation with a young woman from West Virginia. Her response to reading Richard Herrnstein's "IQ" article in *The Atlantic* was that soon intelligence testers would test hillbillies from West Virginia, and find them, and her, stupid. She could not be reassured; after all, Herrnstein was a Harvard professor. Cottle's point was to show how those IQ arguments could have such a nega-tive effect on one's "sense of identity and possibility" (p. 50).

303. Cowley, Geoffrey. "A Confederacy of Dunces." *Newsweek* 112 (21): 80+, May 22, 1989.

Cowley reports on a recent *Atlantic* article by Richard Herrnstein (entry #316) in which Herrnstein warns of the declining birth rate among the intelligent. This trend, in con-junction with the trend of poor and less intelligent women having too many children, will lead to a gradual decline in the population's average IQ, says Herrnstein. This could damage our society's economic standing. Herrnstein suggests some policies to encourage the intelligent to have more chil-dren. Employers could be more accommodating to bright women, encouraging them both to have families and to pursue their careers. Also, governments could provide larger per-child tax exemptions for the wealthy. Herrnstein would also lower welfare payments for families with dependent children, thus discouraging the poor from having too many low IQ children. Cowley disputes Herrnstein's assumption of declin-ing IQ, citing data showing the long-term increase in average IQ. Herrnstein's suggestions also undermine democratic values, says Cowley.

304. Daniels, Norman. "The Smart White Man's Burden." *Harpers Magazine* 247 (1481): 24+, October 1973.

After addressing the negative social implications of the hereditarian argument on intelligence, Daniels attacks the theory's four assumptions. First, he disputes that IQ measures intelligence. Since intelligence varies over time and with different environments, why should we accept that it is a single, stable, underlying ability? Second, the evidence that intelligence is highly heritable is suspect. The crucial twin studies and adoption studies failed to provide significantly different environments for their subjects. Not all of these studies observed other methodological requirements either, such as having different testers test each twin's IQ. Third, high heritability within a group does not allow one to attribute differences between groups (i.e. blacks and whites) to heredity. Fourth, success is not determined by IQ. Citing Bowles and Gintis, Daniels points out that social class background and years of schooling completed, not IQ, are predictive of success. Daniels questions whether the refutations of Jensenism will receive the attention they deserve.

305. Deutsch, Martin, et al. "Racial Factors in Intelligence--A Rebuttal." *Trans-Action* 6 (7): 6+, June 1969.

Written by the Council of the Society for the Psychological Study of Social Issues, this statement raises a number of objections to the arguments of Arthur Jensen. The authors argue that black/white IQ differences are not innate. In fact, they contend it is not possible to assess the effect of heredity when there are such sizable social inequalities between blacks and whites. They further object to Jensen's categorization of compensatory education as a failure; the failure, they believe, "has been in the planning, size, and scope of the program" (p. 6). Jensen is also accused of oversimplifying the heredity-environment interaction and of underestimating the influence of environment. They also argue that IQ tests are biased against blacks and that much of Jensen's supporting research defines race socially, not genetically. The statement concludes with a call for open scientific inquiry and for "rigorous attention to alternative explanations" (p. 75) of findings.

306. Dobzhansky, Theodosius. "Differences Are Not Deficits." *Psychology Today* 7 (7): 97-101, December 1973.

Dobzhansky believes it is likely that both genes and environment contribute to "individual and group differences in IQ"

(p. 97). However, the degree of genetic contribution is unknown, and the cause of black/white or social class differences in average IQ is not, as yet, determinable. He does argue strongly that even if IQ differences were mostly genetic, this would not preclude the impact or effect of new and improved environments. This is especially important since social classes and races do not share equal educational opportunities. Furthermore, even if interests and aptitudes were strongly influenced by one's genes, this would not have to lead to a genetic elite. Genetic diversity or genetic differences do not have to be rewarded unequally; Dobzhansky argues that an equality of status among different occupations is "ethically desirable" (p. 101).

307. Dolphin, Ric, with Wendy McCann. "Race and Behavior." *Maclean's* 102 (7): 44, February 13, 1989.

This article reports the controversy generated by J. Philippe Rushton's presentation at the American Association for the Advancement of Science conference. Rushton, a professor at the University of Western Ontario, argued that intelligence and other human behaviors are influenced by one's genes. Furthermore, he said that races differed genetically on these characteristics, with Orientals being the most intelligent and law-abiding and blacks being "the least so." Rushton's explanation for this is that the races evolved from their hominid ancestors "at different times," thus creating different traits. Rushton projects that Orientals ultimately will "overtake the Caucasian in North America and Western Europe in economic and scientific performance" (p. 44).

308. Dusek, Val. "Bewitching Science: Twin Studies as Public Relations." *Science for the People* 19 (6): 19-22, November/December 1987.

Dusek is critical of recent reports of twin studies conducted by the University of Minnesota's Thomas Bouchard. Bouchard claims to have evidence that a wide range of behavioral traits, including intelligence, are attributable to genes. Dusek points out, however, that so far Bouchard has not published any research data in refereed scholarly journals. Instead, Bouchard's alleged findings have been reported mostly in the popular media. As a result, Dusek says, one of the primary safeguards of science, peer review, has not been allowed to operate.

309. Egerton, John. "The Misuse of IQ Testing." *Change* 5 (8): 40-43, October 1973.

In this interview conducted by Egerton, Leon Kamin argues that there is no convincing evidence that intelligence is heritable. However, he says that politicians cite alleged evidence in order to rationalize political decisions they have already made (e.g. cutting back on compensatory education). Kamin argues further that those scientists studying the heritability of intelligence historically have been predisposed toward believing that position. Their research, though biased, can have harmful social consequences, as evidenced by the immigration and sterilization laws of the early 20th century. He also criticizes Hans Eysenck for relying on the biased and unscientific data collected by Sir Cyril Burt. Kamin suggests that differences in IQ scores are attributable to differences in environments. In conclusion, he states that standardized tests do more harm than good, and therefore, could be done away with.

310. Evans, M. Stanton. "A Tale of Two Heretics." *Human Events* 33: 10, July 21, 1973.

Evans discusses some of the ways in which Richard Herrnstein and Arthur Jensen have been harassed by campus radicals. He argues that the real reason for the harassment is not their alleged racism, but rather their heretical views against environmentalism. According to Evans, environmentalism, the belief that social problems are susceptible to social engineering, is a fundamental principle of the liberal left. Herrnstein and Jensen, by suggesting that both educational and social inequality are a consequence of immutable genetic differences, challenge that orthodox belief. Consequently, they are harassed and not allowed complete freedom of expression. Evans argues that these circumstances are analogous to those in the Soviet Union during the dominance of Lysenkoism. There, too, scientists were stifled because their ideas were contrary to the dominant ideology.

311. Eysenck, H. J. "IQ, Social Class and Educational Policy." *Change* 5 (7): 38-42, September 1973.

Eysenck identifies and criticizes two myths about the relationship between social class and intelligence. The first myth

assumes that the higher IQs of the upper middle or professional classes result from their more favorable environments.
However, Eysenck disputes this by citing research confirming
that intelligence differences are approximately 80% due to
heredity, and 20% due to environment. The second myth,
reflected in the writing of Richard Herrnstein, assumes that
differences in inherited intelligence will lead to permanent
social classes based on intelligence (i.e. a hereditary
meritocracy). Eysenck counters this by explaining that
regression to the mean ensures that children of very high or
very low IQ parents will have scores closer to the mean IQ for
the population, thus allowing for social mobility. Eysenck
concludes by questioning the effectiveness of compensatory
programs like Head Start. He suggests making more use of
the findings of Arthur Jensen on associative learning abilities.
Furthermore, the government should support research into
biological factors that may improve learning.

312.   "Furor Over Race and 'I.Q.'- Here's the Latest Chapter." *U.S.
News and World Report* 66 (22): 54-56, June 2, 1969.

The Spring 1969 issue of the *Harvard Educational Review*
published seven scholars' responses to Arthur Jensen's 1969
essay; this article summarizes the comments of each of these
individuals. Lee J. Cronbach criticized Jensen for overstating
the role of heredity in intelligence and for understating the
interplay between environmental and genetic factors. Citing
studies from Harvard and CUNY, Jerome S. Kagan asserted
that Jensen did not adequately consider evidence showing differences in the socialization experiences of low-income and
middle-income children. While James F. Crow praised
Jensen's research, he criticized some of the conclusions,
saying that it is not possible to predict racial differences attributable to genes. J. McV. Hunt pointed out that cultural
bias in IQ tests makes them limited measures of intelligence.
Referring to data from the Virginia department of education,
William Brazziel disagreed with Jensen's assessment of the
success of compensatory education programs. David Elkind,
on the other hand, felt that while the reasons for the lack of
success of these education programs may not be clear, they
are, in fact, unsuccessful. Finally, Carl Bereiter predicted
that differences in intelligence levels would become greater as
new learning tools such as home computers became more
widely used by those of higher intelligence.

313. Garcia, John. "IQ: The Conspiracy." *Psychology Today* 6 (4): 40-43, 92, 94, September 1972.

Garcia argues that comparing social groups on IQ test scores is inappropriate since the comparison ignores the biases and limitations of the tests. The original Stanford-Binet test, as developed by Lewis Terman, incorporated a number of arbitrary and biased assumptions. First, the test was constructed to reveal a single, general intelligence rather than a number of distinct, separate abilities. Second, test items were biased toward the more scholastic abilities of reading, writing, and arithmetic. Third, the tests were standardized on an English-speaking, Anglo-American population, thus disadvantaging ethnic and immigrant populations. Fourth, the tests were adjusted to show neither improvement of intelligence with age nor sexual differences in performance. However, the scores were not adjusted to remove differences in racial and ethnic performance. Garcia argues that testers cannot construct a culture-free IQ test, nor can they separate the influences of heredity and environment.

314. Gould, Stephen Jay. "Jensen's Last Stand." *The New York Review of Books* 27 (7): 38-44, May 1, 1980.

In this essay review of Arthur Jensen's *Bias in Mental Testing*, Gould primarily criticizes two features of Jensen's argument: 1) his narrow, statistical definition of bias; and 2) his case for the existence of a unitary intelligence ("g"). On the first point, Gould accuses Jensen of retreating from the popular, and his own earlier, definition of bias. According to Gould, the statistical definition of bias only means that IQ scores for blacks and whites are equally good predictors of school grades; it says nothing about the possible environmental causes of the lower average black IQ score. On the second point, Gould cites L. L. Thurstone's criticism of the theory of a unitary intelligence ("g"); this criticism demonstrates the arbitrary statistical basis of the theory. Gould also criticizes Jensen for having a naive understanding of evolutionary theory and for ignoring or glossing over inconsistencies in his own data.

315. Hart, Jeffrey. "The Herrnstein Case." *Human Events* 33: 21, May 26, 1973.

Hart reports on the harassment of Richard Herrnstein by campus radicals. While critics have labeled Herrnstein's views on the heritability of intelligence as racist, Hart contends that Herrnstein is simply speculating that equalizing opportunities will maximize "the influence of the genetic factor on social status" (p. 21). However, because of campus protests and the potential threat to his safety, Herrnstein canceled speaking engagements at Princeton and the University of Iowa. Hart argues that liberal university administrators were not really willing to defend Herrnstein's right to speak. Consequently, campus radicals had the final say over who would be allowed to speak.

316. Herrnstein, Richard. "I.Q." *The Atlantic Monthly* 228 (3): 43-64, September 1971.

According to Herrnstein, as environmental barriers to social mobility are removed, social standing will become increasingly dependent upon hereditary differences in intelligence. Ultimately, this will lead to permanent, hereditary social classes. There are a number of related arguments that lead Herrnstein to this conclusion. He reviews evidence that intelligence is inherited and that it is essential for success, which is reflected in earnings and prestige. Given this, he argues further that one's social standing will be a reflection of these innate differences in mental abilities, especially as opportunities are equalized. Because intelligence is highly heritable, parents will pass on this intellectual advantage to their children, and social classes will become "virtual castes."

317. Herrnstein, Richard J. "IQ Encounters with the Press." *New Scientist* 98 (1355): 230-232, April 28, 1983.

Herrnstein believes that there is a press bias against the hereditarian position on IQ. As evidence, he points out that the *New York Times* and other national publications are consistently critical of the hereditarian position, rarely review books written from that perspective, and never have professional psychometricians review books on the subject. The other side of the bias is that stories critical of the environmentalist position are not reported. The result is that the debate is presented in a one-sided manner and the public is misled. In reality, say Herrnstein, the tests ensure that those with ability, including the poor, will be objectively identified and helped to develop their abilities.

318. Herrnstein, R. J.   "IQ and Falling Birth Rates."   *The Atlantic* 263 (5): 72-79, May 1989.

Herrnstein warns of a loss of productivity and economic well-being resulting from the falling birth rates of intelligent, high-status women.   This trend is accompanied by a "redistribution of childbearing toward the lower social strata" (p. 76.), who have lower measured intelligence.   The danger in this, according to Herrnstein, results from the fact that productivity is positively correlated with intelligence.   Consequently, if those with less intelligence are having more children, the population's intelligence may shift downward; this could result in lower productivity.   Herrnstein argues for increased school research on cultivating those intellectual skills related to productivity.   He also recommends public policy aimed at reducing "the tension between parenthood and career" among the intelligent.

319. Herrnstein, R. J.   "On Challenging an Orthodoxy."   *Commentary* 55 (4): 52-62, April 1973.

This article is roughly similar to the beginning of Herrnstein's book, *IQ in the Meritocracy* (entry #65).   Herrnstein's argument is that the study of human behavior is constrained by an environmentalist bias.   This bias helped to create a harsh reaction to Herrnstein's thesis that the equalization of social opportunities is creating a hereditary meritocracy.   The article recounts many of these reactions both by the "radical left" and by environmentally biased liberal academics.   Herrnstein concludes by arguing that the egalitarian orthodoxy "chokes off honest inquiry" relating to "the inescapable limitations and variations of human ability" (p. 62).

320. "Intelligence and Race."   *New Republic* 160 (14): 10-11, April 5, 1969.

This is an editorial response to Arthur Jensen's *Harvard Educational Review* article.   After a brief review of his findings, the editorial indicates both vulnerable arguments and good points in Jensen's article.   Jensen is most vulnerable on the validity of IQ tests (do they "mean anything"), on social class and racial biases in the tests, on the fixedness of IQ scores, on the alleged link "between genes and psychological processes" (p. 10), and on the racist use to which his findings will be

put. However, the editorial also commends Jensen for pointing out problems with compensatory education and for criti-
quing the overreliance on IQ tests. Ultimately, though, what
good is group intelligence data when the teacher teaches individuals? The editorial argues that we need more good
teachers and schools.

321.   "Intelligence: Is There a Racial Difference?" *Time* 93: 54+,
April 11, 1969.

This article reviews the major arguments and some of the
political implications of Arthur Jensen's controversial 1969 article. While his article is considered inflammatory and supportive of racism, Jensen is not considered racist. Rather, he
is described as trying to provide evidence for the genetic contribution to intelligence. This is "a tabooed subject" (p. 54),
says Jensen, who believes his position runs counter to the
dominant environmental bias. His article argues that blacks,
on the average, are less intelligent than whites, as shown on
IQ tests. These tests measure cognitive or reasoning abilities,
and environmental or cultural enrichment generally does not
have a significant effect on these abilities. However, Jensen
also says that blacks are as good as whites on associative or
rote learning abilities, which he says should form the basis for
effective compensatory programs. This article concludes that
in the absence of better IQ tests, the ranking of whites and
blacks on intelligence is politically "mischievous."

322.   "IQ Heritage." *Human Behavior* 4 (6): 32, June 1975.

The article reports the partial results of an adoption study
based on IQ data collected by the Texas Adoption Project. In
the study, researchers compare the IQs of adopted children,
their biological parents, and their adopted parents. Early
results show that the IQs of the adopted children more closely
resemble the IQs of their natural parents, not their adopted
parents. These results refute the idea that one's IQ can be
significantly improved environmentally and suggest that
"heredity fixes a certain range for one's IQ" (p. 32).

323.   Jencks, Christopher. "Intelligence and Race." *New Republic*
161 (10-11): 25-29, September 13, 1969.

Responding to Arthur Jensen's *Harvard Educational Review*
article, Jencks concedes that IQ is a good predictor of aca-

demic success, although family background and personality are probably more influential. However, IQ is a poor predictor of occupational status and income. While Jencks concedes that IQ measures something of "moderate" importance, he does not grant that differences in IQ are genetic in origin. Current research, such as adoption studies or twin studies, does not permit us to draw conclusions about the differences in intelligence between groups. Furthermore, while Jensen controls for socioeconomic status in comparing groups, this does not equalize their environmental differences. Jencks concludes that there is not sufficient evidence to resolve the IQ debate. In any event, IQ does not determine how blacks are treated in America. As Otis Dudley Duncan demonstrated, high IQ blacks are as economically disadvantaged as low IQ blacks.

324. Jensen, Arthur. "The Differences Are Real." *Psychology Today* 7 (7): 80-86, December 1973.

Jensen defends the plausibility of a genetic explanation of black/white differences in intelligence by showing the inadequacy of environmentalist explanations. He also suggests that since racial groups differ on other physical characteristics, it is likely that they would differ on "genetically conditioned behavioral or mental characteristics" (p. 81) as well. The culture-bias of IQ tests cannot explain black/white differences, says Jensen, because blacks do better on the culture-loaded than on the culture-fair questions. Furthermore, IQ tests have "the same reliability and predictive validity for blacks as for whites" (p. 82). Another measure of culture bias, the rank-order difficulty of test items, shows no difference between blacks and whites. Nor does the race of the examiner make a difference on black test performance, according to Jensen's study. He also discounts other explanations, such as verbal deprivation or poor motivation, in accounting for racial differences. Environmental deprivation cannot account for the lower black scores since American Indians and Mexican-Americans, who rate lower than blacks on such variables, do better than blacks on IQ tests. Jensen argues that science, not politics, should resolve the issues.

325. Kagan, Jerome. "The Magical Aura of the IQ." *Saturday Review* 54: 92-93, December 4, 1971.

Kagan argues that power is distributed unequally in every society, and the small group wielding this power requires an ideology that justifies its predominant position. In our society, Kagan says, the quality that legitimates power is intelligence. Those who exercise power, whether in business, government, or universities, are considered innately intelligent and therefore worthy of wielding power.

Kagan finds numerous problems with the IQ test, which underlies this whole ideology of innate intelligence. Not only are the tests made by middle-class, white men, but also the questions reflect their class bias. A number of test sections, such as vocabulary and analogy questions, situational questions (e.g. what would you do if...), and questions asking one to fill in the missing element in a picture, all require exposure to middle-class culture. If "knowledge of Western language, history, and customs" (p. 93) are required for possessing power, says Kagan, we should be honest about this being an arbitrary political, not biological, criterion.

326. Kamin, Leon. "IQ Tests as Instruments of Oppression--From Immigration Quotas to Welfare." *South Today* 4 (9): 6, 10, July 1973.

Kamin discusses the influence of Lewis Terman, Henry Goddard, Carl Brigham, and Robert Yerkes in the intelligence testing movement in the United States. Using direct quotes, he demonstrates that these men had racist attitudes about the intelligence of not only blacks and American Indians, but also immigrants from Slavic and Latin countries. Based upon these attitudes, they supported sterilization of the feeble-minded and restrictions on immigration from certain countries. According to Kamin, current data on "innate intelligence" is no better than the data used to justify those earlier, oppressive social policies.

327. Kamin, Leon. "Text of Dr. Kamin's Presentation Denying That Proof Exists That IQ Test Scores Are Hereditary." *South Today* 4 (8): 1-5, May-June 1973.

Kamin criticizes the twin studies of Burt; Shields; Newman, Freeman and Holzinger; and Juel-Nielsen. Burt's research is said to be ambiguous about the types of intelligence tests administered to subjects; in fact, many of these were simply assessments or estimates made by the interviewers. Furthermore, Burt's twin correlations for IQ remain the same to three decimal places, despite the increasing numbers of twins; this is a statistical impossibility, and therefore raises questions about the validity of the data. The Shields twin data are faulty, says Kamin, because the twins were not always raised in truly separate environments. Also, Shields often administered the intelligence test to both twins, violating the "elementary precaution" of using two testers. The study by Newman, Freeman and Holzinger and the one by Juel-Nielsen were not properly standardized for age. Consequently, the IQ scores of twins may have resembled each other due to their similar age, not to their similar inherited intelligence.

328. "Let There Be Darkness." *National Review* 21 (39): 996-7, October 7, 1969.

The author discusses some of the negative reactions that Arthur Jensen received at Berkeley for his *Harvard Educational Review* article. Some of Jensen's critics even suggested that the study of the relationship between race and IQ be considered off limits. The author draws a parallel between this proposal and the reaction of the Church to critical inquiry during the Enlightenment. Today's liberals, in their suggestion to discontinue research on race and IQ, are criticized for abandoning the goal of the pursuit of truth. Furthermore, they are critical of Jensen, says the author, because his research threatens their environmentalist assumptions about the perfectibility of humans.

329. Lewontin, Richard C. "The Irrelevance of Heritability." *Science for the People* 19 (6): 23+, November/December 1987.

Lewontin agrees with Diane Paul (entry #336) that leftwing critics of hereditarianism have too readily conceded the importance of the heritability of IQ, while only disputing its quantitative value. Since heritability "does not mean fixity" (p. 23), it is irrelevant to social policy considerations. However, the critique of heritability does demonstrate that hereditarians often subordinate their science to ideology. Leftwing critics, too, sometimes succumb to their own ideology concerning change. While the political right sees nature as fixed and unchangeable, the left sees it as changeable and capable of being bettered. As a result, the researchers on the left are more critical of evidence that purports to show nature as fixed than they are of evidence that seems to support their views. Overall, however, Lewontin sees the ideology of the right as more harmful since they have the power to resist change.

330. Luria, S. E. "What Can Biologists Solve?" *The New York Review of Books* 21 (1): 27-28, February 7, 1974.

The question Luria poses centers on the appropriate role of biological research in addressing and solving social problems. How relevant should this research be? Luria's position is that basic research is potentially important in its social consequences and should not be belittled. However, he argues that biologists venture into inappropriate territory when they attempt to provide technical solutions to what are, in effect, social/political problems. Three examples are given to support the argument: the ecological crisis, crime and aggression, and the IQ debate. On the last example, Luria says it is wrong to attribute black/white differences in IQ to differences in inherited intelligence. To counter this argument, he cites Samuel Bowles and Herbert Gintis (entry #295), who show that it is a child's social class background, not IQ score, that is most predictive of economic success.

331. McCall, Robert B. "Genes, IQ, & You." *Parents* 63 (12): 128-132, December 1988.

McCall argues that there are limits on what parents can do to improve their child's IQ. First, genes play an important part in intelligence, accounting for approximately half of the difference between two people's IQs. Second, early childhood tutoring, such as flash-card programs, has not been proven to be effective. McCall points out that most children have IQs similar to those of their parents. However, since environment does play a role in IQ, there are some things that parents can do. Most importantly, they can encourage their children, answer questions and interact with them, and provide them with varied experiences. McCall suggests that parents should neither worry about nor try to hurry their child's intellectual development. "After all, nature is quite flexible, and mental ability is not permanently fixed in the first three to six years" (p. 132).

332. McKean, Kevin. "Intelligence: New Ways to Measure the Wisdom of Man." *Discover* 6: 25-41, October 1985.

This article focuses on a number of theorists who are challenging traditional conceptions of IQ and intelligence. Howard Gardner, Robert Sternberg, and Jon Baron are redefining intelligence in broader terms and expanding its applicability to other cultures.

Gardner's experience working with gifted children and brain-damaged adults led him to identify seven types of intelligence. These include "verbal, mathematical, and spatial...musical ability, bodily skills, adroitness in dealing with others, and self-knowledge" (pp. 28-29). Sternberg's definition of intelligence has three components: planning and problem-solving skills; skill at applying experience to solving familiar problems; and "tacit knowledge" (i.e. practical experience, common sense). Jon Baron defines intelligence as the learned ability to think rationally. All three have not only expanded the skills and abilities considered to comprise intelligence, but also challenged the assumption that such abilities are innate and not learnable. Their arguments are, in many ways, a serious departure from the view of intelligence held by Arthur Jensen.

As explained by McKean, Jensen argues that there is a general mental ability ("g") that is innate, and that racial and ethnic groups differ genetically in their inheritance of this ability. On the average, blacks score worse than whites on IQ tests measuring this ability while Asian-Americans score better. Critics assert 1) that blacks adopted into prosperous white environments score above average on IQ tests; 2) that standard IQ tests are culturally biased; and 3) that high heritability of intelligence does not mean that the differences between blacks and whites are genetic in origin.

Finally, McKean reviews some research on the role of biology in learning and intelligence, specifically focusing on male/female differences in mathematical abilities. However, a number of theorists point out that being able to express one's abilities, however acquired, is dependent upon one's culture, motivation, and other factors.

333. Mead, Margaret. "Sense--and Nonsense--About Race." *Redbook* 133: 35+, September 1969.

According to Mead, the concept of race is a major "stumbling block" in the achievement of an open society. She is specifically critical of the claim that blacks, as a race, are less intelligent than whites. In fact, she points out, they are not a race in any biological, scientific sense of the word; race has meaning only as a social designation. But the belief in racial inferiority, even if ill-founded, could perpetuate discrimination and impede progress to equality. Mead draws a parallel between arguments of the racial inferiority of blacks and the similar claims made about certain immigrants in the late 19th and early 20th centuries. According to Mead, social change toward equality must involve not just education, but the whole society.

334. Mercer, Jane R. "IQ: The Lethal Label." *Psychology Today* 6 (4): 44+, September 1972.

Using research data collected in Riverside, California, Mercer criticizes the use of IQ test scores in identifying the mentally retarded. According to Mercer's data, blacks and Mexican-Americans were disproportionately represented among those identified as retarded by various social service agencies. Mercer argues that the overrepresentation of these two groups is not a function of their limited innate intelligence; they are overrepresented because the IQ tests are Anglocentric or culturally biased. Her research data demonstrate that those blacks and Mexican-Americans most like Anglo-Americans on a variety of cultural factors scored comparably on the IQ test. Mercer argues for a variety of special education programs to help students with varying degrees of retardation. Mainstreaming these students should be the rule, with separate programs only for the extremely retarded.

335. Panati, Charles, with Malcolm MacPherson. "An Epitaph for Sir Cyril?" *Newsweek* 88 (25): 76, December 20, 1976.

This is a report on the suspected fraud of Sir Cyril Burt's research on the IQs of identical twins. Burt is accused of having fabricated data on the IQ correlations of identical twins reared apart. As pointed out by Leon Kamin, these correlations remained the same to the third decimal point despite increasing sample sizes; this is a virtual statistical impossibility. Burt is also accused of having published articles in the journal he edited under the names of fictitious colleagues, Margaret

Howard and J. Conway. Since many of Burt's papers were burned, it will be difficult to determine the extent of the fraud, let alone why he did it.

336. Paul, Diane B. "The Nature-Nurture Controversy: Buried Alive." *Science for the People* 19 (5): 17-20, September/October 1987.

Despite hereditarian claims to the contrary, the nature-nurture debate persists. Paul provides a historical review of the continuity and change in the debate and in the positions of hereditarians and environmentalists. The position of early hereditarians was overwhelmingly in favor of nature. While this has evolved somewhat toward a more interactionist position, it still gives a disproportionately large influence to genes. As recently as the 1960s, according to Paul, environmentalists, too, adopted an interactionist position toward the causes of behavioral differences. However, the appearance of Arthur Jensen's 1969 article changed the nature of the critical perspective on the heritability of intelligence and other behavioral traits. Some critics began focusing on the methodological defects of hereditarian research, while others questioned the political and ideological assumptions of the hereditarians. Paul suggests that left critics unify and acknowledge both their ideological and methodological critiques of hereditarianism.

337. "Race and IQ." *Time* 96 (10): 27, September 7, 1970.

The article reports the results of research by Peter Watson on West Indian secondary school students in East Ham (England) and by Irwin Katz on black students. These researchers found that the students performed better on IQ tests when they believed they were not intelligence tests. The authors attributed this finding to the students' increased anxiety on the IQ test. Katz believed that students "were aware of the judgment of intellectual inferiority of many white Americans," (p. 27) and had low motivation to do well as a result. In addition, Watson found that students performed better with a black (West Indian) tester than with a white tester. The results "undermine" Arthur Jensen's findings; Watson believes that these findings could explain, at least in part, black/white differences on IQ tests.

338. "Race or Class?" *Human Behavior* 3 (2): 35, February 1974.

Reporting on a study of the IQs of English and Irish school children, this article points out that the students' scores varied by social class. Since the students were all white, their social class, not race, must have been the determining factor in the differences in their scores. It is speculated that a similar social class difference would be found among blacks and that an equitable social class distribution for blacks would eliminate their IQ disadvantage. Furthermore, blue collar students in England, Ireland, and the United States do worse on the vocabulary subtest. Therefore, it is possible that their poor verbal development may be restricting their learning.

339. Rice, Berkeley. "The Brave New World of Intelligence Testing." *New Society* 50 (888): 63-66, October 11, 1979.

Rice reviews some of the new alternatives to traditional intelligence tests. These includes measures of a child's brain activity (evoked potential) and heartbeat in response to changes in a sequence of observed events; these tests measure only a limited range of mental abilities, according to Rice. Given that our culture is becoming increasingly audio-visually oriented, some testers are attempting to measure intelligence in a more visual manner; this is called cinepsychometrics. Still others, such as Jane Mercer, are constructing culture-specific intelligence tests and tests of social competence; these reflect the effort to avoid the bias inherent in traditional tests. Finally, researchers are exploring differences in cognitive style, as well as measures of one's learning potential. As yet, however, researchers are unable to "combine all the relevant dimensional measurements into one overall index" (p. 66) of intelligence.

340. Rice, Berkeley. "The High Cost of Thinking the Unthinkable." *Psychology Today* 7 (7): 89-93, December 1973.

Rice chronicles the early social and political reactions to the theories of Arthur Jensen, Richard Herrnstein, William Shockley, and Hans Eysenck. At a general level, all four supported the position that there were hereditary differences in intelligence between races and/or social classes. Because of their beliefs, they were attacked verbally, professionally, and, in some cases, physically. According to Rice, this occurred because their ideas violated the dominant environmental bias that existed within academia. After discussing some of the specific incidents and reactions that each of the four confronted, Rice argues for the freedom to disseminate even unpopular or controversial ideas.

341. Robinson, Lawrence D. "The Trouble with IQ Tests." *Essence* 5: 8, October 1974.

The main trouble with IQ tests, according to Robinson, is that they do not take into account the environmental disadvantages of blacks. These disadvantages fall into three broad areas: biological, cultural, and social-structural. Biological factors include substandard prenatal care and poor nutrition after birth; both factors can adversely affect a child's mental development. The lack of exposure to a variety of cross-cultural experiences is an important cultural disadvantage. The main social-structural factor is the denial of equal educational opportunity to blacks. Robinson recommends improved medical care, better nutrition, good schools, and a "reorientation to the family" (p. 8) as potential remedies for these environmental disadvantages. Improvements in these areas should help black children to realize their potential.

342. Rowan, Carl T. "How Racists Use 'Science' to Degrade Black People." *Ebony* 25 (7): 31-40, May 1970.

According to Rowan, history shows that white supremacist ideas have served to impede progress for blacks. More recently, these cruder forms of racism have been replaced by seemingly scientific evidence of black inferiority (e.g. Jensen). While the real evidence may not support this argument, the danger is that it may be believed anyway. Policymakers may limit or eliminate social programs such as Head Start, believing that they are doomed to be ineffective. Teachers may assume that black students are inherently less educable, thus creating a self-fulfilling prophecy. However, it is poverty that impairs the intellectual development of blacks. The poor health and nutrition of many black women lead to higher rates of premature births and prenatal diseases; both factors cause a higher incidence of mental retardation in their children. After birth, poor blacks are more susceptible to disease and malnutrition; these conditions, too, hurt intellectual development. Rowan counsels blacks to value learning, get involved in their schools, lobby for a war on hunger, and fight for equitable employment and income.

343. Scarr, Sandra, and Richard A. Weinberg. "Attitudes, Interests, and IQ." *Human Nature* 1: 29-36, April 1978.

Scarr and Weinberg argue that human behavior is the result of the interaction of genes and environment, with genes setting the range of possible reactions within which the environment can have an effect. Their evidence shows that there are no genetically determined racial differences in IQ, but that there are "differences between individuals within each race" (p. 30). This was proven by two Minnesota adoption studies. Both black and white adoptees were placed into above average family environments. Their subsequent IQ scores were above average and well above their biological parents' scores, indicating environmental influence. Also, their scores were less than those of the biological children in their families; this implicates genetic factors. To their surprise, the authors also found genetic influence on authoritarian attitudes and vocational interests. Scarr and Weinberg conclude that these facts should not be used to justify conservative social policy; nor do they allow us to believe in the "limitless malleability" of humans.

344. "Scoring Test Scores." *Human Behavior* 2 (8): 32+, August 1973.

This article reports some of David McClelland's criticisms of IQ tests, particularly his criticism that they are not really valid measures of intelligence. McClelland concedes that the tests do correlate with school grades. However, this is because one's IQ score and school grades are measuring the same thing. IQ tests correlate less well with nonacademic measures, such as job success. McClelland contends that one's social class background is "a more important factor determining who gets the prestige jobs" (p. 33). He argues for the use of criterion sampling, where you directly measure the needed skill or ability, as an alternative to the IQ or Scholastic Aptitude Test (SAT).

345. Snyderman, Mark, and Stanley Rothman. "Science, politics, and the IQ controversy." *The Public Interest* no. 83: 79-97, Spring 1986.

Snyderman and Rothman argue that the facts and technical issues of the IQ debate have become increasingly politicized and misrepresented by the media. To prove their point, the authors surveyed over 1,000 testing experts on their opinions about 1) the elements of intelligence, 2) the heritability of intelligence, 3) group differences in intelligence, and 4) the misuse of intelligence tests. The experts agreed on the elements of intelligence, which included abstract thinking and problem-solving ability. Furthermore, their mean figure on the heritability of intelligence was 60%. A majority of the experts believed that both genes and environment are responsible for race (53%) and social class (63%) differences in IQ; only 17% and 14%, respectively, attributed the differences completely to environmental causes. Finally, the experts supported the continued use of IQ tests, except as a basis for making tracking decisions. The authors argue that policymakers need to be informed by the objective opinions of these experts.

346. Talbott, Robert E. "Must There Be An Intelligence Debate?" *The Urban League Review* 1 (2): 5-9, February 1975.

Talbott argues that the measurement of intelligence proceeds without an understanding of what intelligence is. He points out that disputes over the tests usually center around either the percentage contribution of heredity and environment to intelligence or the culture bias of the tests. However, both positions presume the existence and measurability of intelligence; they also assume that "test intelligence and real intelligence are somehow linked" (p. 7). Talbott acknowledges that school and adult success are considered indications of intelligence, which is further verified by intelligence tests. But he disputes that intelligence tests are anything more than tests of learned or social intelligence. The tests can be valuable as indicators of one's possession of the knowledge and skills deemed necessary by the society. However, intelligence has no real existence beyond this arbitrary, cultural definition.

347. Vasgird, Dan. "Oh God, Oh Galton, Mr. Herrnstein!" *The Crisis* 82 (9): 341-348, November 1975.

Vasgird argues that proponents of racial differences in IQ are insensitive to the social damage caused by their speculations. He is particularly critical of Richard Herrnstein, who seems unaware that his writing on IQ might "sustain the actuality of racist thought and practice in society" (p. 342). Vasgird also disputes that it has been proven that intelligence is 80% heritable. He further questions assuming cause and effect in the correlation between IQ and social standing. At a more general level, Vasgird sees the idea of genetic inferiority as a victim-blaming explanation of inequality. Finally, Vasgird questions Herrnstein's vision of a meritocratic society.

348. Voyat, Gilbert. "IQ: God-Given or Man-Made?" *Saturday Review* 52: 73-75+, May 17, 1969.

Voyat compares Jensen's views on intelligence to those of Jean Piaget. He prefers Piaget's conception of four stages of cognitive development because it is process-oriented, developmental and culture-fair. Jensen's view of intelligence is, for Voyat, too static and culture-bound. Jensen draws conclusions about students' abilities to learn, and about the usefulness of compensatory education programs, from IQ test results. According to Voyat, however, it is inappropriate to use such results to limit the experiences of children; he believes we know too little about the learning process to draw such premature conclusions. Voyat maintains that teachers should view a child's current stage of development as an opportunity for further development, not as an inherent limitation.

349. Watson, Peter. "IQ: The Racial Gap." *Psychology Today* 6 (4): 48+, September 1972.

Watson reviews some of the evidence about the effects of the IQ tester's race and other testing circumstances on the performance of blacks. Early research (1936) by H. G. Canady showed that blacks performed better on intelligence tests when they had black, not white, testers. Irwin Katz elaborated upon this research by testing the effect of stress level, student expectation, and race of the tester on performance. His experiments showed that black students did worse when they were under high stress, when they had low expectations of success, when their tester was white, and when they were expecting to be compared to whites. Watson concludes from this that blacks find white environments stressful and that they "have a low expectancy of success" (p. 97); both factors contribute to lower test performance.

8 Newspaper Articles

350. Albee, George W. "I.Q. Tests on Trial." *The New York Times*, February 12, 1978, Section IV, p. 13.

    Albee argues that intelligence tests are biased in favor of white, middle-class students and that they test the verbal and quantitative skills deemed important by that class. This bias provided the basis of a recent California law suit in which black students placed in classes for the educable mentally retarded sued the California Board of Education. Albee also suggests that the tests are biased against rural children. To date, no culture-fair intelligence test has been devised. However, the California suit does not ask that the tests be eliminated, only that educational placement not be determined exclusively by the test results. Albee points out that the "retarded" label usually sticks with the child and becomes a "self-fulfilling prophecy." As a solution, he suggests determining the children's "adaptive skills" and placing them in appropriate educational environments, not just in classes for the retarded.

351. Barker, Geoffrey. "Intelligence and the Color Code." *The Age*, September 12, 1977, p. 9.

    In this interview, Eysenck reiterates his positions on the heritability of intelligence, racial differences in intelligence, and other issues related to the IQ debate. He believes that intelligence differences are approximately 70% to 80% heritable and that this accounts for why American blacks score 15 points below whites on the average. However, these figures are true only for a "given culture at a given time" (p. 9). Eysenck suggests that as opportunities are equalized, genetics will account for even more of the individual differences in intelligence. Environmental deprivation, such as lack of schooling, cannot fully account for these IQ differences; Eskimos are as deprived as blacks, yet they score better on intelligence tests. Despite the average group differences, the overlap in group scores prevents one from judging any individual's intelligence by his or her color. Eysenck denies the accusations that he is a racist and suggests that the intolerant behavior of his more radical opponents may have "a strong genetic basis" (p. 9). Furthermore, he believes that many of his academic opponents are pseudo-Marxists, whose egalitarianism is inspired by a misreading of Marx.

352. Berg, Paul. "Height Linked to Slight IQ Advantage." *The Washington Post*, October 14, 1986, Section HE, p. 5.

In *Pediatrics*, Dr. Darrell Wilson and colleagues reported the results of a study of 14,000 children in which they found a connection between height and IQ. Analyzing the IQ differences in averages, the researchers found that "tall children have slightly higher IQ's than short children" (p. HE5). Two possible explanations for this finding were offered. The first was that short children's lower IQ scores might reflect the fact that adults tend to "baby" short children more than tall children and have lower expectations of their performance. The second explanation was that there might be one "biological factor" that accounts for both shortness and lower IQ.

353. Blum, Howard. "A Visit by Dr. Shockley Shakes Quiet L.I. Village." *The New York Times*, January 27, 1974, p. 88.

Dr. William Shockley's visit to Cold Spring Harbor High School on Long Island, N. Y., resulted in a demonstration and four arrests. Shockley was at the high school to speak at a panel discussion on "Human Quality Problems and Research Taboos." The invitation to speak was extended after members of the Student Organization had read that other places would not let him present his views on IQ differences between blacks and whites. Once it became public that Shockley was going to speak, the school began to receive phone calls about his visit. Some of the callers expressed worry that the image of the village would be damaged by the presence of such a controversial speaker; others worried about possible retaliation by people from outside the community. While Shockley was speaking, a group of demonstrators protested and the police made four arrests. Both the president of the student organization and the superintendent of schools commented later that Shockley was a boring speaker.

354. Brody, Jane E. "Gains Forecast in Genetic Intelligence." *The New York Times*, October 28, 1971, p. 22.

At a meeting on heredity and society sponsored by the New York State Health Department and its Birth Defect Institute, Dr. Carl Bajema, a biologist at Grand Valley State College, predicted that there will be "a genetic upgrading of the general level of intelligence" (p. 22) due to what he sees as a trend for people of greater intelligence to reproduce more than people of lesser intelligence do. Bajema's theory is contrary to the opinion of many experts who feel that less intelligent people are having more offspring than more intelligent people, thereby lowering our society's genetic intelligence. Still other experts believe that, due to insufficient data, it is impossible to predict whether the general level of intelligence in our society is increasing or decreasing.

355. Campbell, Barbara. "Panelists Say Theory on Black I.Q. Harms Students." *The New York Times*, May 12, 1971, p. 53.

At a symposium on intelligence and race sponsored by the Day Care Council of New York, Inc., Drs. John Dill, Lawrence Plotkin, Doxey Wilkerson, and Lamar Miller criticized Jensen's theory of heritability of intelligence, saying that the theory was negatively influencing the way that black children were educated. Dill pointed out that while flawed, Jensen's theory could not be ignored because some educators were using it "to support their own racial bias" (p. 53). Plotkin questioned the scientific validity of Jensen's research and argued that black/white differences on I.Q. tests reflect the cultural and socio-economic biases of the tests. Wilkerson pointed out that the idea that black children were "culturally deprived" still held sway in the field of education; he attributed poor educational performance by blacks to the fact that teachers expect less of them in the classroom. Miller rejected the premise of using genetic factors to explain racial differences by pointing out that the ancestry of blacks and of some whites was interracial.

356. "Campus Totalitarians." *The New York Times*, May 20, 1969, p. 46.

This editorial condemns the harassment of Arthur Jensen by Berkeley's New Left (see entry #358), arguing that both academic freedom and free speech are undermined. The editorial acknowledges that while Jensen's research on black/white IQ differences is being misused by racists, "this was clearly not Dr. Jensen's intention" (p. 46). Although the validity of Jensen's research is disputed, it is still legitimate scientific research. Consequently, it should be protected by the principle of free inquiry and should not be limited by political orthodoxies.

357. "Dartmouth Blacks Bar Physicist's Talk." *The New York Times*, October 16, 1969, p. 37.

At the October 15th meeting of the National Academy of Sciences, held at Dartmouth College, black students prevented William B. Shockley from presenting his paper on racial differences attributable to genes. The students blocked Shockley's paper by clapping nonstop. Faculty and administrators from Dartmouth were unable to convince the students to stop their protest. Before Shockley was introduced to speak, a letter from the Academy was delivered; this letter affirmed that Shockley's membership in the Academy gave him the right to speak before it, but that the Academy did "not endorse his recommendations" (p. 37).

358. Davies, Lawrence E. "Harassment Charged by Author of Article About Negroes' I.Q.'s." *The New York Times*, May 19, 1969, p. 33.

Davies describes the harassment of Arthur Jensen by the Students for a Democratic Society (SDS) at the University of California, Berkeley campus. The harassment ranged from personal threats to the disruption of Dr. Jensen's classes. According to the article, the intent was to get Jensen to quit or to have him fired. However, the faculty chair of the campus academic freedom committee said that "Dr. Jensen's academic freedom was protected" (p. 33). The article also reports Dr. Jensen's complaint that the editors of the *Harvard Educational Review* were not making reprints of his 1969 article readily available. See also the editorial in *The New York Times* (entry #356).

359. Delaney, Paul. "Black Psychologist Fighting Use of Intelligence Tests He Says Reflect White Middle-Class Values." *The New York Times* May 13, 1975, p. 36.

This article describes the efforts of Washington University's Dr. Robert L. Williams to oppose the use of intelligence tests. He argues that the tests are "based on white middle-class values" (p. 36), leading to higher scores for whites than non-whites. According to Williams, the poor performance of blacks on such tests can hinder their achievement. To protest this situation, Williams created his own intelligence test that demonstrates some of the untapped abilities of minorities. Williams also notes that the existing tests are being successfully challenged. For example, intelligence tests have been banned in California and New York City. Also, their use for employment screening has been challenged in court, as in Griggs v. Duke Power Company. The article also quotes Dr. T. Anne Cleary of the College Entrance Examination Board, who believes that intelligence tests are mostly beneficial and useful as predictors of college success.

360. Edson, Lee. "Jensenism, n. The Theory That I.Q. Is Largely Determined by the Genes." *The New York Times*, August 31, 1969, Section VI, p. 10+.

Edson provides a lengthy overview of the initial reaction to and controversy surrounding Arthur Jensen's 1969 article in the *Harvard Educational Review*. He cites a number of the criticisms of Jensen's research and quotes at length many of Jensen's responses to these criticisms. In particular, Jensen disputes the suggestions that such environmental factors as malnutrition, cultural bias, or teacher expectations account for the average IQ differences between blacks and whites. Moreover, Jensen rejects the argument that existing scientific methods are unable to separate the effects of heredity and environment. Edson also provides a biographical sketch of Jensen, covering both his personality and the development of his interest in individual and group differences in intelligence.

361.   Eysenck, Hans. "Sense and Nonsense about IQ." *The Age*, September 22, 1977, p. 9.

Eysenck discusses how he and Arthur Jensen were harassed on their Australian lecture tour. This harassment, which he feels is an infringement on intellectual freedom, came from two quarters. Some radical college students, "stormtroopers of the left," had tried to disrupt the lectures. More insidious, according to Eysenck, is the misrepresentation of facts by academic opponents to the hereditarian position on IQ. Eysenck singles out John Fox, a philosopher, as having distorted documented facts on racial differences in intelligence. In fact, Eysenck argues that the suggestion that there is an IQ debate is false and misleading. He points out that there is, overall, scientific support for the hereditarian position; there are only "minor differences in emphasis" (p. 9) within this consensus. Criticisms, says Eysenck, should be documented and presented in scientific journals, not in the popular media.

362.   Fiske, Edward B. "A New Way to Test Children is Urged." *The New York Times*, February 18, 1976, p. 28.

Fiske reviews Jane Mercer's System of Multicultural Pluralistic Assessment (SOMPA), which is a culturally fair means of testing the intelligence of 5 to 11 year-olds. By this method, children from different social and cultural backgrounds are compared to each other, not to a "universal standard." This allows the tester to separate truly retarded children from those who are just unfamiliar with the cultural values of conventional tests. Mercer's SOMPA system grew out of research in Riverside, California, where she found that a disproportionate percentage of blacks and Mexican Americans were being labeled as mentally retarded. The system compensates for the biases that are inherent in existing intelligence tests by adjusting their scores based upon medical history, social and cultural background, and related experiences. This more fairly identifies children with "latent scholastic potential."

363.   Flaste, Richard. "I.Q. Tests: Parents are Eager to Learn Meaning of Scores." *The New York Times*, March 28, 1975, p. 28.

After reporting on the increased demand by parents for information on their children's IQ scores, Flaste summarizes some of the arguments for and against IQ testing in the schools and provides examples of how the debate has affected the way the tests are used in some school districts. At a conference of the American Orthopsychiatric Association in Washington, some critics of the tests pointed out that there is no agreement on what intelligence is; others argued that the tests discriminate against minorities. Advocates of testing maintained that the tests are only meant to predict school success and to identify when children are not achieving up to their potential. The IQ controversy has prompted some schools to do away with group testing, others not to describe the scores as IQs, others to administer IQ tests only in the earliest grade levels, and still others to de-emphasize the I.Q. scores when assessing children.

364. Fletcher, Ronald. "Speaking up for Burt." *The Times Educational Supplement*, December 4, 1987, pp. 24-25.

According to Fletcher, the charges of fraud leveled against Sir Cyril Burt are unfair and not provable. More specifically, Fletcher suggests that there is reason to believe that Burt did accumulate, and did not fabricate, data on an increasing number of separated twins between 1953 and 1966. Burt has also been criticized for having twin correlations that remained the same to the third decimal place, despite increases in the number of twins. However, Fletcher points out that Burt's findings are consistent with those of other researchers reporting IQ correlations for twins. Burt was also accused of creating fictional coauthors (i.e. Margaret Howard and Jane Conway); Fletcher suggests reasons for believing that these two persons did exist. Regardless of one's position on the twin studies, Fletcher argues that most of Burt's work is "unaffected" and valuable. He calls for a fair and balanced reconsideration of Burt and his work.

365. Flynn, James. "Psychology's Square Peg." *The Times Higher Education Supplement*, July 17, 1987, p. 11.

Flynn reports research from eight countries (France, Belgium, the Netherlands, Norway, East Germany, Australia, Canada, the United Kingdom) showing that 18-year-olds in 1980 scored 18 IQ points higher than 18-year-olds in 1950 on culturally reduced IQ tests. According to Flynn, the "gains are simply too huge to be plausible as intelligence gains" (p. 11).

Consequently, these findings cast serious doubt on the validity of culturally reduced (culture fair) tests; these IQ differences could not be measuring differences in intelligence. Flynn argues that if culturally reduced tests are not valid across generations, then they should also be considered suspect when used to compare nations, racial groups, and ethnic groups.

366. Goleman, Daniel. "An Emerging Theory on Blacks' IQ Scores." *The New York Times*, April 10, 1988, Section 12, EDUC 22-24.

Goleman reviews an increasingly popular theory for explaining the 15 point average IQ difference between blacks and whites. John Ogbu, the theory's popularizer, argues that blacks do worse on such tests because they are a caste-like minority. As such, they suffer certain patterns of discrimination with adverse consequences for their self-images and educational success. To support the theory, Ogbu shows that, relative to the dominant group, caste-like minorities from other societies do as poorly as blacks on IQ tests. Other research, by James Flynn, shows consistent IQ gains from one generation to the next in 14 countries studied. His research in the U.S. shows that Americans' IQ scores improved steadily from 1932 to 1978. In addition, research on caste-like minorities from other countries who have emigrated shows that eventually their "IQ scores and school performance tend to match those of other children in the new country" (p. EDUC 24). All of this research supports the argument that it is one's environment, not one's genes, that has the greatest influence on IQ scores.

367. Goleman, Daniel. "New Scales of Intelligence Rank Talent for Living." *The New York Times*, April 5, 1988, Section C, p. 1.

Because traditional IQ tests are not considered good at measuring practical intelligence or "success in living," some researchers are developing tests for these neglected aspects of intelligence. Goleman reviews some of the research of Seymour Epstein, Robert Sternberg, David McClelland, Howard Gardner, and Albert Bandura. All are attempting to measure more practical life skills which, they believe, require intelligence. For example, Epstein's test of constructive thinking "predicts a great range of life success, from salaries and promotions, to happiness with friendships, families and romantic relationships, to physical and emotional health" (p. 1). These successes were not predicted by individuals' IQ scores. Sternberg and his colleagues, as well as David McClelland, have attempted to measure other aspects of practical intelligence, such as general sales or managerial abilities. Albert Bandura of Stanford has developed measures of one's feelings of self-efficacy, which can influence how effectively a person makes use of his or her existing abilities.

368. Goleman, Daniel. "Rethinking the Value of Intelligence Tests." *The New York Times*, November 9, 1986, ED 23-27.

This article examines the criticism that existing IQ tests measure an unnecessarily narrow range of abilities and talents (i.e. primarily mathematical and verbal). The critics discussed here argue that intelligence is comprised of many talents and abilities not tapped by conventional IQ tests. In fact, they argue that there is no single intelligence; rather, there are many or multiple intelligences.

These critics, such as Howard Gardner or Robert Sternberg, concede that intelligence tests are good at predicting academic performance. However, these same tests do not do well in predicting job performance or success after school. This is because other important aspects of intelligence are not tested. Consequently, Gardner and Sternberg are broadening the definition and measurement of intelligence to include these neglected abilities.

Gardner's expanded definition of intelligence includes such things as "the spatial abilities of good architects, the body grace of the superb athlete or dancer, musical gifts" (p. 24) and other abilities. Sternberg's redefinition includes the broadly defined abilities to "learn from context," to be flexible and adaptable in responding to novel situations, and to have insight into problems. A number of critics also point out the crucial role of motivation and persistence in intelligent behavior in the real world.

Both Gardner and Sternberg are developing new intelligence tests in cooperation with the Educational Testing Service and the Psychological Corporation, respectively. These tests will identify a broader range of intellectual abilities and talents.

Once identified, abilities could be cultivated and weaknesses could be improved through the school curriculum.

369. Goodman, George. "I.Q. Scores Linked to Environment." *The New York Times*, January 22, 1974, p. 16.

According to the findings of a 1971 study carried out by Dr. Peggy Sanday, an anthropologist at the University of Pennsylvania, the differences in IQ scores of white and nonwhite students can be attributed to environmental rather than genetic factors. After analyzing data for 3,762 ninth grade students, Sanday concluded that the amount and type of social integration with the middle class were important factors in determining IQ score differences between groups.

370. Harris, Art. "The Shockley Suit: In Atlanta, Debating IQ Ideas in a Libel Case." *The Washington Post*, September 12, 1984, Section B, p. 1.

This article reports on William B. Shockley's $1.25 million libel suit against Cox Enterprises, Inc. In his suit, Shockley alleges that Roger Witherspoon, a former reporter with the *Atlanta Constitution*, libeled him in a 1980 article entitled "Designer Genes by Shockley." In that article, Witherspoon drew a comparison between Shockley's Voluntary Sterilization Bonus Plan (VSBP) and the genetic experiments conducted by the Nazis during World War II. Shockley's plan is to offer monetary bonuses to people with an IQ under 100 or with a genetically transmittable disease if they agree to be sterilized. Shockley, who is taking advantage of the court appearances as a way to publicize his views, argues that the comparison is similar to branding him a mass murderer.

371. Hechinger, Fred M. "Further Proof That I.Q. Data Were Fraudulent." *The New York Times*, January 30, 1979, p. Section C, p. 4.

Hechinger reports that Oliver Gillie, a British investigator, found evidence that Sir Cyril Burt's data were fabricated. These findings raise further doubts about the validity of Burt's theory that genes play a more important role in determining intelligence than the environment does and that some groups of people are genetically inferior to others. Hechinger discusses the dangerous implication of Burt's views--that it is futile to try to raise the potential of those groups of children who were thought to be genetically inferior--and the fact that Burt's research had been used to justify educational policies such as segregation. He also suggests that Burt's theory was attractive to policy-makers who wished to find excuses for the failures of public education or for the failures of government to solve the economic plight of poor people. Hechinger concludes that Gillie's findings may represent a "victory" for those who feel that the potential of children, rather than being a fixed capacity determined by genes, can be raised through compensatory education programs like Head Start.

372. "Intelligence Tests Will Be Tested." *The New York Times*, October 16, 1976, Section IV, p. 6.

In a court case in San Francisco, lawyers for six black children were suing the State Department of Education for using intelligence tests, which the plaintiffs contended were unfair to minorities. The schools had placed the children in classes for the educable mentally retarded (EMR) based upon their IQ scores. However, when tested later with a culture-fair test administered by black psychologists, the students "scored 17 to 38 points higher" (p. 6). Previously, a Federal judge had temporarily banned the use of IQ tests because blacks comprised 27% of EMR students, but were only 9% of the student population. The state contended that the black students did worse on the tests partly because of a "poorer genetic pool."

373. "I.Q. Study Scored By Psychologists." *The New York Times*, May 11, 1969, p. 31.

This article reports that the council of the Society for the Psychological Study of Social Issues unanimously disagreed with Arthur Jensen's position on racial differences in intelligence. The Society argued that current scientific knowledge did not warrant Jensen's conclusion that average black/white differences on IQ tests reflected hereditary differences. Furthermore, they argued that Jensen's position lent itself to misinterpretation and that it could adversely affect social policy decisions. The society contended that persistent black/white social inequalities had to be taken into account when explaining observed differences between the races.

374.   Kaplan, Paul S. "It's the Group I.Q. Tests That Flunk." *The New York Times*, March 13, 1977, Section XXI, p. 26.

Dr. Paul S. Kaplan, assistant professor of psychology at Suffolk County Community College in Selden, New York, criticizes the practice of using group I.Q. tests in the schools and advocates a "critical review and reform of educational testing policies on a district level" (p. 26). Kaplan outlines several problems with the administration, interpretation and use of group I.Q. tests. He points out that the group context puts inexperienced test takers at a disadvantage and does not provide any opportunity for the children to receive individual attention. Moreover, because of the group setting, the logic of each child's answers cannot be analyzed; thus, valuable information about a child's thinking processes is overlooked. Addressing the problems of misinterpretation and misuse of the test results, Kaplan cites the widespread yet mistaken belief among both teachers and parents that I.Q. scores indicate an individual's potential. Kaplan concludes that I.Q. tests "serve no valid educational need" (p. 26), but they have the potential to do harm.

375.   Knickerbocker, Brad. "What Can Schools Use to Replace I.Q. Testing?" *The Christian Science Monitor*, October 24, 1979, p. 4.

This article reports on U.S. District Judge Robert Peckham's ruling in California, which prohibited the use of IQ tests to determine the placement of students in special education classes for the mentally retarded. Peckham found that the IQ tests used for placement were culturally biased; as such, their use resulted in a disproportionate number of black children being enrolled in the special education classes. The case was filed by the NAACP Legal Defense Fund and by Public Advocates, Inc., a San Francisco law firm.

376.   Lichtenstein, Grace. "Fund Backs Controversial Study of 'Racial Betterment.'" *The New York Times*, December 11, 1976, p. 76.

Lichtenstein provides information on the activities of the Pioneer Fund, a foundation that supports research into the genetic inferiority of blacks. The Fund has supported research by William Shockley, Arthur Jensen, and Audrey

Shuey, among others, on such topics as immigration restriction, eugenics, and the intelligence of blacks. According to the article, the Fund and its founder, the late Wycliffe P. Draper, "have had long-standing ties to conservative causes or political candidates" (p. 76). More recently, the political activity of one funded researcher, who was active in opposition to school busing and integration, has raised questions about the Fund's tax-exempt status. Officers in the Genetics Society of America and the American Society of Human Genetics said they supported the right to conduct this kind of genetic research. However, they also said they believed there was no "convincing evidence" for an "appreciable genetic difference in intelligence between races" (p. 76).

377. Lyons, Richard. "Scientists Shun Confrontation on Causes of Differences in I.Q." *The New York Times*, May 3, 1970, p. 58.

Drs. William Shockley and Arthur Jensen presented their views on the role of genetics and environment in intelligence at a meeting of the National Academy of Sciences in Washington. Their ideas have sparked a great deal of controversy, which may explain why many of their colleagues at the session did not participate in the discussion. Shockley argued that black/white differences in earning power resulted from genetic differences between the races. While proposing that his theory "accounts for about 50 per cent of the income variance" (p. 58), he did not discount the role that discrimination might play in that variance. Jensen discussed some of the studies of identical twins, asserting that the small differences in the I.Q. scores of twins might be attributed to differences in the pre-natal environment of each twin.

378. McKnight, David. "'Bright' or 'Dull': the IQ tag sticks." *The Sydney Morning Herald*, May 8, 1986, p. 19.

McKnight discusses some of the arguments in the Australian debate on IQ testing. Many critics believe that the tests are biased and that they do not fully measure intelligence (whatever it is). In fact, the New South Wales Teachers' Federation opposed mass intelligence testing in that state, with the tests ultimately being discontinued. Other critics find fault with the streaming or tracking which results from intelligence testing; this streaming is particularly harsh on poor students and those from other ethnic groups, who are considered less educable and therefore given a more restricted education. Defenders of the test point out its usefulness as a diagnostic tool for identifying students needing remedial help. They also argue that cultural bias results not from the test itself, but from its misuse. Furthermore, a certain amount of cultural bias is unavoidable since there is a common, cultural knowledge that all students must acquire.

379.   Newell, Peter. "Jensen Defends His Views on Race, Class and Intelligence." *The Times Educational Supplement*, July 24, 1970, p. 9.

Newell reports on two speaking engagements by Arthur Jensen in Cambridge, England. The first, to the Brain Research Association, was a routine talk to a group of specialists. The second, to the Cambridge Society for Social Responsibility in Science, was marked by more debate and controversy. Jensen not only reiterated his personal opposition to school segregation and racial prejudice, but also emphasized the validity of studying racial differences in intelligence. Furthermore, he argued that the data supporting his position were "established." Jensen's critics at this meeting included Jerry Hirsch, Steven Rose, and Liam Hudson. They and others argued that heritability estimates were "trivial" because they did not indicate how one "might have developed" under different environmental circumstances. They also accused Jensen of using data selectively to support his position. Others pointed out that there was no culture-free intelligence test and defended compensatory education programs.

380.   Page, Jake. "Does Genius Come in Seven Flavors?" *The Washington Post*, December 14, 1986, Section H, p. 3.

This article reports on some new approaches to intelligence that challenge the notion that intelligence is what IQ tests measure. One approach, suggested by Robert Sternberg of Yale, synthesizes the work of Paul Bohannan and Jean Piaget and views intelligence as a "system of checks and balances" among a persons's "internal world of brain function," "external world of cultural bias," and "real world of experience" (p. H3). Another approach, neurobiological rather than psychological, measures brain activity directly with equipment like electroencephalographs. The article focuses on still another approach, that of Harvard's Howard Gardner, which draws on psychology and neurobiology. Gardner proposes that human's have seven intelligences, each with its own location in the brain. These intelligences are linguistic, musical, logical-mathematical, spatial, bodily-kinesthetic, perception of self, and sense of others. The article presents some of Gardner's supporting evidence, some of which is cross-cultural.

381. "Panelists Assail View on Black I.Q." *The New York Times*, November 23, 1969, p. 88.

At a meeting of the American Anthropological Association in New Orleans, the members considered a resolution denouncing the ideas put forth by Jensen in his article "Race and Intelligence." At this same meeting, a special session was held to discuss Jensen's views. The five anthropologists on the panel - Drs. Alland, Brace, John, Cohen and Washington - criticized every aspect of Jensen's work: "his data, assumptions and conclusions, as well as his writing style" (p. 88). According to the panel members, Jensen's assertion that differences in intelligence resulted mainly from differences in genes was "dangerous." One anthropologist in attendance illustrated this point by remarking that Jensen's conclusions had "discouraged" black teachers in Little Rock, Arkansas.

382. Reinhold, Robert. "Psychologist Arouses Storm by Linking I.Q. to Heredity." *The New York Times*, March 30, 1969, p. 52.

Reinhold reviews the controversy generated by Arthur Jensen's contention that intelligence is mostly hereditary and that blacks are, on the average, less intelligent than whites. On the hereditary nature of intelligence, Jensen cites studies of identical twins reared apart. He further points out that: 1) blacks do worse than whites on "culture-fair" tests; 2) blacks score worse than American Indians, who are more disadvantaged; 3) upper-class blacks have many times more retarded children than their white counterparts; and 4) improvements from compensatory programs are short-lived. For Jensen, this evidence casts doubt on environmental explanations of intelligence differences and makes a genetic explanation "not unreasonable." Jensen's critics are concerned that his research may support racist claims of black inferiority. Others suggest that the science of genetics has no firm evidence supporting Jensen's position.

383. Rensberger, Boyce. "Briton's Classic I.Q. Data Now Viewed as Fraudulent." *The New York Times*, November 28, 1976, p. 26.

According to Rensberger, scholars now believe that Sir Cyril Burt faked crucial data in his study of identical twins reared apart. This belief is based on that fact that even with increasing sample sizes of twins reared apart, the reported correlations of their IQ's remained the same to the third decimal place. This is considered a virtual statistical impossibility. It is also believed that Burt invented two collaborators so that he could publish more of his ideas under their names. Arthur Jensen believes that the loss of Burt's data, which he agrees is flawed, does no real harm to the hereditarian argument; other twin studies verify the strong hereditary component in intelligence differences. Leon Kamin and Richard Lewontin, on the other hand, argue that the loss of Burt's data is a critical blow to the hereditarian position.

384. Rensberger, Boyce. "Data on Race Role in I.Q. Called False." *The New York Times*, November 8, 1978, p. 9.

Critics have accused the late Sir Cyril Burt of having fabricated his data on genetic differences in intelligence. Burt's defenders, on the other hand, have argued that the mistakes were simply carelessness. However, a recent article in *Science* by D. D. Dorfman (see #168) demonstrates intentional fabrication on Burt's part. Dorfman found that Burt copied 30 year-old data into a 1961 publication and passed it off as the results of recent research. According to Dorfman, Burt obtained IQ's for subjects by selecting scores off of a normal curve distribution and assigning them to people, not by testing them; Burt believed that intelligence was distributed in the population along the lines of the normal curve. Burt used his data to argue that the lower classes were less intelligent than the upper classes, that women were less intelligent than men, and that "Jews and the Irish were less intelligent than the English" (p. 9).

385. Schanberg, Sydney H. "New Patterns." *The New York Times*, October 12, 1982, Section A, p. 29.

A College Entrance Examination Board report showed that the gap between the SAT scores of black and white students decreased significantly when the family income of the two groups was about the same. Seeing this as counterevidence to the genetic theorists, Schanberg suggests that differences in socioeconomic status may be the pattern that accounts for differences in IQ. Schanberg anticipates what the genetic theorists would say in response to the findings of the Board: first, that only the "hereditarily superior" blacks are socially mobile, so it is their children who are getting higher test scores; second, that, while it is decreasing, the gap in black/white scores still exists. Dismissing these arguments, he suggests that people in the middle class achieve in a middle-class way and that a group of people who have been excluded from that class in the past "need a chance to catch up" before they can perform at the same level as those for whom the middle-class "habits and rituals of achievement are more deeply ingrained" (p. A29).

386. Schmeck, Harold M., Jr. "Science Group Balks at Study of Race." *The New York Times*, April 29, 1971, p. 24.

The National Academy of Sciences accepted a report by a special committee that had been appointed to consider "genetic factors in human performance" (p. 24). The committee, whose formation had been pressed for by Dr. William Shockley, affirmed the scientific value and social relevance of research into racial differences in humans and made three recommendations, two of which were rejected by the Academy. The accepted recommendation called for more collaboration between the fields of study that comprise behavioral genetics, that is, human genetics, education, psychology and neurobiology. The rejection of the other two recommendations was "a rebuff" for Shockley. One of these recommendations, that the National Science Foundation work with other agencies on "the possible educational implications of human behavioral genetics" (p. 24), was rejected for being ambiguous. The other, calling for a feasibility study of a research project into the interaction of nature and nurture in human performance, was found to be unnecessary.

387. Sowell, Thomas. "New Light on Black I.Q." *The New York Times*, March 27, 1977, Section VI, p. 57+.

Sowell argues that the "level or the pattern of black I.Q.'s" (p. 57) is not appreciably different from that of other immigrant groups. Historically, many immigrant groups had initial IQ scores similar to those of blacks. However, as they assimilated into American society and became more upwardly mobile, their scores improved to be equal to or, in some cases, better than the national average. Sowell suggests that black IQ's should be viewed in light of this historical pattern. As for IQ tests, Sowell points out that while they can be used in a biased manner, they still have a valid predictive use. However, they should not be used to label some students as inferior, and consequently "to justify providing inferior education to children from disadvantaged backgrounds" (p. 62).

388. Stevens, Wallace K. "Doctor Foresees an I.Q. Caste System." *The New York Times*, August 29, 1971, p. 34.

The September 1971 issue of *Atlantic* reported the conclusions of Dr. Richard Herrnstein (entry #316), a psychologist at Harvard, who asserted that the U.S. is liable to become a caste system in which people are stratified because of their inherited intelligence. Herrnstein reviewed the scientific literature and concluded that genes accounted for 85% of the difference between people's I.Q. scores. He felt that the U.S. was becoming more successful in providing equal opportunities for everyone and that the differences in people's success reflected "biologic stratification." Herrnstein did not address the issue of racial differences in I.Q. scores.

389. Sullivan, Walter. "Scientists Debate Question of Race and Intelligence." *The New York Times*, February 23, 1976, p. 23.

The existence of racial and ethnic differences in intelligence was debated at the American Association for the Advancement of Science conference. Bernard Davis argued that since the human brain has evolved under different environmental conditions, it is likely that races have different potentials for acquiring various behavioral traits. Arguing the other side, Richard Lewontin said that one's genetic potential did not act as a limit on one's learning ability. Rather, individuals respond differently to stimuli and environments. "Hence, society...should make it possible for those with diverse inherited mental qualities to develop them to the fullest possible extent" (p. 23). Lewontin also pointed out that black children adopted by white parents had IQs comparable to whites and that the degree of white ancestry had no effect on black IQ.

This demonstrates the lack of genetic racial differences in intelligence. Davis rejected the position argued by some audience members that one's genes had no influence on the brain.

390. Wade, Nicholas. "The Shadow Over Race and I.Q." *The New York Times*, September 10, 1982, Section A, p. 22.

In this editorial, Wade summarizes Richard Herrnstein's complaint, presented in the August 1982 issue of the *Atlantic*, that the national press does not adequately cover the hereditarian view of intelligence. Wade argues that this "lack of attention is richly deserved" (p. 22). Referring to the fraudulent work of Sir Cyril Burt, which had served as the basis for Jensen's and Herrnstein's views, and to the misinterpretation of mental test scores of Army recruits in WWI, Wade questions the credibility of the psychometric research which has been used to support the theory of the heritability of intelligence. He also notes that the inferences drawn from the theory - that I.Q. is fixed and that some groups of people are more intelligent than others - are "fallacious" and disputable. Wade maintains that while the scientific community has not monitored its own research carefully enough, reporters and others have.

391. Weinraub, Bernard. "Children of Retarded Mothers Learn Well in a Wisconsin Study." *The New York Times*, August 20, 1970, p. 31.

At a symposium of the Maudsley Institute of Psychiatry in London, Rick Heber, of the Department of Studies in Behavioral Disabilities at the University of Wisconsin, presented the results of a study designed to determine the effect of "intensive training" on the development of children of retarded mothers. The children of 40 mothers with IQ's under 70 were studied. The children who started the training program shortly after birth were beginning to read and learn arithmetic by 3 years of age. The children who did not receive the training were less "verbal, energetic and intellectually curious" (p. 31) than their counterparts in the experimental group. Arthur Jensen, who spoke at the same conference, asserted that "there are large and important differences" between individuals and groups that are not "due simply to the social structure or to poverty..." (p. 31). As a result, the causes of these differences must be considered when establishing educational policy.

9　ERIC Documents

392.　Alford, David W.　"IQ Test Controversy:　Past, Present, and Future Trends."　1984.　24p.　(ERIC microfiche ED 259 026).

Alford reviews the controversy over both the definition of intelligence and the relative influence of heredity and environment.　Despite disagreements, there are some environmental influences that are confirmed, such as the prenatal environment, birth weight, child rearing practices, birth order, and socioeconomic level.　Other external factors can affect IQ scores too, such as examiner bias, age of the test taker, and score interpretation.　Regardless of its problems, the IQ test provides a valuable diagnostic service and can help in the proper labeling and classification of students.　Recent efforts at improving the tests have focused on developing culture-fair and culture-specific tests, eliminating age/sexual/racial bias, correcting biased test content, and developing alternative forms of assessment.　Others have focused on physiological measures reflecting intelligence, such as evoked potentials, or measures of cognitive style.　Despite the tests' problems, Alford feels that our energy is better spent improving them, rather than banning them.

393.　Cancro, Robert.　"Race, Reification, and Responsibility."　1974.　18p.　(ERIC microfiche ED 106 398).

In 1972, a number of academics signed a resolution in favor of freedom of inquiry on investigations into the genetic basis of behavior (e.g. intelligence differences).　Cancro, a signee of that resolution, reviews some of the negative reactions that he and other signees received. He systematically addresses what he sees as the false distinction between environment and heredity; these are incorrectly portrayed as competing, rather than complementary, explanations of behavior. Cancro discusses the strengths, such as their predictive power, and the limitations of IQ tests. He questions whether anyone could doubt the influence of genetics on behavior, but also points out the genetic similarity of groups and the variety of gene-environment combinations that can lead to the same behavioral outcome. In any event, he sees no clear policy implications of the behavior geneticists' findings. Cancro concludes by reaffirming the importance of free inquiry both within the university and the society.

394. Gartner, Alan, and Frank Riessman. *The Lingering Infatuation with I.Q. COP Bulletin No. 4.* New York, Queens College, City University of New York, New Careers Training Lab, 1973. 14p. (ERIC microfiche ED 106 305).

Gartner and Riessman cite evidence that contradicts the hereditarian explanation of racial differences in IQ scores. They show that training students in test taking and conceptual thinking and eliminating test examiner bias reduce racial and social class differences in intelligence. Furthermore, in half of the twin pairs studied by Sir Cyril Burt and James Shields, the twins were not raised in significantly different environments. They also question whether IQ tests measure intelligence, noting that the tests include many achievement test items and that the results correlate poorly with measures of creativity. Finally, the authors argue that educational programs building on the strengths of the poor have been much more successful than the compensatory programs, which are based on a deficit model. While the policy implications of the hereditarian position are funding cutbacks and resignation by blacks, Gartner and Riessman argue for environmental improvements that are commensurate with the problem.

395. Hunt, J. McVicker. "Relevance to Educability: Heritability or Range of Reaction." 1977. 33p. (ERIC microfiche ED 154 922).

Hunt argues that there is plasticity in early childhood development, which offers opportunities to redress some of the experiential inequalities of the poor in our society. This was the basis of project Head Start. The alleged failure of Head Start gave rise to the ideas of innate intelligence and fixed development, as represented by Arthur Jensen's work. However, one's rate of development or ultimate level of achievement is not constrained by heritability. "Educability depends on the ingenuity of those who try to invent development-fostering experiences through child-rearing procedures and those who set about to improve pedagogic technology" (p. 10). This follows from the genetic concept of range of reaction, which says that a given genotype is capable of producing many different phenotypes (traits, behaviors), depending on environmental circumstances. Hunt illustrates this argument with data from a study he conducted in a Tehran orphanage, as well as with related research findings.

396. Jensen, Arthur R. "Political Ideologies and Educational Research." 1982. 14p. (ERIC microfiche ED 216 028).

Jensen applauds the "growing awareness" that ideology can influence scientific research. This awareness confirms the challenge and value of scientific objectivity; the "researchers' primary concern should be in discovering and representing the educational realities that prevail despite shifting politics and policies" (p. 4). Contrary to the claims of Marxist sociologists of knowledge, Jensen argues that it is possible to separate facts from values or ideology. For example, in his own specialization, IQ theory, there is research from Eastern European communist countries demonstrating that intelligence is highly heritable, this despite the fact that the evidence runs counter to their political ideologies. Jensen sees this as confirmation of an educational reality which can be studied scientifically and objectively.

397. Jensen, Arthur R. "Test Bias and Construct Validity." 1975. 31p. (ERIC microfiche ED 114 415).

Jensen examines the cultural bias of intelligence tests as indicated by measures of their construct validity. Specifically, he compares the Raven's Progressive Matrices and Peabody Picture Vocabulary Test on a number of internal characteristics reflecting construct validity; these two tests are considered "widely separated on the culture-loading continuum" (p. 10). Using data collected on black and white California school

children, Jensen finds no indications of cultural bias on the
"correlation of raw scores with age,...rank order of item difficulty" (p. 29), and other measures. Research on other tests,
such as the Stanford-Binet and the Wechsler Intelligence Scale
for Children, also shows a lack of racial bias on the rank order of item difficulty. Furthermore, Jensen finds that the g-
loading of many standard intelligence tests is similar for
blacks and whites; this is another indication of construct
validity and lack of cultural bias. Based upon these data,
Jensen concludes that the intelligence tests he examined, and
others like them, are not culturally biased.

398. Morris, Frank L. *The Jensen Hypothesis: Social Science Re-
search or Social Science Racism? Center Monograph Series,
No. 2.* Los Angeles, UCLA Center for Afro-American
Studies, 1971. 72p. (ERIC microfiche ED 186 526).

This critique of Jensen focuses on three major areas:
weaknesses in Jensen's assumptions, methodology, and interpretation of data; problems with the social and political uses
to which his findings could be put; and the racial biases that
permeate Jensen's arguments. Among other points, Morris
criticizes Jensen for incorrectly assuming that high heritability
of intelligence within races also means high heritability for
between-race differences. Jensen also mistakenly assumes
"that environmental differences *between* races are comparable
to environmental variation *within* them" (p. 26). Morris raises
doubts about Jensen's assertion that IQ tests measure intelligence, citing the "narrow range" of abilities measured and
the tests' poor correlation with tests of creativity or divergent
thinking. Since Jensen's theory assumes a genetic limitation
on the cognitive abilities of blacks and the poor, it essentially
blames the victims for their plight and justifies a more
neglectful social policy. Morris further criticizes Jensen for
his unconscious "white perspective" and inability to understand the environmental and cultural differences of blacks.
Finally, a social scientist's research responsibilities require
complete disclosure of one's values, biases, and data limitations when doing research on issues related to race.

399. Ogbu, John. "Social Structure and Cognitive Behavior: A
Critique of the Heredity-Environment Hypothesis and an
Alternative Interpretation of Black-White Differences in IQ."
1974. 43p. (ERIC microfiche ED 097 401).

According to Ogbu, a group's cognitive skills are adaptations to the cognitive demands of their techno-economic environment. This environment is different for blacks and whites in this country. Historically, blacks have been a pariah minority group with correspondingly limited opportunities. As a result, they have developed cognitive skills (i.e. concrete, nonabstract thinking) consistent with the demands and opportunities of their environment and different from the skills required of middle and upper-class whites. The various socializing institutions (e.g. family, school) have helped black and white children adapt to these different environmental demands. IQ tests tap this difference in adaptation to one's macroenvironment, not differences in innate ability. Blacks' cognitive behavior will change as the society's occupational and opportunity structure becomes more open.

400. Richman, Charles L., Harlan Wichelhaus, and James Feldman. "Teacher Attitudes Concerning the Nature of Intelligence." no date. 10p. (ERIC microfiche ED 167 923).

Do teachers believe that students' IQs are genetically determined? To answer this question, samples of teachers in the northeast and southeast were questioned, with their answers analyzed for differences by age (over or under 30) and type of school (public vs. private). The authors hypothesized that teachers who were over 30 or in private schools would be more supportive of a genetic explanation of IQ. The data confirmed these hypotheses and also indicated that teachers in private schools were more likely to have entered the school with those beliefs. The authors suggest that low teacher expectations, affected by a belief in genetically determined IQ, could harm a student's education.

401. Scarr, Sandra. "Heritability and Educational Policy: Genetic and Environmental Effects on IQ, Aptitude and Achievement." 1979. 43p. (ERIC microfiche ED 193 333).

Scarr compares older adopted and biological children on IQ, aptitude, and achievement scores in order to determine the relative influence of family background and heredity. She finds that for whites who come from "humane environments" (i.e. working-class to upper middle-class, not environmentally deprived), "there is little evidence for differential environmental effects" (p. 22). Scarr also finds that IQ tests seem to be more culture-fair than achievement tests, which are more subject to social class bias. She finds a consistent genetic effect across all three types of tests. There are also genetic differences across social classes, indicating that the upper classes are genetically more able. As for educational policy, Scarr suggests the continued use of IQ tests as opposed to achievement tests, which are more biased. Because of genetic differences between social classes in IQ and test scores, Scarr questions whether it is appropriate to expect all schools to show comparable achievement levels for their students. For some groups, more time and resources may be required.

402. Scarr, Sandra. "Intelligent Intervention." 1986. 48p. (ERIC microfiche ED 272 778).

Within the normal range of humane environments (i.e. working-class to upper-class families), individual differences in intelligence and personality are about equally the result of genetics and within-family environmental differences. Differences in between-family variables (e.g. socioeconomic status) account for little. Yet, according to Scarr, there is no theory to explain specifically what the relevant environmental variables are. Consequently, we have no basis for effective intervention programs. Despite this gap in our knowledge, interventionists often construct programs based more on wishful thinking than on the scientific testing of competing explanations. Scarr illustrates the problem by taking a few factors, such as peer relations or parent-child relations, and demonstrating the various explanations for their correlation with intelligence and personality. Ultimately, "a theory can be tested by the usefulness of the intervention it implies" (p. 27). Scarr is more optimistic about our ability to change specific behaviors than "our abilities to change more pervasive aspects of people's functioning" (p. 28).

403. Willhelm, Sidney M. "The Race and Racism of the I.Q. Argument." 1975. 16p. (ERIC microfiche ED 120 332).

Willhelm criticizes IQ theory as being one of a number of ideologies that historically have justified racism and the oppression of blacks. For example, Christianity was used to justify slavery, while Social Darwinism rationalized racial inequality in the post-slavery era. More recently, the concept of equality is racist because it ignores the fact that blacks lack "the economic resources to compete on equal terms with whites" (p. 12). IQ theory, too, is racist for a number of reasons. First, comparisons of intelligence are "invidious" and are undertaken for social, not biological, reasons. Second, research into intelligence has a long and racist scholarly history. Third, IQ theory is defended by the concept of academic freedom; this principle is given more importance than the damage IQ theory does to blacks. Fourth, IQ theory is racist because it blames the victims for their plight. Given a history of genocide against blacks, Willhelm questions whether whites can be trusted to preserve the integrity of blacks.

10　Media Materials

404. *The I.Q. Myth.* New York, Carousel Films, 1975. film and videotape. 51 minutes.

   Hosted by Dan Rather, this "CBS Reports" television program provides a critical examination of the history, current uses, and implications of intelligence testing. After pointing out how important IQ scores can be to one's future opportunities, Rather presents criticisms by Jerome Kagan, Kenneth Clark, and others that the tests do not measure general intelligence, that they narrowly focus on facts, and that they are biased against non-middle class groups. William Shockley and Arthur Jensen are identified as proponents of the controversial position that blacks are innately inferior to whites in intelligence. Jensen doubts the ability of compensatory education programs to alter this fact. However, Leon Kamin advocates for the importance of environment, and Rather refers to a Long Island intervention program that has produced long-lasting improvements in IQ. Finally, Rather warns of the danger of labeling or stigmatizing on the basis of IQ; educational tracking and lower performance can result. Agreeing with David McClelland, Rather points out that achievement motivation is more important than IQ and that parents should not see a child's low IQ score as a sign of limited potential.

405. Jensen, Arthur Robert. *An Interview with Arthur Jensen: Intelligence, Race, and Heredity, Part 1 and 2.* New York, Harper and Row, 1976. 2 audiocassettes. 125 minutes.

Jensen provides a broad overview of his position on the IQ debate in this interview with Charles Harris of Fordham University. He begins by discussing the evolution of his interest in the subject and talks about some of the early psychologists who influenced his thinking. He then reviews the evidence (e.g. kinship, twin, and adoption studies) supporting the high heritability of intelligence and defends the definition and measurement of general intelligence ("g"). Jensen also reviews the evidence suggesting that intelligence differences between blacks and whites are highly heritable. He cites research evidence to rebut the charges that intelligence tests are culturally biased against blacks and talks about the minimal impact of existing environmental manipulations on IQ differences. Jensen discusses the educational implications of this line of research and speculates about the direction of future inquiry into intelligence.

406. Jensen, Arthur Robert, and Donald McDonald. *A Matter of Genes*. Santa Barbara, Calif., The Center for the Study of Democratic Institutions, 1971. audiocassette. 29 minutes.

In this conversation with Donald McDonald of The Center for the Study of Democratic Institutions, Jensen reiterates many of the major points he made in his *Harvard Educational Review* article. He suggests that it is a "not unreasonable hypothesis" that genetic differences account for average IQ differences between whites and blacks. This is likely since so many other physiological and behavioral characteristics vary between geographically isolated groups. Various environmental explanations do not adequately account for this average black IQ deficit. Jensen reviews some of the negative reactions to his theory by, for example, students at Berkeley and by the Society for the Psychological Study of Social Issues. He discusses some of the pedagogical implications of his theory, suggesting that instructional techniques should be more individualized, varied, and geared to individual differences. He mentions computer assisted instruction as one new technique for providing this individualized instruction. The key is to gear instruction to the student's individual profile of ability.

407. *The Speaker...a film about freedom*. Chicago, American Library Association, 1977. 16mm film. 42 minutes.

This is a fictional account of a high school controversy surrounding an invited speaker who was arguing that blacks were genetically less intelligent than whites. While the film is intended to explore issues of freedom of speech and censorship, it also reflects many of the circumstances, issues, and debates that have accompanied some speeches by Arthur Jensen, William Shockley, and Hans Eysenck, among others.

408. *White or Black Superiority? A Controversial Debate: Dr. Francis Welsing vs. Dr. William B. Shockley.* North Hollywood, Calif., Center for Cassette Studies, 1974. audiocassette. 56 minutes.

This is an audiocassette recording of one program of Tony Brown's "Black Journal." The program consisted of both a debate between and phoned-in questions for the two guests, Francis Welsing and William B. Shockley. Shockley expressed his concern over dysgenic trends within, primarily, the black community. By this he meant that the intellectually least able blacks were reproducing far more than the more able blacks, thus lowering the overall genetic intelligence of the group. One of his suggestions for addressing the problem was that the genetically least able be offered cash incentives to undergo sterilization. Welsing argued that racism reflects white people's fears of blacks, who are genetically superior to whites, and that it serves to protect white people's social, political, and economic advantages. Arguments like Shockley's rationalized racism, Welsing said, by laying the blame for inequality on black people's allegedly inferior genetic makeup.

Glossary

adoption studies -
> studies in which adopted children's IQs are compared to both their adoptive parents and their biological parents. If the IQs are more similar to the biological parents, this is considered evidence of the influence of heredity, rather than of the adoptive environment, on intelligence.

assortative mating -
> the tendency to marry someone like yourself (i.e. in terms of intelligence, social background, etc.).

compensatory education -
> these are educational programs intended to compensate for deficiencies in a child's previous learning or in a child's values, attitudes, and behaviors.

concurrent validity -
> determining the validity of a test or research instrument by seeing how well it correlates with other similar instruments or measures whose validity is already established.

correlation –

a measure of the strength of relationship between two variables.

dizygotic twins –

twins who may have only 50% of their genes in common because they are produced from two separate eggs.

dysgenics –

the belief by some that increased numbers of offspring by the genetically less intelligent can cause a lowering of the genetic intelligence of the population as a whole.

eugenics –

the belief in the betterment of human populations through selective breeding. Some hereditarians in the IQ debate, particularly during the early years, were eugenicists.

g –

general intelligence, which is supposed to be the largest source of difference in intelligence between individuals.

g-loading –

the degree to which an intelligence test's items measure general intelligence ("g"), as opposed to more specific intelligence factors.

genotype –

the genetic or hereditary influences that contribute to some behavior or trait.

heritable -

that which can be inherited. When intelligence is said to be "80% heritable," that means that 80% of the individual differences within a population are supposedly attributable to genetic, not environmental, differences.

ideology -

a set of theories and beliefs that justify a particular social and political position.

kinship studies -

studies attempting to determine the heritability of intelligence by correlating the IQ scores of various relatives. If intelligence is highly heritable, then it is assumed that scores of close relatives should be more highly correlated than scores of distant relatives.

meritocracy -

a situation in which success is said to depend on one's ability and effort.

metacognitive processes -

these are strategies and techniques individuals use to go about problem solving. In the IQ debate, some people argue that individuals with low IQ scores are not less intelligent but have poor problem solving strategies.

monozygotic twins -

twins who are genetically identical because they are produced from the same egg (zygote).

normal curve –

otherwise known as the bell-shaped curve. It represents a distribution of values or scores (e.g. IQ scores) in which most scores cluster around the average or middle of the distribution (e.g. IQ of 100), with smaller percentages of scores at the high or low extremes.

phenotype –

the observable behavior or trait which can be the result of the influence of the genotype, the environment, and their interaction.

postnatal environment –

all of the environmental influences that occur after birth.

predictive validity –

determining the validity of a test (e.g. IQ) or research instrument by seeing how well it predicts some other variable (e.g. scholastic achievement).

prenatal environment –

this is the environment in the mother's womb, which can include such important factors as the mother's diet and nutrition.

psychometrics –

the study and measurement of behavioral differences between individuals.

range of reaction –

the full range of ways in which a particular genotype (e.g. intelligence) may manifest itself. For example, intelligence, even if it is mostly heritable, may still be manifested by a wide range of scores, depending on environmental influences.

regression to the mean -

in the IQ debate, this refers to the tendency of parents who are above or below the intelligence mean or average to produce children whose measured intelligence is closer to that mean.

reification -

treating an abstract concept as if it were a real thing. Some critics of IQ testing have argued that "intelligence" is an abstraction that hereditarians have treated as a real entity.

reliability -

the requirement that repeated administrations of a test give similar results.

self-fulfilling prophecy -

the process by which one's expectation contributes to that expectation becoming a reality. For example, a teacher who believes that a student is incapable of learning much might interact with the student consistent with that belief, and contribute to lower student achievement as a result.

standardization -

the process of developing methods and procedures for administering and evaluating the results of a test. This is usually done by administering the test to a representative sample of the population on which it will be used. In the IQ debate, some argue that the test has been standardized on middle-class whites, thus making it inappropriate for testing blacks and other non-white or culturally different groups.

twin studies –

studies in which genetically identical (monozygotic) twins have been separated at a young age and raised in significantly different environments. If, despite being raised in different environments, their subsequent IQ scores are similar, then this is considered evidence of the influence of heredity on intelligence.

validity –

the requirement that a test or research instrument (e.g. IQ test) measure what it is supposed to measure (e.g. intelligence).

variance –

the amount of spread or variation that exists in a collection of scores.

Name Index

Arabic numbers refer to entry numbers; roman numerals refer to page numbers in the Introduction.

Adams, Phillip, 137
Adesso, Vincent J., 147
Albee, George W., 350
Alford, David W., 392
Anastasiow, Nicholas, 138
Armor, D.J., reference to, 105
Aronowitz, Stanley, 26, 59

Bajema, Carl, reference to, 354
Bandura, Albert, reference to, 367
Bane, Mary Jo, 30, 292
Barker, Geoffrey, 351
Baron, Jon, reference to, 332
Beck, Clive, 139
Bereiter, Carl, 27, 30, 102, 141, 142; reference to, 312
Berg, Paul, 352
Berger, Brigitte, 293
Bernstein, Richard, reference to, 268

Berube, Maurice R., 294
Biesheuvel, S., 28
Biggs, J.B., 143
Binet, Alfred, x; references to, 3, 25, 52, 60, 75, 81, 90, 103, 169, 176, 221
Blau, Zena Smith, xiv, 29
Block, N.J., 30
Blum, Howard, 353
Blum, Jeffrey M., 31, 144
Bodmer, Walter F., 32, 62, 107, 145
Bohannan, Paul, reference to, 380
Boone, James A., 146, 147
Boozer, Bernard, 148
Bortowski, John G., 149
Bouchard, Thomas J., Jr., 150; reference to, 308
Bowles, Samuel, xv, 33, 34, 59, 295; references to, 97, 304, 330
Brace, C. Loring, 35

Brazziel, William F., 277;
   references to, 235, 312
Bridger, Wagner, 189
Brigham, Carl C., 36;
   references to, 41, 60, 271,
   326
Brody, Jane E., 354
Bronfenbrenner, Urie, 37
Brown, A.E., 151
Brown, Frederick G., 277
Brown, Tony, 408
Brown, Wayne Curtis, 100,
   114
Buchanan, Patrick, 296
Buckley, William, 297
Burnham, Dorothy, 298
Buros, Oscar Krisen, 18
Burt, Cyril, vii, xi, xiv, 135,
   152, 153, 154, 155;
   references to, 25, 50, 52,
   60, 61, 63, 76, 86, 161,
   168, 169, 178, 188, 193,
   206, 210, 211, 218, 268,
   309, 327, 335, 364, 371,
   383, 384, 390, 394
Burton, Andrew, 107
Buss, A.R., reference to, 179

Cameron, Howard K., 277
Campbell, Barbara, 355
Canady, H.G., reference to,
   349
Cancro, Robert, 38, 130, 393
Capron, Christiane, 156
   reference to, 232
Cattell, James McKeen,
   references to, 3, 52
Cattell, Raymond B., 38, 135,
   160
Cavalli-Sforza, Luigi, 145
Ceci, Stephen J., 169
Chapman, Paul Davis, 39
Chomsky, Noam, 30, 40, 59,
   300

Cinzio, Steve, 157
Clark, Cedric X., 158
Clark, Kenneth, 404
Cleary, T. Anne, reference
   to, 359
Cohen, David K., 301
Colman, Andrew M., 159
Conoley, Jane Close, 19
Conway, Jane, references to,
   188, 335, 364
Conwill, William L., 161
Corsini, Raymond J., 24
Cottle, Thomas J., 302
Cowley, Geoffrey, 303
Cravens, Hamilton, 41
Cronbach, Lee J., 162
   reference to, 312
Crouse, James, 243
Crow, James F., 163
   reference to, 312

Daniels, John, 107
Daniels, Norman, 304
Davies, Lawrence E., 358
Davis, Bernard, reference to,
   389
DeFries, J.C., 251
Delaney, Paul, 359
Delgado, Richard, 164
Dent, Harold E., 165, 166
Deutsch, Martin, 167, 305
Dill, John, reference to, 355
Dobzhansky, Theodosius, 306
Dolphin, Ric, 307
Dorfman, D.D., 168
   reference to, 384
Doris, John L., 169
Douglas, John H., 170
Draper, Wycliffe P.,
   reference to, 376
Drucker, Ernest, 130
Duncan, Otis Dudley,
   reference to, 323
Dusek, Val, 308

Duyme, Michel, 156
    reference to, 232
Dworkin, Gerald, 30
Dyer, Henry, reference to,
    253

Ebel, Robert L., 171
Eckberg, Douglas Lee, 42
Eckland, Bruce K., 38, 43,
    172
Edel, Abraham, 130
Edson, Lee, 360
Egerton, John, 309
Ehrlich, Paul R., 44
Elkind, David, 173 references
    to, 235, 312
Elliott, Rogers, 45
Engles, Friedrich, reference
    to, 179
Epps, Edgar G., 174
Epstein, Seymour, reference
    to, 367
Erlenmeyer-Kimling L., 175
Ertis, B.P.A., 176
Evans, Brian, 46
Evans, M. Stanton, 310
Evans, Ross A., 59
Eysenck, Hans, 9, 47, 48, 49,
    50, 51, 102, 160, 177, 178,
    179, 311, 361, 407;
    references to, 116, 137,
    190, 264, 276, 279, 309,
    340

Fancher, Raymond E., 52
Farber, Susan L., 53, 150
Fehr, F.S., 180
Fine, Benjamin, 54
Fischbein, Siv, 181
Fiske, Edward B., 362
Flaste, Richard, 363
Fletcher, Ronald, 364
Florissant, Belle Gibson, 182
Flynn, James R., 55, 102,
    365; references to, 366

Fox, John, reference to, 361
Freeman, Frank N., xi, 104,
    150; references to, 116,
    180, 210, 327
Friedrichs, Robert W., 183
Furby, Lita, 184

Gage, N.L., 185
Galton, Francis, vii, ix, 56,
    135; references to, 3, 25,
    47, 52, 81, 110, 169, 176,
    268
Garber, Howard L., 57, 58;
    references to, 284
Garcia, John, 313
Gardner, Howard, 186;
    references to, 272, 332,
    367, 368, 380
Garrett, Henry, reference to,
    239
Gartner, Alan, 59, 394
Garza, Blas M., 245
Gill, C.E.R. Jardine, 187
Gillie, Oliver, 188; reference
    to, 371
Gintis, Herbert, xv, 33, 34,
    59, 295; references to, 97,
    304, 330
Goddard, Henry, references
    to, 3, 25, 52, 60, 78, 221,
    326
Golden, Mark, 189
Goleman, Daniel, 366, 367,
    368
Goodman, George, 369
Gordon, Edmund W., 38,
    190, 191
Gordon, Robert A., 192
Gould, Stephen Jay, 60, 61,
    314
Gray, J., 192
Green, Derek, 190
Green, Herman, 267
Green, Robert L., 194

Greer, Colin, 59
Greg, Andrews, 139
Griffore, Robert J., 194
Grubb, Henry Jefferson, 195, 196
Gutterman, Stanley S., 197

Hall, G. Stanley, reference to, 268
Halsey, A.H., 62
Hambley, John, 107
Harris, Art, 370
Harris, Charles, 405
Hart, Jeffrey, 315
Haskins, Ron, 254
Hearnshaw, L.S., 63
Heber, Rick, 57, 58; references to, 159, 284, 391
Hechinger, Fred M., 371
Henderson, Paul, 64
Herrnstein, Richard J., xiii, 30, 65, 160, 271, 316, 317, 318, 319; references to, 40, 116, 129, 130, 162, 176, 190, 264, 278, 296, 300, 302, 303, 310, 311, 315, 340, 347, 388, 390
Hilliard, Asa G., III, 198, 199
Hirsch, Jerry, 38, 66, 200; reference to, 379
Hitler, Adolf, reference to, 235
Holzinger, Karl I., xi, 104, 150; references to, 116, 180, 210, 327
Horn, Joseph M., 201
Houghton, Vincent, 107
Howard, Margaret, references to, 188, 335, 364
Hudson, Liam, references to, 379

Hunt, J. McVicker, 38, 67, 135, 202, 203, 395; references to, 235, 312
Hyde, Elizabeth M., 247

Jacobsen, L., reference to, 162
James, T., 62, 118
Jarvik, Lissy F., 175
Jencks, Christopher, 30, 114, 292, 323; references to, 82, 105, 190
Jensen, Arthur R., vii, ix-xiv, 9, 30, 62, 68, 69, 70, 71, 72, 73, 74, 102, 112, 135, 160, 204, 205, 206, 207, 208, 209, 210, 211, 212, 213, 214, 215, 216, 217, 324, 396, 397, 404, 405, 406, 407; references to, 1, 2, 27, 28, 32, 35, 52, 55, 60, 61, 82, 84, 85, 96, 103, 105, 110, 116, 123, 126, 129, 130, 131, 137, 138, 141, 143, 158, 161, 162, 163, 167, 170, 174, 176, 180, 183, 185, 189, 190, 200, 219, 225, 226, 227, 234, 235, 239, 241, 249, 252, 257, 258, 268, 273, 274, 276, 277, 279, 286, 290, 294, 296, 297, 298, 299, 305, 310, 311, 312, 314, 320, 321, 323, 328, 336, 337, 340, 342, 348, 355, 356, 358, 360, 361, 373, 376, 377, 379, 381, 382, 383, 390, 391, 395, 398
Jones, F.L., 218
Joseph, Andre, 75
Joynson, Robert B., xiv, 76
Judd, Charles, reference to, 268

Juel-Nielsen, Niels, 77, 150; references to, 210, 327

Kagan, Jerome S., 59, 219, 220, 325, 404; references to, 235, 312
Kamin, Leon J., xiii, 9, 30, 50, 51, 78, 79, 112, 221, 222, 223, 326, 327, 404; references to, 52, 61, 309, 335, 383
Kaplan, Paul S., 374
Karier, Clarence, 30, 224
Katz, Irwin, references to, 337, 349
Kilgore, William J., 225
Klineberg, Otto, 252
Knickerbocker, Brad, 375
Kramer, Jack J., 19
Krasner, William, 80
Krause, Audrey, 149

Lawler, James M., 81
Layzer, David, 82, 114, 130
Lenin, Vladimir, reference to, 179
Lewontin, Richard C., 9, 30, 83, 84, 85, 86, 113, 114, 329; references to, 73, 383, 389
Lichtenstein, Grace, 376
Light, Richard J., 226
Lindsey, Richard A., 227
Lindzey, Gardner, 95
Lippmann, Walter, vii, x, 30, 87, 88, 89, 90, 91, 92, 93, 125; reference to, 129
Liungman, Carl G., 94
Livingston, Frank B., 35
Loehlin, John C., 95
Lohman, David F., 129
Lowe, Roy A., 228
Luria, S.E., 330
Lyons, Richard, 377

Machock, Bernadine J., 247
Mackenzie, Brian, 229
Mackintosh, N.J., 230
MacPherson, Malcolm, 335
Madaus, George F., 249
Marcus, Laurence R., 273
Marks, Russell, 96, 231
Martin, N.G., 187
Marx, Karl, reference to, 179
Matthews, Michael R., 97; reference to, 258
Mayeske, G.W., reference to, 257
McCall, Robert B., 331
McCann, Wendy, 307
McClelland, David C., 30, 59, 98, 404; references to, 344, 367
McDonald, Donald, 406
McGue, Matt, 232
McKean, Kevin, 332
McKnight, David, 378
McNeil, Nathaniel D., 233
Mead, Margaret, 333
Mercer, Jane R., xiv, 99, 100, 114, 334; references to, 80, 257, 339, 362
Mill, John Stuart, reference to, 52
Miller, Douglas R., 234
Miller, Lamar, reference to, 355
Miller, M. Sammy, 235
Milofsky, Carl, 101
Mitchell, James V., Jr., 20
Modgil, Celia, 102
Modgil, Sohan, 102
Montagu, Ashley, 103
Moore, Clifford L., 236
Moore, Elsie G.J., xiv, 237, 238
More, Thomas, reference to, 235
Morgan, Harry, 239

Morris, Frank L., 398
Muir, Sharon Pray, 240
Munro, Ella, 216
Murphy, Claudia M., 241

Newell, Peter, 379
Newman, Horatio H., xi, 104,
    150; references to, 116,
    180, 210, 327

Ogbu, John U., 242, 399;
    reference to, 366
Olneck, Michael R., 243
Ornstein, Allan, 244;
    reference to, 194

Padilla, Amado M., 245
Page, Jake, 380
Panati, Charles, 335
Paul, Diane B., 336;
    reference to, 329
Peckham, Robert, reference
    to, 375
Peers, John, 246
Perney, Lawrence R., 247
Persell, Caroline Hodges, 248
Pezzullo, Thomas R., 249
Piaget, Jean, references to,
    53, 67, 173, 235, 348, 380
Piel, Gerard, 130
Pine, Patricia, 250
Plomin, Robert, 251
Plotkin, Lawrence, 105, 252;
    reference to, 355
Prohansky, Harold M., 130
Purvin, George, 59, 253

Radford, John, 107
Ramey, Craig, 254
Rather, Dan, xix, 296, 404
Reinhold, Robert, 382
Rensberger, Boyce, 383, 384
Retish, Paul M., 236
Rex, John, 107

Rice, Berkeley, 339, 340
Richards, Graham, 255
Richards, Martin, 107
Richardson, Ken, 107, 108
Richman, Charles L., 400
Riessman, Frank, 59, 394
Robinson, David Z., 109, 114
Robinson, Lawrence D., 341
Rose, Hilary, 110
Rose, Steven, 107, 110;
    reference to, 379
Rosenfield, Geraldine, 2
Rosenthal, R., reference to,
    162
Rotatori, Anthony F., 267
Rothman, Stanley, 119, 345
Rowan, Carl T., 342
Rubain, Tresmaine J., 191
Rudert, Eileen, 192
Rushton, J. Philippe,
    reference to, 307
Ryan, Joanna, 107

Samuda, Ronald J., 111, 256
Sanday, Peggy R., 257;
    reference to, 369
Sanders, James T., 258
Scarr, Sandra, 9, 30, 112,
    259, 260, 261, 262, 263,
    264, 343, 401, 402;
    references to, 181, 273,
    279
Scarr-Salapatek, Sandra. *See*
    Scarr, Sandra.
Schanberg, Sydney H., 385
Schiff, Michel, 113
Schmeck, Harold M., Jr., 386
Schoenfeld, William N., 265
Schwartz, Judah L., 266
Schwenn, John, 267
Selden, Steven, xxvi, 268
Senna, Carl, 114
Shields, James, 115, 150;
    references to, 210, 327,
    394

Shockley, William, xiii, 116, 269, 404, 407, 408; references to, 158, 176, 190, 225, 235, 286, 296, 340, 353, 356, 370, 376, 377, 386
Shuey, Audrey M., vii, 117; references to, 49, 227, 376
Sidel, Victor, 130
Simmons, Cassandra, 194
Skeels, Harold M., 270
Skodak, Marie, 270
Smith, G., 62, 118
Smith, Paul V., 226
Snyderman, Mark, 119, 271, 345
Sowell, Thomas, 387
Spearman, Charles, 135; references to, 52, 60, 76, 128, 176, 212
Spears, David, 107, 108
Spuhler, J.N., 95
Stern, William, reference to, 52
Sternberg, Robert J., 102, 120, 272; references to, 272, 332, 367, 368, 380
Stevens, Wallace K., 388
Stickney, Benjamin D., 241, 273
Stinchcombe, Arthur L., 274
Stoddard, Ann H., 275
Stoddard, Lothrop, reference to, 90
Storfer, Miles D., 121
Stott, D.H., 276
Strickland, Stephen P., 114, 122
Sullivan, Barbara, 225
Sullivan, Walter, 389
Swift, Donald, 107

Talbott, Robert E., 346
Taylor, Howard F., 123, 150, 278, 279

Terman, Lewis, vii, x, 30, 88, 89, 91, 92, 124, 125; references to, 3, 25, 39, 52, 60, 78, 81, 86, 90, 93, 103, 129, 144, 176, 221, 313, 326
Thoday, J.M., 126, 127
Thomas, William B., 280, 281, 282
Thorndike, Edward Lee, references to, 3, 268
Thorndike, Robert L., 128, 160
Thorndike, Robert M., 129
Thorsen, Eric E., 249
Thurstone, L.L., references to, 60, 176, 314
Tobach, Ethel, 130
Tobias, Phillip V., 62, 131
Trotman, Frances Keith, 283

van den Haag, Ernest, reference to, 297
Vasgird, Dan, 347
Vernon, Philip E., 102, 132, 133, 135, 160, 284
Vetta, Atam, 285
Voyat, Gilbert, 348

Wade, Nicholas, 390; reference to, 63
Waites, Bernard, 46
Wallace, Bruce, 286
Wallen, Norman E., 287
Watson, Peter, 107, 348; reference to, 337
Watson, Robert I.,Sr., 3
Wechsler, David, 38, 134, 160; reference to, 52
Weinberg, Richard A., 260, 261, 262, 263, 343
Weinraub, Bernard, 391
Welsing, Francis, 408
White, Sheldon H., 288

Wilkerson, Doxey, reference
    to, 355
Willhelm, Sidney M., 403
Williams, Paul, 291
Williams, Robert L.,
    reference to, 359
Wilson, Darrell, reference to,
    352
Wiseman, Stephen, 135
Witherspoon, Roger,
    reference to, 370
Wolff, Joseph, 222
Wolman, Benjamin B., 23, 25
Wright, Logan, 4

Yagerman, Howard, 2
Yerkes, Robert M., vii, 136;
    references to, 3, 25, 41,
    52, 60, 78, 221, 326
Yoakum, Clarence S., 136

Zach, Lillian, 289, 290
Zoref, Leslie, 291

Subject Index

Arabic numbers refer to entry numbers; roman numerals refer to page numbers in the Introduction.

Aborigines, 126
Abstract learning abilities, xii, 73, 143, 207, 249, 299, 321, 399
Achievement tests, 68, 187, 266, 401. *See also specific tests*
ADC. *See* Aid to Dependent Children
Adolescent Adoption Study, 263
Adoption studies, xi, 48, 50, 55, 71, 95, 132, 133, 154, 178, 189, 201, 256, 260, 261, 270, 284, 299, 322, 323, 405; criticisms of, xiii, 35, 46, 79, 86, 106, 111, 145, 304; meritocracy argument and, 65; race and, 44, 237, 238, 262, 263, 273, 332, 343, 389; socioeconomic status and, 113, 156, 232, 401. *See also specific studies*

AEP (Average evoked potentials), 169
Age, 131, 313, 392
Aid to Dependent Children (ADC), 247
American Anthropological Association, 381
American Association for the Advancement of Science, 389
American Indians, xiv, 73, 99, 167, 324, 326, 382
American Orthopsychiatric Association, 363
American Society of Human Genetics, 376
Animal studies, 67, 214
Aptitude tests, 68. *See also specific tests*
Army intelligence tests, x, 36, 39, 41, 60, 86, 89, 90, 91, 125, 129, 136, 162, 221, 223, 231, 289, 390
Asian-Americans, 332

Associative learning. *See*
Rote learning
Assortative mating, 43, 141
Australian Scholastic Ap-
titude Test, 187

BEAT. *See* Black Environ-
mental Adjustment Test
Biological stratification, 388
Birth rates, 318
BIT. *See* Black Intelligence
Test
BITCH. *See* Black In-
telligence Test of Cultural
Homogeneity
Black Environmental Adjustment Test (BEAT), 146
Black Intelligence Test (BIT),
147
Black Intelligence Test of
Cultural Homogeneity
(BITCH), 233
Blacks, ix, xii, xiv-xv, 29,
59, 61, 72, 82, 84, 85,
100, 106, 109, 111, 117,
121, 145, 159, 163, 167,
183, 184, 185, 192, 195,
208, 209, 212, 217, 219,
235, 239, 242, 247, 252,
256, 257, 264, 265, 269,
273, 274, 276, 277, 278,
283, 286, 290, 292, 296,
297, 298, 299, 304, 305,
306, 307, 314, 321, 323,
324, 326, 330, 333, 337,
338, 341, 351, 353, 355,
356, 357, 359, 360, 366,
373, 376, 377, 381, 382,
387, 397, 398, 399, 403,
404, 405, 406, 407, 408;
adoption studies of, 237,
238, 262, 332, 343, 389;
culture-fair tests and, 191,
362, 372; culture-specific

tests and, 146, 147, 191,
233; early criticisms of
tests by, 280, 281; education and, 49, 69, 99, 126,
138, 190, 282; effect of
examiners on, 236, 349;
executive system and, 149;
General Systems Theory
and, 158; litigation on be-
half of, 166, 350, 372,
375; mental retardation
and, 196, 334, 342, 350,
362, 372; migration and,
222; SAT scores of, 385;
social allocation model
and, 226; social policy
and, 105
Brain Research Association,
379
Brown v. Board of Education
96, 105

Cambridge Society for Social
Responsibility in Science,
379
Capitalism, 231
Cinepsychometrics, 339
Cognitive learning abilities.
See Abstract learning
abilities
Cognitive style mapping, 148,
392
Cold Spring Harbor High
School, 353
Compensatory education, xii,
73, 138, 141, 163, 167,
309, 321, 371, 379; alleged
failure of, ix, xiv, 85,
106, 159, 202, 203, 204,
207, 227, 235, 241, 290,
299, 305, 311, 320, 348,
382, 394, 404
Concurrent validity, 97
Constitutional factors, 132

Construct validity, 97, 397
Content-free tests, 213
Court cases, 45, 165, 166, 199, 259, 350, 359, 370, 372
Cox Enterprises, Inc., 370
Crime, 41, 48
Criterion sampling, 98, 191, 344
Cultural bias, 28, 69, 86, 133, 146, 191, 192, 204, 209, 212, 220, 233, 242, 244, 250, 253, 265, 273, 275, 277, 298, 324, 332, 334, 350, 355, 360, 378, 397, 405
Culture fairness, xiii, 14, 75, 128, 159, 171, 191, 227, 267, 279, 324, 362, 365, 382, 392, 401
Culture-free tests, 171, 245, 252, 279, 313
Culture-specific tests, 146, 147, 191, 233, 339, 392

Dartmouth College, 357
Deviation from the mean, 83
Differential theories, 267
Divergent thinking, 249
Dizygotic twins. *See* Fraternal twins

Ecological intervention, 118
Education, 9, 11, 12, 16, 27, 39, 70, 93, 94, 133, 141, 177, 186, 187, 213, 292, 295; eugenics and, 228; IQ test ban and, 165, 166, 259, 375; labeling of students and, 80; litigation and, 45, 165, 166, 199, 259, 350, 372; Marxist theory on, 97; meritocracy and, 224; race and, 28, 44, 49, 69, 99, 101, 110, 126, 138, 139, 174, 190, 282, 306; socioeconomic status and, 33, 34, 113, 139, 224, 311; teacher bias and, 290; test misuse and, 54, 87, 99, 101, 151, 198, 275, 374. *See also* Compensatory education; Intervention programs
Educational Testing Service, 368
English children, 338
Environmentalism, 26, 319
Eskimos, 351
Eugenics, xi, 31, 46, 75, 78, 81, 96, 110, 116, 163, 221, 223, 228, 269, 303, 318, 354, 376
Eugenics Education Society, 228
Evoked potentials, xii, 47, 132, 230, 339, 392; average, 169
Examiner bias, 392, 394
Executive system, 149

Family environment, 37, 44, 86, 93, 94, 113, 121, 225, 243, 260, 283, 323, 402
Fraternal twins, 104, 115, 249

General intelligence, 32, 46, 60, 74, 128, 153, 205, 208, 212, 213, 216, 258, 313, 314, 332, 404
General Systems Theory, 158
Genetics Society of America, 376
Genius, 56, 124, 144
Gifted children, 124, 144, 332
G-loadings, 212, 397

Griggs v. Duke Power Company, 359

Head Start program, 1, 118, 132, 159, 161, 219, 239, 276, 311, 342, 371, 395
Height and IQ, 40, 300, 352
Hispanics, 99, 245. *See also* Mexican-Americans

Identical twins, xi, 53, 61, 65, 77, 104, 111, 115, 150, 152, 154, 175, 210, 211, 218, 219, 249, 269, 279, 299, 335, 377, 382, 383
Immigrants, x, 36, 39, 59, 78, 79, 96, 129, 161, 242, 282, 309, 313, 376, 387
Immigration Restriction Act of 1924, x, 60, 61, 78, 86, 105, 221, 223, 258, 271
Indians. *See* American Indians
Information-processing theories, 267, 272
Inspection time, 132, 169, 230
Intelligence testers, 3, 52, 78, 79, 135, 221, 271. *See also specific individuals*
Intelligence tests, x-xi, 4, 6, 9, 11, 14, 17, 18, 19, 23, 74, 75, 86, 91, 94, 128, 194, 212, 240, 287, 341; alternatives to, 148, 165, 339, 344, 362, 367; ban on, 165, 166, 259, 375; culture-free, 171, 245, 252, 279, 313; culture-specific, 146, 147, 191, 233, 339, 392; distinction between achievement tests and, 266; early criticisms of, 280, 281; examiner bias and, 392, 394; history of, 39, 46, 52, 129; improvements on, 368; labeling and, 80, 157; legal issues and, 45, 165, 166, 223, 259, 372, 375; misconceptions about, 250; misuse of, 57, 87, 88, 99, 101, 151, 198, 275, 374; opposition to use of, 54, 140, 359; overemphasis on, 182; role of in meritocracy, 40, 59. *See also specific tests*; Army intelligence tests; Culture fairness; Test bias; Test reliability; Test validity
Intervention programs, 37, 118, 132, 167, 239, 264, 276, 284, 402, 404; for infants, 254; for mentally retarded, 57, 58, 122, 391; *See also specific programs*; Compensatory education
Intrauterine environment. *See* Prenatal influences
Irish, 338, 384

Japanese, 265
Jews, 294, 384

Kalamazoo Brothers study, 243
Kibbutzim, 159, 170, 294
Kinship correlations, xi, 50, 71, 74, 132, 133, 152, 175, 405; alleged fraud in, 76; criticisms of, xiii, 46, 79, 106, 211
Kuhlman-Anderson Test of Intelligence, 247

Labeling, 80, 157
Language problems, 44, 72, 273, 287

Larry P. v. Wilson Riles, 45, 166, 199

Lawsuits. *See* Court cases

Level I/II theory, 102, 143, 207, 208, 214, 249. *See also* Abstract learning abilities; Rote learning abilities

Lorge-Thorndike test, 233

Lysenkoism, 310

Marxism, 81, 97, 179, 258, 396

Media, 119. *See also* Press bias

Mental age, x, 14, 90, 125

Mental illness, 48, 53

Mental retardation, 23, 70; intervention programs and, 57, 58, 122, 391; race and, 45, 80, 99, 101, 116, 165, 166, 196, 199, 334, 342, 350, 362, 372, 375, 382

Mental tests, 41, 162, 213, 282; bias in, 68, 191; defense of, 74; early criticisms of, 280; eugenics and, 228; history of, 39, 46, 129. *See also specific types*

Meritocracy, 65, 96, 141, 177, 243, 301, 319, 347; role of IQ tests in, 40, 59; school system as, 224; socioeconomic status and, 33, 43, 243, 278, 316

Mexican-Americans, 100, 159, 324, 334, 362. *See also* Hispanics

Migration, 222

Milwaukee Project, 57, 58, 122, 159, 170

Minnesota Adoption Studies, 55, 263, 343

Monozygotic twins. *See* Identical twins

Movement time, 216

Mulatto hypothesis, 281

NAACP (National Association for the Advancement of Colored People), 375

National Academy of Sciences, 357, 377, 386

Nazism, xi, 370

New South Wales Teachers' Federation, 378

Nonverbal tests, 128

Nutrition, 28, 35, 44, 55, 95, 131, 217, 256, 341, 342, 360

Occupational status, 155, 301

Opportunity School, 282

Orientals, 307

Orphanage studies, 154, 395

Parent-offspring studies, 251

PASE v. Hannon, 45, 199

Peabody Picture Vocabulary Test, 397

Personality, 48, 53, 77, 104, 115, 323

Pioneer Fund, 376

Prenatal influences, 79, 121, 131, 133, 156, 210, 225, 276, 341, 377, 392

Press bias, 317. *See also* Media

Princeton University, 315

Programmed instruction, 27

Project Talent, 243

Pseudoscience, 31

Psychological Corporation, 368

Psychometric theories, 272

Public Advocates, Inc., 375

Quick Test, 197

Race, ix, xiii, xv, 23, 26, 31,
32, 35, 36, 37, 41, 42, 44,
50, 55, 60, 62, 66, 68, 73,
74, 75, 81, 86, 94, 95,
102, 103, 107, 108, 112,
116, 120, 127, 130, 131,
132, 133, 135, 148, 189,
203, 205, 207, 214, 220,
221, 223, 227, 229, 230,
240, 248, 253, 259, 275,
279, 283, 287, 291, 293,
300, 310, 312, 314, 320,
328, 332, 334, 337, 340,
342, 345, 347, 361, 362,
369, 373, 379, 386, 390,
392, 393, 394; adoption
studies and, 44, 237, 238,
262, 263, 273, 332, 343,
389; attempt to restrict research on, 164; early testing movement and, 78, 79;
education and, 28, 44, 49,
69, 99, 101, 110, 126, 138,
139, 174, 190, 282, 306;
labeling and, 80; litigation
and, 45, 165, 166, 199,
350, 372, 375; Marxism
on, 258; media and, 119;
mental retardation and,
45, 80, 99, 101, 116, 165,
166, 196, 199, 334, 342,
350, 362, 372, 375, 382;
meritocracy argument and,
40. *See also specific racial and ethnic groups*
Racial admixture, 44, 55, 69,
95, 227, 229, 281, 389
Rat breeding studies, 214
Raven's Standard Progressive
Matrices, 216, 397
Reaction time, xx, 47, 102,
132, 169, 170, 213, 216,
230

Regression to the mean, 50,
155, 178, 285, 311
Rote learning abilities, xii,
27, 73, 143, 167, 207, 208,
249, 299, 321

SAT. *See* Scholastic Ap-
titude Test
Scholastic Aptitude Test
(SAT), 344, 385
School system. *See* Educa-
tion
SDS. *See* Students for a
Democratic Society
Self-fulfilling prophecies, 54,
275
SES. *See* Socioeconomic
status
Sex, 26, 68, 128, 131, 275,
291, 313, 384
Shipley Institute of Living
Scale, 146, 147
Sibling studies, 251, 261
Slavery, 185
Social allocation model, 226
Social class. *See*
Socioeconomic status
Social competence tests, 339
Society for the Psychological
Study of Social Issues,
373, 406
Socioeconomic status (SES),
xv, xvi, 26, 41, 48, 64, 69,
73, 75, 93, 94, 95, 102,
112, 121, 128, 131, 132,
133, 135, 146, 147, 159,
168, 172, 184, 189, 190,
193, 197, 203, 204, 208,
215, 219, 225, 227, 248,
259, 264, 274, 276, 279,
283, 293, 295, 306, 320,
323, 330, 338, 340, 344,
345, 392, 402; adoption
studies on, 113, 156, 232,

401; education and, 33,
34, 113, 139, 224, 311;
Marxist theory of, 97;
meritocracy argument and,
33, 43, 243, 278, 316; SAT
scores and, 385; twin
studies on, 181
SOMPA. *See* System of
Multicultural Pluralistic
Assessment
Specificity doctrine, 213
Stanford-Binet Intelligence
Scale, 75, 89, 90, 106,
125, 128, 209, 221, 313,
397
Sterilization, xiii, 116, 235,
269, 309, 326, 370
Students for a Democratic
Society (SDS), 358
System of Multicultural
Pluralistic Assessment
(SOMPA), 80, 362
Systems theories, 272

Teacher bias, 400
Tertiary Admission Examination, 187
Test bias, 44, 68, 72, 74, 100,
102, 191, 197, 273, 291,
313, 350, 378, 397, 401,
404. *See also* Cultural
bias
Test reliability, 92
Test validity, 31, 74, 125;
concurrent, 97; construct,
97, 397
Texas Adoption Project, 322
Translated tests, 245
Transracial adoption, 44, 237,
238, 262, 263, 273, 332,
389
Transracial Adoption Study,
263
Triarchic theory, 120

Twin studies, xi, xiii, 44, 48,
50, 52, 53, 70, 71, 74, 77,
95, 104, 115, 116, 133,
150, 152, 154, 171, 175,
178, 180, 189, 210, 214,
234, 251, 256, 269, 284,
294, 299, 323, 364, 377,
382, 405; on achievement
tests, 187; alleged fraud
in, 76, 188, 218, 335, 383,
384; criticisms of, xiii, 46,
61, 63, 79, 82, 86, 106,
111, 123, 145, 161, 185,
190, 211, 219, 225, 278,
279, 292, 304, 308, 327,
394; level I/II theory and,
249; meritocracy argument
and, 65; socioeconomic
status and, 181

University of California
Berkeley, 358, 406
University of Iowa, 315

Variance, analysis of, 83
Verbal deprivation, 324
Voluntary Sterilization Bonus
Plan (VSBP), 370
VSBP. *See* Voluntary
Sterilization Bonus Plan

WAIS. *See* Wechsler Adult
Intelligence Scale
Wechsler Adult Intelligence
Scale (WAIS), 128
Wechsler Intelligence Scale
for Children (WISC), 106,
128, 209, 397
Wechsler Preschool and Pri-
mary Scale of Intelligence
(WPPSI), 236
Wechsler Scale, 220. *See also*
specific tests
West Indians, 337

WISC. *See* Wechsler In-
telligence Scale for Children
WPPSI. *See* Wechsler Preschool and Primary Scale
of Intelligence

About the Compiler and the Assistant

STEPHEN H. ABY has a Ph.D. in Foundations of Education from the State University of New York at Buffalo and is currently the Education Bibliographer at the University of Akron. His previous book, *Sociology: A Guide to Reference and Information Sources* (1987), was a *Choice* award winner for 1987-1988.

MARTHA J. MCNAMARA is the writing curriculum coordinator and an Instructor in the English Language Institute at the University of Akron.